SOLUTIONS MANUAL
TO ACCOMPANY

MODELS
FOR
QUANTIFYING RISK
(THIRD EDITION)

ROBIN J. CUNNINGHAM, FSA, PH.D.
THOMAS N. HERZOG, ASA, PH.D.
RICHARD L. LONDON, FSA

ACTEX PUBLICATIONS, INC.
WINSTED, CONNECTICUT

Copyright © 2006, 2008, by ACTEX Publications, Inc.

All rights reserved. No portion of this textbook may be reproduced by any means without prior written permission from the copyright owner.

Requests for permission should be addressed to
    ACTEX Publications
    P.O. Box 974
    Winsted, CT 06098

Manufactured in the United States of America

ISBN: 978-1-56698-676-2

Table of Contents

Chapter 3	Survival Models	1
Chapter 4	The Life Table	15
Chapter 5	Contingent Payment Models	33
Chapter 6	Contingent Annuity Models	49
Chapter 7	Funding Plans for Contingent Contracts	73
Chapter 8	Contingent Contract Reserves	89
Chapter 9	Models Dependent on Multiple Survivals	111
Chapter 10	Multiple Contingencies with Applications	125
Chapter 11	Claim Frequency Models	143
Chapter 12	Claim Severity Models	159
Chapter 13	Models for Aggregate Payments	197
Chapter 14	Process Models	223

CHAPTER THREE
SURVIVAL MODELS
(CONTINUOUS PARAMETRIC CONTEXT)

3-1 (a) $S(x) = \exp\left[-\int_0^x \lambda(y)\, dy\right] = \exp\left[-\int_0^x a+by\, dy\right] = e^{-(ax+bx^2/2)}$

(b) $f(x) = S(x) \cdot \lambda(x) = (a+bx) \cdot e^{-ax-bx^2/2}$

(c) We seek the value of x which maximizes $f(x)$. Consider the derivative

$$\frac{d}{dx} f(x) = (a+bx) \cdot (e^{-ax-bx^2/2})(-a-bx) + b \cdot e^{-ax-bx^2/2}$$

$$= b \cdot e^{-ax-bx^2/2} - (a+bx)^2 \cdot e^{-ax-bx^2/2} = 0.$$

Then

$$b = (a+bx)^2 = a^2 + 2abx + b^2x^2,$$

or

$$b^2x^2 + 2abx + (a^2 - b) = 0.$$

Then

$$x = \frac{-2ab \pm \sqrt{(2ab)^2 - 4b^2(a^2-b)}}{2b^2}$$

$$= \frac{-2ab \pm 2b^{3/2}}{2b^2} = \frac{-a + b^{1/2}}{b} = b^{-1/2} - ab^{-1}.$$

Note: The positive square root is taken here, since otherwise the mode would be negative, which is impossible.

1

3-2 We have $S(0) = b = 1$ and $S(k) = ak^2 + 1 = 0$. Thus $a = \frac{-1}{k^2}$, so $S(x) = 1 - \frac{x^2}{k^2}$. Then

$$E[X] = \int_0^k S(y)\,dy = k - \frac{k^3}{3k^2} = k - \frac{1}{3}k = \frac{2}{3}k = 60,$$

so $k = 90$, and thus $a = \frac{-1}{8100}$. Finally, $S(m) = 1 - \frac{m^2}{8100} = \frac{1}{2}$, which leads to $m^2 = 4050$, and $m = 45\sqrt{2}$.

3-3 $S(x) = \exp\left[-\int_0^x e^{-ry}\,dy\right] = \exp\left[\frac{e^{-rx} - 1}{r}\right]$

Then $S(0) = 1$, as required, but $\lim_{x \to \infty} S(x) = e^{-1/r} \neq 0$, as required for a survival distribution.

3-4 To be a valid survival model, we require $S_X(0) = 1$, $\lim_{x \to \infty} S_X(x) = 0$, and that $S_X(x)$ be a non-increasing function.

(a) This $S_X(x)$ does not qualify; although $S_X(0) = 1$ and $\lim_{x \to \infty} S_X(x) = 0$, as required, we find

$$S'_X(x) = e^{[x - .70(2^x - 1)]} \cdot \left(1 - .70(2^x)(\ln 2)\right)$$

and

$$S'_X(0) = 1 - .70(\ln 2) = .5148,$$

so $S_X(x)$ is an increasing function near $x = 0$.

(b) This $S_X(x)$ does qualify, since
$$S_X(0) = 1^{-2} = 1,$$
$$\lim_{x \to \infty} S_X(x) = \lim_{x \to \infty} (1+x)^{-2} = 0,$$
and
$$S'_X(x) = -2(1+x)^{-3} < 0,$$
so $S_X(x)$ is a decreasing function.

Chapter Three

(c) This $S_X(x)$ also qualifies, since

$$S_X(0) = e^0 = 1,$$

$$\lim_{x \to \infty} S_X(x) = \lim_{x \to \infty} e^{-x^2} = 0,$$

and

$$S_X'(x) = -2x \cdot e^{-x^2} < 0,$$

so $S_X(x)$ is a decreasing function.

3-5 If X is uniform over $(1,3)$, then $f(x) = \frac{1}{2}$ and $E[X] = 2$.

$$E[X^2] = \int_1^3 x^2 \cdot f(x)\,dx = \frac{1}{2}\int_1^3 x^2\,dx = \frac{1}{6}x^3 \Big|_1^3 = \frac{13}{3}$$

Then $Var(X) = \frac{13}{3} - (2)^2 = \frac{13}{3} - \frac{12}{3} = \frac{1}{3}$.

3-6 (a) $S_Y(y) = Pr(Y > y)$

$ = Pr(X_1 > y \text{ and } X_2 > y)$

$ = Pr(X_1 > y) \cdot Pr(X_2 > y) = S_{X_1}(y) \cdot S_{X_2}(y)$

(b) $F_Z(z) = Pr(Z \le z) = Pr(X_1 \le z \text{ and } X_2 \le z)$

$ = Pr(X_1 \le z) \cdot Pr(X_2 \le z)$

$ = F_{X_1}(z) \cdot F_{X_2}(z)$

(c) If $S_{X_1}(y) = e^{-\lambda_1 y}$ and $S_{X_2}(y) = e^{-\lambda_2 y}$, then $S_Y(y) = e^{-(\lambda_1 + \lambda_2)y}$, which is clearly an exponential distribution. We also have $F_{X_1}(z) = 1 - e^{-\lambda_1 z}$ and $F_{X_2}(z) = 1 - e^{-\lambda_2 z}$. Then

$$F_z(z) = 1 - e^{-\lambda_1 z} - e^{-\lambda_2 z} + e^{-(\lambda_1 + \lambda_2)z},$$

which is *not* the CDF of an exponential distribution.

3-7 Using the results of Exercise 3-6, where $S_Y(y)$ and $S_Z(z)$ were defined, we have
$$S_Y(2) = e^{-2(\lambda_1+\lambda_2)} = .24$$
and
$$S_Z(2) = e^{-2\lambda_1} + e^{-2\lambda_2} - e^{-2(\lambda_1+\lambda_2)} = .86.$$

To simplify notation, let $e^{-2\lambda_1} = a$ and $e^{-2\lambda_2} = b$. Then our two equations are $ab = .24$ (so that $b = \frac{.24}{a}$), and $a+b-ab = .86$. Then
$$.86 = a + b(1-a) = a + \frac{.24}{a}(1-a),$$
so that
$$.86a = a^2 + .24(1-a).$$

This quadratic solves for $a = .30$ or $a = .80$. If $a = .80$, then $b = \frac{.24}{a} = .30$, and if $a = .30$, then $b = .80$. We know that $\lambda_1 > \lambda_2$, so therefore $a < b$, so we must have $a = .30$. Thus $a = e^{-2\lambda_1} = .30$, so $-2\lambda_1 = \ln(.30)$, and $\lambda_1 = -\frac{1}{2}\ln(.30) = .60199$.

3-8 The information we seek about $_m|q_0$ is revealed by the sign of $\frac{d}{dm}{_m|q_0}$. Since $_m|q_0 = S(m) - S(m+1)$, then
$$\frac{d}{dm}{_m|q_0} = \frac{d}{dm}[S(m) - S(m+1)] = f(m+1) - f(m).$$

(a) For uniform, $f(x) = \frac{1}{\omega}$, a constant, so $f(m+1) - f(m) = 0$, so $_m|q_0$ is constant.

(b) For exponential $f(x) = \lambda e^{-\lambda x}$, so
$$f(m+1) - f(m) = \lambda e^{-\lambda(m+1)} - \lambda e^{-\lambda m} = \lambda e^{-\lambda m}(e^{-\lambda}-1).$$
Since $\lambda > 0$, then $e^\lambda > 1$, so $e^{-\lambda} < 1$, so $(e^{-\lambda}-1) < 0$, so $_m|q_0$ is decreasing.

(c) $f(x) = .00125x$, so clearly $f(m+1) - f(m) = .00125 > 0$, so $_m|q_0$ is increasing.

3-9 (a) (i) $E[X] = \int_0^\infty x \cdot f(x)\,dx = \int_0^\infty \frac{1}{2^{r/2}\Gamma\left(\frac{1}{2}r\right)} x^{r/2} e^{-x/2}\,dx$

Now $x^{r/2} = x^{1/2(r+2)-1}$, $2^{r/2} = 2^{1/2(r+2)-1}$, and

$\Gamma\left(\frac{1}{2}r\right) = \dfrac{\Gamma\left(\frac{1}{2}r+1\right)}{\frac{1}{2}r}$, so we have

$E[X] = \int_0^\infty \dfrac{1}{2^{1/2(r+2)} \cdot 2^{-1} \cdot \frac{\Gamma\left(\frac{1}{2}r+1\right)}{\frac{1}{2}r}} x^{1/2(r+2)-1} e^{-x/2}\,dx$

$= (2)\left(\dfrac{r}{2}\right)\int_0^\infty \dfrac{1}{2^{1/2(r+2)}\Gamma\left(\frac{1}{2}r+1\right)} x^{1/2(r+2)-1} e^{-x/2}\,dx.$

We recognize the integrand as $f(x)$ for a Chi-square distribution with $r+2$ degrees of freedom, so the integral must be one. Thus $E[X] = r$.

(ii)

$E[X^2] = \int_0^\infty x^2 \cdot f(x)\,dx = \int_0^\infty \dfrac{1}{2^{r/2}\Gamma\left(\frac{1}{2}r\right)} x^{(r/2)+1} e^{-x/2}\,dx$

This time $x^{(r/2)+1} = x^{1/2(r+4)-1}$, $2^{r/2} = 2^{1/2(r+4)-2}$, and

$\Gamma\left(\frac{1}{2}r\right) = \dfrac{\Gamma\left(\frac{1}{2}r+2\right)}{\left(\frac{1}{2}r+1\right)\left(\frac{1}{2}r\right)}$, so we have

$E[X^2] = \int_0^\infty \dfrac{1}{2^{1/2(r+4)} \cdot 2^{-2} \cdot \frac{\Gamma\left(\frac{1}{2}r+2\right)}{\left(\frac{1}{2}r+1\right)\left(\frac{1}{2}r\right)}} x^{1/2(r+4)-1} e^{-x/2}\,dx$

$= 2^2 \left(\dfrac{1}{2}r\right)\left(\dfrac{1}{2}r+1\right)\int_0^\infty f(x)$ for χ^2 with $r+4$ d.f.

$= (r)(r+2)\cdot 1 = r^2 + 2r.$

Then $Var(X) = r^2 + 2r - (r)^2 = 2r.$

(iii) $E[X^{-1}] = \int_0^\infty x^{-1} \cdot f(x)\,dx = \int_0^\infty \dfrac{1}{2^{r/2}\,\Gamma\left(\frac{1}{2}r\right)}\, x^{(r/2)-2} e^{-x/2}\,dx$

This time
$$x^{(r/2)-2} = x^{1/2(r-2)-1},\quad 2^{r/2} = 2^{1/2(r-2)+1},$$
and
$$\Gamma\!\left(\tfrac{1}{2}r\right) = \left(\tfrac{1}{2}r-1\right)\cdot\Gamma\!\left(\tfrac{1}{2}r-1\right),$$
so we have

$$E[X^{-1}] = \int_0^\infty \dfrac{1}{2^{1/2(r-2)}\cdot 2\!\left(\frac{1}{2}r-1\right)\cdot\Gamma\!\left(\frac{1}{2}r-1\right)}\, x^{1/2(r-2)-1} e^{-x/2}\,dx$$

$$= \dfrac{1}{2\!\left(\frac{1}{2}r-1\right)}\int_0^\infty f(x)\,dx,\ \text{for } \chi^2 \text{ with } r-2 \text{ d.f.}$$

$$= \dfrac{1}{r-2}\cdot 1 = \dfrac{1}{r-2}.$$

(b) If $r = 2$, then $f(x) = \dfrac{1}{2^1\cdot\Gamma(1)}\,x^0 e^{-x/2} = \tfrac{1}{2}\cdot e^{-x/2}$, since $\Gamma(1) = x^0 = 1$. Now we recognize this as the PDF for an exponential distribution with $\lambda = \tfrac{1}{2}$. Since, for that distribution, $\lambda(x) = \lambda$, then we have $\lambda(x) = \tfrac{1}{2}$.

3-10 We recognize the Weibull distribution of Section 3.2.5, with SDF given by
$$S_X(x) = \exp\!\left[-\dfrac{k\cdot x^{n+1}}{n+1}\right].$$
The median is 22, so
$$S_X(22) = \exp\!\left[-\dfrac{k\cdot 22^{n+1}}{n+1}\right] = .50,$$
or
$$-\dfrac{k\cdot 22^{n+1}}{n+1} = \ln.50 = -.69315.$$

We are also given $\lambda(22) = k \cdot 22^n = 1.26$. Substituting, we have

$$.69315 = (k \cdot 22^n)\left(\frac{22}{n+1}\right) = (1.26)\left(\frac{22}{n+1}\right),$$

which solves for $n = 38.99$.

3-11 If X is uniform, then so is T_{16}. Given $T_{16} = \frac{\omega - 16}{2} = 42$ tells us that $\omega = 100$. Then

$$Var(T_{16}) = \frac{(100-16)^2}{12} = 588.$$

3-12 Recall that $q_{50} = \frac{S(50) - S(51)}{S(50)}$. Here we have

$$S(50) = \frac{9000 - 10(50) - (50)^2}{9000} = .66667$$

and

$$S(51) = \frac{9000 - 10(51) - (51)^2}{9000} = .65433,$$

so

$$q_{50} = \frac{.66667 - .65433}{.66667} = .01850.$$

Then recall that $\mu_{50} = \left.\frac{-\frac{d}{dx}S(x)}{S(x)}\right|_{x=50}$. Here we have

$$\frac{d}{dx}S(x) = \frac{-10 - 2x}{9000},$$

so

$$\mu_{50} = \frac{\frac{10+2(50)}{9000}}{.66667} = .01833.$$

Finally

$$q_{50} - \mu_{50} = .01850 - .01833 = .00016 = \frac{1}{6000}.$$

3-13 Recall that
$$_tp_x = e^{-\int_0^t \mu_{x+r}\, dr} = e^{-\int_0^{x+t} \mu_y\, dy}.$$

Here
$$_{10}p_{35} = .81 = e^{-\int_{35}^{45} ky\, dy}$$
$$= e^{-\left[\frac{1}{2}k(45)^2 - \frac{1}{2}k(35)^2\right]} = e^{-400k},$$

and
$$_{20}p_{40} = e^{-\int_{40}^{60} ky\, dy}$$
$$= e^{-\left[\frac{1}{2}k(60)^2 - \frac{1}{2}k(40)^2\right]}$$
$$= e^{-1000k}$$
$$= \left(e^{-400k}\right)^{2.5} = (.81)^{2.5} = .59049.$$

3-14 First note that
$$\mu_y = \frac{-\frac{d}{dy}S(y)}{S(y)} = \frac{\frac{r}{\omega}\left(1 - \frac{y}{\omega}\right)^{r-1}}{\left(1 - \frac{y}{\omega}\right)^r} = \frac{r}{\omega - y}$$

and
$$\overset{o}{e}_y = \int_0^{\omega-y} {}_tp_y\, dt$$
$$= \int_0^{\omega-y} \frac{S(y+t)}{S(y)}\, dt$$
$$= \int_0^{\omega-y} \frac{(\omega-y-t)^r}{(\omega-y)^r}\, dt = -\frac{(\omega-y-t)^{r+1}}{(r+1)(\omega-y)^r}\bigg|_0^{\omega-y} = \frac{\omega-y}{r+1}.$$

Then we have $\frac{r}{\omega-y} = .10$, so $\omega - y = 10r$, and
$$\overset{o}{e}_y = \frac{\omega-y}{r+1} = \frac{10r}{r+1} = 8.75,$$

which solves for $r = \frac{8.75}{1.25} = 7$.

CHAPTER THREE

3-15 The median of the distribution of T_{20} is the value of t for which ${}_tp_{20} = .50$. Here we have

$${}_tp_{20} = e^{-\int_{20}^{20+t}(80-x)^{-1/2}\,dx}$$

$$= e^{2(80-x)^{1/2}\big|_{20}^{20+t}} = e^{2(60-t)^{1/2} - 2(60)^{1/2}} = .50.$$

Then

$$2(60-t)^{1/2} - 2(60)^{1/2} = \ln .50$$

or

$$(60-t)^{1/2} = \frac{\ln .50 + 2(60)^{1/2}}{2} = 7.39939$$

or

$$t = 60 - (7.39939)^2 = 5.24898.$$

3-16 First recall that

$${}_tp_x = \frac{S(x+t)}{S(x)} = \frac{(k^2 - x - t)^{1/2}}{(k^2 - x)^{1/2}} = \left(1 - \frac{t}{k^2 - x}\right)^{1/2}.$$

Then

$$\overset{\circ}{e}_x = \int_0^{k^2 - x} {}_tp_x\,dt$$

$$= \int_0^{k^2 - x} \left(1 - \frac{t}{k^2 - x}\right)^{1/2} dt$$

$$= -\frac{2}{3}\left(1 - \frac{t}{k^2 - x}\right)^{3/2} (k^2 - x)\Big|_0^{k^2 - x} = \frac{2}{3}(k^2 - x).$$

Now we use $\overset{\circ}{e}_{40} = 2 \cdot \overset{\circ}{e}_{80}$ to write

$$\frac{2}{3}(k^2 - 40) = \frac{4}{3}(k^2 - 80),$$

which solves for $k^2 = 120$. Finally,

$$\overset{\circ}{e}_{60} = \frac{2}{3}(k^2 - 60) = \frac{2}{3}(120 - 60) = 40.$$

3-17 First we seek the median, which is the value of m such that $S(m) = 1 - \frac{m^2}{10,000} = \frac{1}{2}$. This gives $m^2 = 5000$, or $m = 50\sqrt{2}$. We now need the survival distribution truncated below at m, which is

$$S(x \mid X > m) = \frac{S(x)}{S(m)} = \frac{10,000 - x^2}{10,000 - m^2},$$

from which we find

$$f(x \mid X > m) = -\frac{d}{dx} S(x \mid X > m) = \frac{2x}{10,000 - m^2}.$$

Then the expected age at death is

$$E[X \mid X > m] = \int_m^{100} x \cdot f(x \mid X > m)\, dx$$

$$= \int_m^{100} \frac{2x^2}{10,000 - m^2}\, dx = \frac{\frac{2}{3}(1,000,000 - m^3)}{10,000 - m^2}.$$

Since $m = 50\sqrt{2}$, this evaluates to

$$E[X \mid X > m] = \frac{\frac{2}{3}(1,000,000 - 250,000\sqrt{2})}{5000} = 86.19288.$$

Finally, the expected future lifetime at m is the expected age at death, minus m, producing 15.4822.

3-18 Note first that $S(0) = b = 1$. Then $_2p_0 = S(2) = 2a + 1 = .75$, so $a = -.125$, and thus $S(x) = 1 - \frac{x}{8}$. Now

$$f(x) = S(x) \cdot \lambda(x) = -\frac{d}{dx} S(x) = \frac{1}{8}.$$

Then from (5.58),

$$_2m_3 = \frac{\int_3^5 S(y) \cdot \lambda(y)\, dy}{\int_3^5 S(y)\, dy} = \frac{\int_3^5 \frac{1}{8}\, dy}{\int_3^5 \left(1 - \frac{y}{8}\right) dy} = \frac{\frac{1}{4}}{2 - \frac{25}{16} + \frac{9}{16}} = \frac{1}{4}.$$

CHAPTER THREE

3-19 If X is uniform, then $\mu_x = \frac{1}{\omega - x}$ and

$$_tp_x = \frac{S(x+t)}{S(x)} = 1 - \frac{t}{\omega - x},$$

so that $_tp_x \cdot \mu_{x+t} = \frac{1}{\omega - x}$. From Equation (3.62) we have

$$m_x = \frac{\int_0^1 {}_tp_x \mu_{x+t}\, dt}{\int_0^1 {}_tp_x\, dt}$$

$$= \frac{\int_0^1 \frac{1}{\omega - x}\, dt}{\int_0^1 \frac{\omega - x - t}{\omega - x}\, dt}$$

$$= \frac{\int_0^1 dt}{\int_0^1 (\omega - x - t)\, dt} = \frac{1}{\omega - x - .50}.$$

Then

$$\frac{m_x}{1 + .50 m_x} = \frac{1}{\frac{1}{m_x} + .50} = \frac{1}{\omega - x - .50 + .50} = \frac{1}{\omega - x} = \mu_x,$$

as required.

3-20 The numerator of Equation (3.62) is $_nq_x$, so we have

$$_nm_x = \frac{{}_nq_x}{\int_0^n {}_tp_x\, dt}.$$

Since $_tp_x \leq 1$, then $\int_0^n {}_tp_x\, dt \leq n$, so

$$_nm_x \geq \frac{{}_nq_x}{n},$$

as required. If no failures could occur between ages x and $x+n$, then $_tp_x = 1$ and the denominator equals n and the equality holds.

3-21 First note that $S(0) = a = 1$, so we have $S(x) = 1 - \left(\frac{x}{b}\right)^2$. The PDF of X is $-\frac{d}{dx}S(x) = \frac{2x}{b^2}$, so from Equation (5.61) we have

$$m_2 = \frac{\int_2^3 \frac{2y}{b^2} dy}{\int_2^3 \frac{b^2 - y^2}{b^2} dy}$$

$$= \frac{y^2 \big|_2^3}{b^2 y - \frac{1}{3} y^3 \big|_2^3}$$

$$= \frac{5}{b^2 - \frac{1}{3}(19)} = \frac{15}{3b^2 - 19} = \frac{15}{24,281},$$

so $3b^2 - 19 = 24,281$ which solves for $b = 90$.

3-22 First note that

$$S(x) = e^{-\int_0^x \lambda(y) dy}$$
$$= e^{-\int_0^x \frac{2}{y+1} dy}$$
$$= e^{-\ln(y+1)^2 \big|_0^x} = e^{-\ln(x+1)^2} = (x+1)^{-2},$$

so that $S(x) \cdot \lambda(x) = 2(x+1)^{-3}$. Then from Equation (3.61) we have

$$_a m_a = \frac{\int_a^{2a} 2(x+1)^{-3} dx}{\int_a^{2a} (x+1)^{-2} dx}$$

$$= \frac{-(x+1)^{-2} \big|_a^{2a}}{-(x+1)^{-1} \big|_a^{2a}}$$

$$= \frac{(a+1)^{-2} - (2a+1)^{-2}}{(a+1)^{-1} - (2a+1)^{-1}} = \frac{3a+2}{(a+1)(2a+1)}.$$

CHAPTER THREE

3-23 (a) $\;_4p_{[30]} = S_T(4;30) = 1 - \dfrac{4}{40-30} = .60$

(b) $\overset{\circ}{e}_{[30]} = \displaystyle\int_0^{10} S_T(t;30)\, dt$

$= \displaystyle\int_0^{10} \left(1 - \dfrac{t}{10}\right) dt$

$= \left. t - \dfrac{t^2}{20} \right|_0^{10} = 5$

(c) $\mu_{[20]+t} = \dfrac{-\frac{d}{dt} S_T(t;20)}{S_T(t;20)} = \dfrac{-\frac{d}{dt}\left(1 - \frac{t}{20}\right)}{1 - \frac{t}{20}} = \dfrac{\frac{1}{20}}{1 - \frac{t}{20}} = \dfrac{1}{20 - t}$

3-24 In general,

$$S_T(t;x) = \exp\left[-\int_0^t \lambda_T(u;x)\, du\right].$$

Here we have

$S_T(t;x) = \exp\left[-\displaystyle\int_0^t B \cdot r^u \cdot c^{x+u}\, du\right]$

$= \exp\left[-\displaystyle\int_0^t B \cdot c^x \cdot (rc)^u\, du\right]$

$= \exp\left[-\left(\dfrac{B \cdot c^x \cdot (rc)^u}{\ln(rc)}\right)_0^t\right]$

$= \exp\left[-\left(\dfrac{B \cdot c^x \cdot (rc)^t - B \cdot c^x}{\ln r + \ln c}\right)\right]$

$= \exp\left[\dfrac{B}{\ln r + \ln c}\left(c^x - r^t c^{x+t}\right)\right],$

as required.

CHAPTER FOUR
THE LIFE TABLE
(DISCRETE TABULAR CONTEXT)

4-1 (a) Each $S(x)$ is calculated by $S(x) = S(x-1) \cdot p_{x-1}$, with $S(0) = 1$. Then $S(1) = p_0 = .90$, $S(2) = S(1) \cdot p_1 = .72$, and so on.

(b) Each ℓ_x is found from $\ell_x = \ell_0 \cdot S(x)$, where $\ell_0 = 10,000$. Then $\ell_1 = (10,000)(.90) = 9000$, $\ell_2 = (10,000)(.72) = 7200$, and so on. Each d_x is found from $d_x = \ell_x - \ell_{x+1}$. Then $d_0 = \ell_0 - \ell_1 = 1000$, $d_1 = \ell_1 - \ell_2 = 1800$, and so on.

(c) $S(x) = 0$ is first reached age $x = 5$, and that defines $\omega = 5$.

(d) From the answers,
$$\sum_{x=0}^{4} d_x = (1000+1800+2880+3024+1296) = 10,000.$$

4-2 (a) $_3d_0 = \ell_0 - \ell_3 = 5680$

(b) $_2q_1 = \dfrac{\ell_1 - \ell_3}{\ell_1} = .52$

(c) $_3p_1 = \dfrac{\ell_4}{\ell_1} = .144$

(d) $_3q_2 = \dfrac{\ell_2 - \ell_5}{\ell_2} = 1.00$, since $\ell_5 = 0$.

4-3 (a) This probability is given by $\int_x^{x+1} f(y)\,dy$, which is $F(x+1) - F(x) = S(x) - S(x+1)$. Since $\ell_x = \ell_0 \cdot S(x)$, then $S(x) = \dfrac{\ell_x}{\ell_0}$, so $_x|q_0 = \dfrac{\ell_x - \ell_{x+1}}{\ell_0} = \dfrac{d_x}{\ell_0}$.

(b) $\sum_{x=0}^{\omega-1} {}_x|q_0 = \sum_{x=0}^{\omega-1} \frac{d_x}{\ell_0}$. Since $\sum_{x=0}^{\omega-1} d_x = \ell_0$ (from Exercise 4-1(d)),

then $\sum_{x=0}^{\omega-1} {}_x|q_0 = 1$. (Note that the values of ${}_x|q_0$ are the probabilities of mutually exclusive events.)

4-4 (a) First we see that $\ell_{35} = \ell_0 \cdot S(35) = (100,000)\left(\frac{c-35}{c+35}\right) = 44,000$.
Thus $c - 35 = .44(c+35)$, so $c = \omega = 90$.

(b) This probability is given directly by $S(60) = \frac{90-60}{90+60} = .20$.

(c) This probability is given by

$${}_{20}|_{15}q_{10} = \frac{S(30) - S(45)}{S(10)} = \frac{\frac{60}{120} - \frac{45}{135}}{\frac{80}{100}} = \frac{1/6}{4/5} = \frac{5}{24}.$$

4-5 First we find, in general,

$$-\int_0^x \mu_y \, dy = -\int_0^x \frac{2}{y+1} + \frac{2}{100-y} \, dy$$

$$= -2 \cdot \ln(y+1) + 2 \cdot \ln(100-y)\Big|_0^x$$

$$= \ln\left(\frac{100-y}{y+1}\right)^2 \Big|_0^x = \ln\left(\frac{100-x}{100(x+1)}\right)^2.$$

From (4.10), $\ell_x = \ell_0 \cdot \exp\left[-\int_0^x \mu_y \, dy\right]$. Thus $\ell_1 = 10,000\left(\frac{99}{200}\right)^2$
and $\ell_4 = 10,000\left(\frac{96}{500}\right)^2$. Then

$${}_3d_1 = \ell_1 - \ell_4 = 10,000\left[(.495)^2 - (.192)^2\right] = 2081.61.$$

4-6 (a) From (4.8a), $-\frac{d}{dt}\ell_{x+t} = \ell_{x+t}\mu_{x+t}$, so, dividing both sides by $-\ell_x$, $\frac{d}{dt}{}_tp_x = -{}_tp_x\mu_{x+t}$.

(b) $\frac{d}{dx}{}_tp_x = \frac{d}{dx}\frac{\ell_{x+t}}{\ell_x} = \frac{\ell_x \cdot \frac{d}{dx}\ell_{x+t} - \ell_{x+t} \cdot \frac{d}{dx}\ell_x}{(\ell_x)^2}$

$= \frac{\ell_x(-\ell_{x+t}\mu_{x+t}) - \ell_{x+t}(-\ell_x\mu_x)}{(\ell_x)^2}$

$= \frac{\ell_{x+t}\mu_x - \ell_{x+t}\mu_{x+t}}{\ell_x}$

$= {}_tp_x(\mu_x - \mu_{x+t})$

4-7 $\frac{d}{dx}\ell_x \approx \frac{\ell_{x+1} - \ell_{x-1}}{2}$, so $\mu_x = \frac{-\frac{d}{dx}\ell_x}{\ell_x} \approx \frac{\ell_{x-1} - \ell_{x+1}}{2 \cdot \ell_x}$.

Then $\mu_2 \approx \frac{\ell_1 - \ell_3}{2 \cdot \ell_2} = \frac{248}{2(97,259)} = .0012749$.

4-8 Recall that ${}_tp_x = e^{-\int_0^t \mu_{x+r}\, dr}$. Here

$${}_{.40}p_0 = e^{-\int_0^{40}(k+e^{2x})\, dx}$$

$$= e^{-(kx + .50e^{2x})\big|_0^{40}}$$

$$= e^{-(.40k + .50e^{80} - .50)}$$

$$= e^{-(.40k + .61277)} = .50.$$

Then
$$-(.40k + .61277) = \ln .50 = -.69315,$$
so
$$k = \frac{.69315 - .61277}{.40} = .20094.$$

4-9 (a) Note that $\omega = 80$ and $\ell_0 = 2500(64)^{1/3} = 10,000$. From (4.11), we have

$$f(x) = \frac{\ell_x \mu_x}{\ell_0} = \frac{-\frac{d}{dx}\ell_x}{\ell_0}$$

$$= \frac{1}{10,000}\left[-\frac{1}{3}(2500)(64-.80x)^{-2/3}(-.80)\right]$$

$$= \frac{1}{15}(64-.80x)^{-2/3}.$$

(b) We find

$$T_0 = \int_0^{80} \ell_x \, dx = 2500(64-.80x)^{4/3}\left(\frac{3}{4}\right)\left(-\frac{10}{8}\right)\Big|_0^{80}$$

$$= \left(\frac{3}{4}\right)\left(\frac{10}{8}\right)(2500)(64)^{4/3} = 600,000.$$

Then $E[X] = \overset{\circ}{e}_0 = \dfrac{T_0}{\ell_0} = 60.$

(c) $T_x = \int_x^{80} \ell_y \, dy = (2343.75)(64-.80x)^{4/3}.$ Then

$$Y_0 = \int_0^{80} T_x \, dx = (2343.75)\left(\frac{3}{7}\right)(64-.80x)^{7/3}\left(-\frac{10}{8}\right)\Big|_0^{80}$$

$$= (2343.75)\left(\frac{3}{7}\right)\left(\frac{10}{8}\right)(64)^{7/3} = 20,571,429,$$

and from (4.22), $\mathrm{Var}(X) = \dfrac{2 \cdot Y_0}{\ell_0} - (\overset{\circ}{e}_0)^2 = 514.2875.$

4-10 (a) $\dfrac{d}{dx}\left(\dfrac{T_x}{\ell_x}\right) = \dfrac{\ell_x \cdot \frac{d}{dx} T_x - T_x \cdot \frac{d}{dx}\ell_x}{(\ell_x)^2}$

$$= \frac{(\ell_x)(-\ell_x) - T_x(-\ell_x \mu_x)}{(\ell_x)^2} = -1 + \frac{T_x \mu_x}{\ell_x}.$$

(b) $\dfrac{d}{dx}(\ln T_x) = \dfrac{1}{T_x} \cdot \dfrac{d}{dx} T_x = \dfrac{1}{T_x} \cdot -\ell_x = -\dfrac{\ell_x}{T_x} = -\dfrac{1}{\overset{\circ}{e}_x}.$

CHAPTER FOUR

4-11 The survival model is uniform. The fact that $\overset{\circ}{e}_0 = 25$ tells us that $\omega = 50$. Then T_{10} is uniform over $(0, 40)$, so its variance is
$$\frac{(40)^2}{12} = 133.3\dot{3}.$$

4-12 First we note that $p_{x+1} = \dfrac{\ell_{x+2}}{\ell_{x+1}} = .80$, so $\ell_{x+1} = \dfrac{\ell_{x+2}}{.80} = \dfrac{6.40}{.80} = 8.00$.

Then
$$\ell_y = \ell_{x+1} \cdot {}_{y-x-1}p_{x+1} = 8(.80)^{y-x-1},$$

so
$$T_{x+1} = \int_{x+1}^{\infty} \ell_y \, dy = 8\int_{x+1}^{\infty} (.80)^{y-x-1} \, dy$$
$$= \frac{8(.80)^{y-x-1}}{\ln(.80)}\bigg|_{x+1}^{\infty}$$
$$= \frac{-8}{\ln(.80)} = 35.85.$$

4-13 We are given
$$_{1|}q_{x+1} = p_{x+1}(1-p_{x+2}) = p_{x+1} - p_{x+1} \cdot p_{x+2} = .095$$

and
$$_{2|}q_{x+1} = p_{x+1} \cdot p_{x+2} \cdot q_{x+3} = .171.$$

Substituting $q_{x+3} = .200$ in the second equation gives
$$p_{x+1} \cdot p_{x+2} = \frac{.171}{.200} = .855.$$

Substituting this value in the first equation gives
$$p_{x+1} = .095 + .855 = .950,$$

so
$$p_{x+2} = \frac{.855}{.950} = .900.$$

Finally,
$$q_{x+1} + q_{x+2} = (1-.950) + (1-.900) = .15.$$

4-14 Note the first that $_sp_x = \dfrac{\ell_{x+s}}{\ell_x} = \dfrac{[64-.8(x+s)]^{1/3}}{(64-.8x)^{1/3}} = \left(1 - \dfrac{.8s}{64-.8x}\right)^{1/3}$,

so that $_sp_{70} = (1-.1s)^{1/3}$. From (4.28a),

$$\overset{\circ}{e}_{70} = \int_0^{10} {}_sp_{70}\, ds = \left(\dfrac{3}{4}\right)(1-.1s)^{4/3}(-10)\Big|_0^{10} = \left(\dfrac{30}{4}\right)(1)^{4/3} = 7.50.$$

From Exercise 4-9, $T_x = 2343.75(64-.80x)^{4/3}$. From (4.30),

$$Y_{70} = \int_{70}^{80} T_x\, dx = (2343.75)\left(\dfrac{3}{7}\right)\left(\dfrac{-10}{8}\right)(64-.80x)^{7/3}\Big|_{70}^{80}$$

$$= (2343.75)\left(\dfrac{3}{7}\right)\left(\dfrac{10}{8}\right)(8)^{7/3} = 160,714.29.$$

Then

$$Var(T_{70}) = \dfrac{2 \cdot Y_{70}}{\ell_{70}} - (\overset{\circ}{e}_{70})^2 = \dfrac{2(160,714.29)}{5000} - (7.50)^2 = 8.03571.$$

4-15 $\overset{II\,\circ}{e}_x = \int_0^\infty {}^{II}_t p_x\, dt = \int_0^\infty \left[\exp\left(-\int_x^{x+t} {}^{II}\mu_y\, dy\right)\right] dt$

$\phantom{\overset{II\,\circ}{e}_x} = \int_0^\infty \left[\exp\left(-\int_x^{x+t} {}^{I}\mu_y + \dfrac{{}^I\ell_y}{{}^IT_y}\, dy\right)\right] dt$

$\phantom{\overset{II\,\circ}{e}_x} = \int_0^\infty \left[{}^I_t p_x \cdot \exp\left(-\int_x^{x+t} \dfrac{-\frac{d}{dy}{}^IT_y}{{}^IT_y}\, dy\right)\right] dt$

$\phantom{\overset{II\,\circ}{e}_x} = \int_0^\infty \left[\dfrac{{}^I\ell_{x+t}}{{}^I\ell_x} \cdot \dfrac{{}^IT_{x+t}}{{}^IT_x}\right] dt$

$\phantom{\overset{II\,\circ}{e}_x} = \dfrac{-1}{{}^I\ell_x \cdot {}^IT_x} \int_0^\infty {}^IT_{x+t}(-{}^I\ell_{x+t})\, dt$

$\phantom{\overset{II\,\circ}{e}_x} = \dfrac{-\frac{1}{2}({}^IT_{x+t})^2}{{}^I\ell_x \cdot {}^IT_x}\Big|_0^\infty = \dfrac{\frac{1}{2} \cdot {}^IT_x}{{}^I\ell_x} = \dfrac{1}{2} \cdot {}^I\overset{\circ}{e}_x.$

CHAPTER FOUR

4-16 Under the existing model, $\overset{\circ}{e}_{30} = 35$, since T_{30} is uniform with $\omega = 100$. Under the revised model, $\overset{\circ}{e}_{30} = 39$ and T_{30} is still uniform. Thus the maximum future lifetime is $2(39) = 78$ so the limiting age is $\omega = 30+78 = 108$.

4-17 When μ_x is constant, then ${}_tp_x = e^{-\mu t}$ since the future lifetime is exponential. Here we have ${}_tp_{25} = e^{-.04t}$, for $0 < t \leq 15$, and

$${}_tp_{25} = {}_{15}p_{25} \cdot {}_{t-15}p_{40} = e^{-(.04)(15)} \cdot e^{-(.05)(t-15)},$$

for $t > 15$. Then

$$\begin{aligned}
\overset{\circ}{e}_{25:\overline{25|}} &= \int_0^{25} {}_tp_{25}\, dt = \int_0^{15} e^{-.04t}\, dt + \int_{15}^{25} e^{-.60} \cdot e^{-(.05)(t-15)}\, dt \\
&= \int_0^{15} e^{-.04t}\, dt + e^{-.60} \cdot e^{.75} \int_{15}^{25} e^{-.05t}\, dt \\
&= \left.\frac{e^{-.04t}}{-.04}\right|_0^{15} + e^{.15}\left(\left.\frac{e^{-.05t}}{-.05}\right|_{15}^{25}\right) \\
&= \frac{1-e^{-.60}}{.04} + e^{.15}\left(\frac{e^{-.75} - e^{-1.25}}{.05}\right) \\
&= 11.27971 + (1.16183)(3.71724) = 15.59852.
\end{aligned}$$

4-18 From (4.33), $e_x = \sum_{k=1}^{\infty} {}_kp_x = p_x + {}_2p_x + {}_3p_x + \cdots$

$$= p_x + p_x \cdot p_{x+1} + p_x \cdot {}_2p_{x+1} + \cdots$$

$$= p_x\left[1 + \sum_{k=1}^{\infty} {}_kp_{x+1}\right] = p_x(1+e_{x+1}).$$

4-19 Since $\dfrac{1+e_x}{1+e'_x}=1+k$ for all x, then $\dfrac{1+e_{x+1}}{1+e'_{x+1}}=1+k$ as well. Using the identity from Exercise 4-18, we have

$$\dfrac{1+p_x(1+e_{x+1})}{1+p'_x(1+e'_{x+1})} = 1+k = \dfrac{1+e_{x+1}}{1+e'_{x+1}}.$$

Then

$$(1+e'_{x+1}) + p_x(1+e_{x+1})(1+e'_{x+1}) = (1+e_{x+1}) + p'_x(1+e'_{x+1})(1+e_{x+1}).$$

Then

$$(p_x - p'_x)(1+e_{x+1})(1+e'_{x+1}) = e_{x+1} - e'_{x+1},$$

so

$$p_x - p'_x = \dfrac{e_{x+1} - e'_{x+1}}{(1+e_{x+1})(1+e'_{x+1})} = 1 - q_x - 1 + q'_x.$$

Then

$$q'_x = q_x + \dfrac{e_{x+1} - e'_{x+1}}{(1+e_{x+1})(1+e'_{x+1})}.$$

Now

$$k = \dfrac{1+e_{x+1}}{1+e'_{x+1}} - 1 = \dfrac{e_{x+1} - e'_{x+1}}{1+e'_{x+1}},$$

so we have

$$q'_x = q_x + \dfrac{k}{1+e_{x+1}}.$$

4-20 Note that

$$\dfrac{d}{dx} L_x = \dfrac{d}{dx}(T_x - T_{x+1}) = -\ell_x + \ell_{x+1} = -d_x.$$

Then

$$m_x = \dfrac{d_x}{L_x} = \dfrac{-\frac{d}{dx}L_x}{L_x} = -\dfrac{d}{dx}\ln L_x,$$

so

$$d\ln L_x = -m_x\, dx,$$

and

$$\int_x^{x+1} d\ln L_y = -\int_x^{x+1} m_y\, dy.$$

The left side becomes

$$\ln L_{x+1} - \ln L_x = \ln \frac{L_{x+1}}{L_x},$$

so we have

$$\ln \frac{L_{x+1}}{L_x} = -\int_x^{x+1} m_y \, dy,$$

and

$$L_{x+1} = L_x \cdot \exp\left[-\int_x^{x+1} m_y \, dy\right].$$

4-21 $_{10}m_{70} = \dfrac{_{10}d_{70}}{_{10}L_{70}} = \dfrac{\ell_{70} - \ell_{80}}{T_{70} - T_{80}} = \dfrac{\ell_{70}}{T_{70}}$, since $\ell_{80} = T_{80} = 0$. Clearly

$_{10}m_{70}$ is the reciprocal of $\overset{\circ}{e}_{70}$, as found in Exercise 4-14, so

$$_{10}m_{70} = \frac{1}{7.50} = \frac{2}{15}.$$

4-22 (a) $\dfrac{\partial}{\partial x} {}_nL_x = \dfrac{\partial}{\partial x}[T_x - T_{x+n}] = -\ell_x + \ell_{x+n} = -{}_nd_x$

(b) $\dfrac{\partial}{\partial n} {}_nL_x = \dfrac{\partial}{\partial n}[T_x - T_{x+n}] = 0 + \ell_{x+n} = \ell_{x+n}$

4-23 From Equation (4.26) we have

$$\mu_{x+r} = \frac{-\dfrac{d}{dr} {}_rp_x}{{}_rp_x} = -\frac{d}{dr} \ln {}_rp_x.$$

Integrating both sides from 0 to t we have

$$\int_0^t \mu_{x+r} \, dr = -\int_0^t d\ln {}_rp_x,$$

so $-\int_0^t \mu_{x+r} \, dr = \ln {}_rp_x\Big|_0^t = \ln {}_tp_x - \ln {}_0p_x = \ln {}_tp_x,$

since $\ln {}_0p_x = \ln 1 = 0$. Finally,

$$_tp_x = e^{-\int_0^t \mu_{x+r} \, dr}.$$

4-24 (a) Under the linear assumption, $_{1/2}q_x = \frac{1}{2} \cdot q_x$ and

$$_{1/2}q_{x+1/2} = \frac{\frac{1}{2} \cdot q_x}{1 - \frac{1}{2} \cdot q_x}.$$ Since $1 - \frac{1}{2} \cdot q_x < 1$, it follows that

$_{1/2}q_x < {}_{1/2}q_{x+1/2}$.

(b) $_{1-t}p_x \cdot {}_t q_{x+1-t} = [1-(1-t)q_x] \cdot \frac{t \cdot q_x}{1-(1-t)q_x}$, and $_t q_x = t \cdot q_x$, so the relationship is clearly true.

(c) $\mu_{x+t} = \frac{q_x}{1 - t \cdot q_x}$ and $_t q_x = t \cdot q_x$. The denominator of μ_{x+t} is less than one, so $\mu_{x+t} > q_x$. Since $0 < t < 1$, then $_t q_x < q_x$, so $\mu_{x+t} > {}_t q_x$.

4-25 Let T_x be the random variable for the complete future lifetime of a person aged x, and let $K = K(x)$ be the random variable for the curtate future lifetime. Then $T_x = K+S$, from (3.59b). Under UDD, we know from (4.48) that $E[T_x] = E[K] + \frac{1}{2}$. We also know that $Var(T_x) = Var(K) + \frac{1}{12}$, since S is uniform over $(0,1)$. From (4.33) we have $E[K] = \sum_{k=1}^{\infty} {}_k p_x = \sum_{k=0}^{\infty} {}_{k+1} p_x$. By a similar development we can show that $E[K^2] = \sum_{k=0}^{\infty} (2k+1) \cdot {}_{k+1} p_x$. Therefore, under UDD, we have

$$\begin{aligned}
Var(T_x) &= Var(K) + \frac{1}{12} = E[K^2] - \{E[K]\}^2 + \frac{1}{12} \\
&= E[K^2] - \left\{ E[T_x] - \frac{1}{2} \right\}^2 + \frac{1}{12} \\
&= E[K^2] - \{E[T_x]\}^2 + E[T_x] - \frac{1}{4} + \frac{1}{12} \\
&= E[K^2] + E[T_x] - \frac{1}{6} - \{E[T_x]\}^2.
\end{aligned}$$

Chapter Four

Of course it is also true that $Var(T_x) = E[T_x^2] - \{E[T_x]\}^2$. Equating these two expressions for $Var(T_x)$, and solving for $E[T_x^2]$, we have

$$\begin{aligned}
E[T_x^2] &= E[K^2] + E[T_x] - \frac{1}{6} \\
&= E[K^2] + E[K] + \frac{1}{2} - \frac{1}{6} \\
&= \sum_{k=0}^{\infty} (2k+1) \cdot {}_{k+1}p_x + \sum_{k=0}^{\infty} {}_{k+1}p_x + \frac{2}{6} \\
&= 2 \cdot \sum_{k=0}^{\infty} (k+1) \cdot {}_{k+1}p_x + \frac{2}{6} \\
&= \frac{2}{\ell_x} \left[\sum_{k=0}^{\infty} (k+1) \cdot \ell_{x+k+1} + \frac{1}{6} \cdot \ell_x \right].
\end{aligned}$$

But, from (4.29), we have $E[T_x^2] = \frac{2 \cdot Y_x}{\ell_x}$. Equating this to our last expression for $E[T_x^2]$ directly gives us

$$Y_x = \sum_{k=0}^{\infty} (k+1) \cdot \ell_{x+k+1} + \frac{1}{6} \cdot \ell_x.$$

4-26 $\overset{o}{e}_{45:\overline{1}|} = \int_0^1 {}_t p_{45}\, dt = \int_0^1 (1 - t \cdot q_{45})\, dt = 1 - \frac{1}{2} \cdot q_{45}$

To find q_{45}, recall that

$$\mu_{45.5} = \frac{q_{45}}{1 - \frac{1}{2} \cdot q_{45}} = .50,$$

which solves for $q_{45} = .40$. Then

$$\overset{o}{e}_{45:\overline{1}|} = 1 - \frac{1}{2}(.40) = .80.$$

4-27 This time we have

$$\overset{o}{e}_{70:\overline{1.5|}} = \int_0^{1.5} {}_tp_{70}\, dt$$

$$= \int_0^1 {}_tp_{70}\, dt + p_{70}\int_0^{.50} {}_tp_{71}\, dt$$

$$= \int_0^1 (1-t\cdot q_{70})\, dt + p_{70}\int_0^{.50} (1-t\cdot q_{71})\, dt$$

$$= \left(t - \frac{1}{2}t^2\cdot q_{70}\right)\Big|_0^1 + p_{70}\left(t - \frac{1}{2}t^2\cdot q_{71}\right)\Big|_0^{.50}$$

$$= 1 - .50q_{70} + p_{70}(.50 - .125\, q_{71})$$

$$= 1 - (.50)(.040) + (.96)[.50 - (.125)(.044)]$$

$$= 1 - .02 + (.96)(.4945) = 1.45472.$$

4-28 First we use $\mu_{80.5} = \dfrac{q_{80}}{1 - .50 q_{80}} = .0202$ to solve for $q_{80} = .02$. Similarly we find $q_{81} = .04$ and $q_{82} = .06$. Arbitrarily let $\ell_{80} = 1000$, so

$$\ell_{81} = (.98)(1000) = 980,$$

$$\ell_{82} = (.96)(980) = 940.80,$$

and

$$\ell_{83} = (.94)(940.80) = 884.352.$$

Then

$$_2q_{80.5} = 1 - \frac{\ell_{82.5}}{\ell_{80.5}} = 1 - \frac{\frac{1}{2}(940.80 + 884.352)}{\frac{1}{2}(1000 + 980)}$$

$$= 1 - \frac{912.576}{990} = .07821.$$

4-29 This is the same as Exercise 4-27. We have

$$\overset{o}{e}_{1:\overline{1.5|}} = \int_0^{1.5} {}_tp_1\, dt = \int_0^1 {}_tp_1\, dt + p_1\int_0^{.50} {}_tp_2\, dt$$

$$= (t-.50t^2\cdot q_1)\Big|_0^1 + p_1(t-.50t^2\cdot q_2)\Big|_0^{.50}$$

$$= 1-.50q_1 + p_1[.50-.125q_2]$$

$$= 1-(.50)(.10)+(.90)[.50-(.125)(.05)]$$

$$= 1-.05+(.90)(.49375)$$

$$= 1.394375.$$

4-30 The exponential interpolation is given by (4.52a). Taking logs, we have $\log \ell_{x+t} = t\cdot \log \ell_{x+1} + (1-t)\cdot \log \ell_x$, which is clearly linear interpolation on the log of the ℓ_x function.

4-31 Exactly, $\mu_x = \dfrac{-\frac{d}{dx}\ell_x}{\ell_x} = \dfrac{500(100-x)^{-1/2}}{1000(100-x)^{1/2}} = \tfrac{1}{2}(100-x)^{-1}$. Then

$$\mu_{36.25} = \tfrac{1}{2}(63.75)^{-1} = .0078431.$$

Next note that
$$\ell_{36} = 1000(64)^{1/2} = 8000$$
and
$$\ell_{37} = 1000(63)^{1/2} = 7937.$$
Then
$$p_{36} = .992125 \text{ and } q_{36} = .007875.$$

Under linear, $\mu_{36.25} = \dfrac{q_{36}}{1-\frac{1}{4}\cdot q_{36}} = .0078905.$

Under exponential, $\mu_{36.25} = \mu = -\ln p_x = .0079061.$

Under hyperbolic, $\mu_{36.25} = \dfrac{q_{36}}{1-\frac{3}{4}\cdot q_{36}} = .0079218.$

4-32 $_2q_{x+1/2} = 1 - \dfrac{\ell_{x+5/2}}{\ell_{x+1/2}} = 1 - \dfrac{\ell_{x+2}(p_{x+2})^{1/2}}{\ell_x (p_x)^{1/2}}$, using exponential interpolation. Now

$$\ell_{x+2} = \ell_{x+1}(1-q_{x+1}) = (8100)(.75) = 6075,$$

and

$$d_{x+2} = L_{x+2} \cdot m_{x+2} = (6000)(.3645) = 2187.$$

Then

$$\ell_{x+3} = \ell_{x+2} - d_{x+2} = 3888.$$

This gives us

$$p_x = \dfrac{\ell_{x+1}}{\ell_x} = .81$$

and

$$p_{x+2} = \dfrac{\ell_{x+3}}{\ell_{x+2}} = .64.$$

Then $_2q_{x+1/2} = 1 - \dfrac{(6075)(.64)^{1/2}}{(10,000)(.81)^{1/2}} = 1 - \dfrac{(6075)(.80)}{(10,000)(.90)} = .46.$

4-33 We start with

$$\overset{\circ}{e}_{x:\overline{3}|} = \int_0^3 {}_tp_x\, dt$$

$$= \int_0^1 {}_tp_x\, dt + p_x \int_0^1 {}_tp_{x+1}\, dt + p_x \cdot p_{x+1} \int_0^1 {}_tp_{x+2}\, dt.$$

Under the constant force assumption,

$$\int_0^1 {}_tp_x\, dt = \int_0^1 (p_x)^t\, dt = \dfrac{(p_x)^t}{\ln p_x}\bigg|_0^1 = \dfrac{1-p_x}{-\ln p_x}.$$

But

$$p_x = e^{-\mu_x} \text{ and } \dfrac{1-p_x}{-\ln p_x} = \dfrac{1-e^{-\mu_x}}{\mu_x},$$

so

$$\overset{\circ}{e}_{x:\overline{3}|} = \dfrac{1-e^{-\mu_x}}{\mu_x} + e^{-\mu_x}\left(\dfrac{1-e^{-\mu_{x+1}}}{\mu_{x+1}}\right) + e^{-\mu_x} \cdot e^{-\mu_{x+1}}\left(\dfrac{1-e^{-\mu_{x+2}}}{\mu_{x+2}}\right)$$

$$= .9754 + (.9512)(.9744) + (.9512)(.9493)(.9730) = 2.78084.$$

CHAPTER FOUR

4-34 We seek the value of y such that $\dfrac{\ell_y}{\ell_{50}} = .50$, so $\ell_y = .50\ell_{50} = 40,000$. This shows us that $75 < y < 76$.

(a) Under uniform,

$$y = 75 + \frac{40,280 - 40,000}{40,280 - 37,480} = 75.10,$$

so the median future lifetime is 25.10.

(b) Under exponential,

$$\ell_{75+t} = (\ell_{76})^t \cdot (\ell_{75})^{1-t} = 40,000.$$

Then

$$t \cdot \ln \ell_{76} + (1-t) \cdot \ln \ell_{75} = \ln 40,000$$

and

$$t = \frac{\ln 40,000 - \ln 40,280}{\ln 37,480 - \ln 40,280} = .096811,$$

so the median future lifetime is 25.096811.

4-35 The given values of ℓ_x are calculated under the linear assumption, so all $\ell_{x+.50}$ values are midway between ℓ_x and ℓ_{x+1}. This tells us that $\ell_{97} = 360$ and $\ell_{98} = 216$. Then under the exponential assumption we have

$$\begin{aligned}
\ell_{97.5} &= (\ell_{97})^{.50} \cdot (\ell_{98})^{.50} \\
&= (360)^{.50}(216)^{.50} \\
&= (18.97367)(14.69694) \\
&= 278.85486.
\end{aligned}$$

4-36 The probability of failure is $q = 1-e^{-\mu}$, where μ is a realization of the random variable M which is uniform over (0,2). Therefore

$$\begin{aligned} q &= \int_0^2 (1-e^{-\mu}) \cdot f_M(\mu) \, d\mu \\ &= \frac{1}{2} \int_0^2 (1-e^{-\mu}) \, d\mu \\ &= \frac{1}{2} \left[\mu + e^{-\mu} \right]_0^2 \\ &= \frac{1}{2} (2 + e^{-2} - 1) = .56767. \end{aligned}$$

4-37 From Equation (3.59a) we have $T_x = K_x - 1 + S_x$, and from Equation (4.51b) we know that K_x and S_x are independent under the UDD assumption, so it follows that

$$Var(T_x \mid X > x) = Var(K_x \mid X > x) + Var(S_x \mid X > x).$$

But S_x has a uniform distribution over (0,1], with variance $\frac{1}{12}$, so the desired relationship follows.

4-38 Using Equation (4.62) we find

$$_{1-t}p_{x+t} = \frac{\ell_{x+1}}{\ell_{x+t}} = \ell_{x+1} \left[\frac{t}{\ell_{x+1}} + \frac{1-t}{\ell_x} \right] = t + (1-t) \cdot p_x,$$

so

$$_{1-t}q_{x+t} = 1 - {}_{1-t}p_{x+t} = 1 - t - (1-t)(1-q_x) = (1-t) \cdot q_x,$$

as required.

CHAPTER FOUR

4-39 $\mathring{e}_{[20]} = \dfrac{1}{\ell_{[20]}} \left[\int_0^4 \ell_{[20]+s} \, ds + \int_4^\infty \ell_{20+s} \, ds \right]$

$\qquad = \int_0^4 {}_sp_{[20]} \, ds + \dfrac{1}{\ell_{[20]}} \int_0^\infty \ell_{24+t} \, dt,$

by making the variable change $t = s - 4$ in the second integral. Then

$\mathring{e}_{[20]} = \int_0^4 {}_sp_{[20]} \, ds + \dfrac{1}{\ell_{[20]}} \int_0^\infty {}_tp_{24} \cdot \ell_{24} \, dt$

$\qquad = \int_0^4 {}_sp_{[20]} \, ds + \dfrac{\ell_{24}}{\ell_{[20]}} \int_0^\infty {}_tp_{24} \, dt = \mathring{e}_{[20]:\overline{4}|} + {}_4p_{[20]} \cdot \mathring{e}_{24}.$

4-40 First we diagram a three-year select table for reference:

$\ell_{[0]} \qquad\qquad \ell_{[0]+1} \qquad\qquad \ell_{[0]+2}$

$\qquad\qquad\qquad\qquad\qquad\qquad\qquad\qquad \ell_3$

$\qquad\qquad\qquad\qquad\qquad\qquad\qquad\qquad \ell_4$

$\qquad\qquad\qquad\qquad\qquad\qquad\qquad\qquad \ell_5$

$\qquad\qquad\qquad\qquad\qquad\qquad\qquad\qquad \ell_6$

Then ${}_5p_{[1]} = \dfrac{\ell_6}{\ell_{[1]}} = \dfrac{4}{5}$, so $\ell_{[1]} = \dfrac{5}{4} \cdot \ell_6 = 112{,}500.$

Next, ${}_3p_{[0]+1} = \dfrac{\ell_4}{\ell_{[0]+1}} = \dfrac{9}{10} \cdot \dfrac{\ell_4}{\ell_{[1]}},$

so $\ell_{[1]} = \dfrac{9}{10} \cdot \ell_{[0]+1}$, so $\ell_{[0]+1} = \dfrac{10}{9} \cdot \ell_{[1]} = 125{,}000.$ Finally,

$\ell_{[0]} \cdot p_{[0]} = \ell_{[0]+1}$, so $\ell_{[0]} = \dfrac{\ell_{[0]+1}}{1 - q_{[0]}} = \dfrac{125{,}000}{\frac{5}{6}} = 150{,}000.$

4-41 $.90q_{[60]+.60} = .40q_{[60]+.60} + (1-.40q_{[60]+.60}) \cdot .50q_{[60]+1}$

$$= \frac{.40q_{[60]}}{1-.60q_{[60]}} + \left(1 - \frac{.40q_{[60]}}{1-.60q_{[60]}}\right) \cdot .50q_{[60]+1}$$

Here

$$q_{[60]} = 1 - \frac{\ell_{[60]+1}}{\ell_{[60]}} = 1 - \frac{79,954}{80,625} = .00832248$$

and

$$q_{[60]+1} = 1 - \frac{\ell_{62}}{\ell_{[60]+1}} = 1 - \frac{78,839}{79,954} = .01394552,$$

so

$$.90q_{[60]+.60} = \frac{(.40)(.00832248)}{1-(.60)(.00832248)}$$

$$+ \left(1 - \frac{(.40)(.00832248)}{1-(.60)(.00832248)}\right)(.50)(.01394552)$$

$$= .0033457 + (1-.0033457)(.50)(.01394552) = .01029.$$

4-42 The person is age 61 on 1/1/01, so selection on 1/1/00 must have been at age 60. Thus we seek the value of

$$_5p_{[60]+1} = p_{[60]+1} \cdot p_{[60]+2} \cdot p_{63} \cdot p_{64} \cdot p_{65}$$

$$= (.89)(.87)(.85)(.84)(.83) = .45886.$$

CHAPTER FIVE
CONTINGENT PAYMENT MODELS
(INSURANCE MODELS)

5-1 From Equation (5.18) we have

$$Cov(Z^1_{x:\overline{n}|}, {}_n|Z_x) = \frac{1}{2}\Big[Var(Z_x) - Var(Z^1_{x:\overline{n}|}) - Var({}_n|Z_x)\Big]$$

$$= \frac{1}{2}\Big[{}^2A_x - A_x^2 - {}^2A^1_{x:\overline{n}|} + {A^1_{x:\overline{n}|}}^2 - {}^2{}_n|A_x + {}_n|A_x^2\Big]$$

$$= \frac{1}{2}\Big[{A^1_{x:\overline{n}|}}^2 + {}_n|A_x^2 - A_x^2\Big],$$

since ${}^2A_x - {}^2A^1_{x:\overline{n}|} - {}^2{}_n|A_x = 0$ by Equation (5.17).

5-2 We start with the right-hand side of Equation (5.19a) and substitute for A_x from Equation (5.16), obtaining

$$\frac{1}{2}\Big[{A^1_{x:\overline{n}|}}^2 + {}_n|A_x^2 - (A^1_{x:\overline{n}|} + {}_n|A_x)^2\Big]$$

$$= \frac{1}{2}\Big[{A^1_{x:\overline{n}|}}^2 + {}_n|A_x^2 - ({A^1_{x:\overline{n}|}}^2 + 2 \cdot A^1_{x:\overline{n}|} \cdot {}_n|A_x + {}_n|A_x^2)\Big]$$

$$= -A^1_{x:\overline{n}|} \cdot {}_n|A_x, \text{ as required.}$$

5-3 From Equation (5.19b) we directly have

$$Cov(Z^1_{x:\overline{3}|}, {}_3|Z_x) = -A^1_{x:\overline{3}|} \cdot {}_3|A_x$$

$$= -(.686227)(.286867)$$

$$= -.19686,$$

where the values of $A^1_{x:\overline{3}|}$ and ${}_3|A_x$ are found in Examples 5.2 and 5.3, respectively.

5-4 When $i=0$ the present value factor is $v=1$, so the present value random variable $Z=1$ as well. Then

$$E[Z] = 1 \cdot q_x + 1 \cdot p_x \cdot q_{x+1} = .50 + .50 q_{x+1}.$$

The second moment is the same (since $Z=1$), so the variance is

$$\begin{aligned}Var(Z) &= (.50+.50q_{x+1})-(.50+.50q_{x+1})^2 \\ &= (.50+.50q)-(.25+.50q+.25q^2) \\ &= .25-.25q^2 = .1771,\end{aligned}$$

which solves for $q = q_{x+1} = .54$.

5-5 The present value of payment is $b \cdot v$ if (x) fails, which happens with probability q_x, or $e \cdot v$ if (x) survives, which happens with probability p_x. Then we have

$$E[Z] = bv \cdot q_x + ev \cdot p_x$$

and

$$E[Z^2] = b^2 v^2 \cdot q_x + e^2 v^2 \cdot p_x,$$

so

$$\begin{aligned}Var(Z) &= b^2 v^2 \cdot q_x + e^2 v^2 \cdot p_x - (bv \cdot q_x + ev \cdot p_x)^2 \\ &= b^2 v^2 \cdot q_x + e^2 v^2 \cdot p_x - b^2 v^2 \cdot q_x^2 - 2be \cdot v^2 \cdot q_x \cdot p_x - e^2 v^2 \cdot p_x^2 \\ &= b^2 v^2 \cdot q_x (1-q_x) + e^2 v^2 \cdot p_x (1-p_x) - 2be \cdot v^2 \cdot q_x \cdot p_x \\ &= b^2 v^2 \cdot q_x \cdot p_x - 2be \cdot v^2 \cdot q_x \cdot p_x + e^2 v^2 \cdot q_x \cdot p_x \\ &= v^2 (b-e)^2 \cdot q_x \cdot p_x, \text{ as required.}\end{aligned}$$

CHAPTER FIVE

5-6 From Equation (5.2),

$$A_x = \sum_{k=1}^{\infty} v^k \cdot {}_{k-1|}q_x = v \cdot q_x + \sum_{k=2}^{\infty} v^k \cdot {}_{k-1|}q_x.$$

Letting $j = k-1$ we then have

$$A_x = v \cdot q_x + \sum_{j=1}^{\infty} v^{j+1} \cdot {}_{j|}q_x = v \cdot q_x + v \cdot p_x \sum_{j=1}^{\infty} v^j \cdot {}_{j-1|}q_{x+1}$$
$$= v \cdot q_x + v \cdot p_x \cdot A_{x+1}, \text{ as required.}$$

5-7 Recall from Exercise 5-6 that $A_{50} = v \cdot q_{50} + v \cdot p_{50} \cdot A_{51}$. Then

$$A_{51} - A_{50} = A_{51} - v \cdot q_{50} - v \cdot p_{50} \cdot A_{51}$$
$$= A_{51}(1 - v \cdot p_{50}) - v \cdot q_{50}$$
$$= A_{51}\left(1 - \frac{.98}{1.02}\right) - \frac{.02}{1.02} = .004,$$

which implies $A_{51} = .60199$.

Similarly,

$$^2A_{51} - {}^2A_{50} = {}^2A_{51} - v' \cdot q_{50} - v' \cdot p_{50} \cdot {}^2A_{51}$$
$$= {}^2A_{51}(1 - v' \cdot p_{50}) - v' \cdot q_{50}$$
$$= {}^2A_{51}\left(1 - \frac{.98}{(1.02)^2}\right) - \frac{.02}{(1.02)^2} = .005,$$

which implies $^2A_{51} = .41725$.

Then

$$Var(Z_{51}) = {}^2A_{51} - A_{51}{}^2 = .41725 - (.60199)^2 = .05486.$$

5-8 Recall that

$$Var(Z_1 + Z_2) = Var(Z_1) + Var(Z_2) + 2 \cdot Cov(Z_1, Z_2),$$

and, in turn,

$$Cov(Z_1, Z_2) = E[Z_1 \cdot Z_2] - E[Z_1] \cdot E[Z_2].$$

The insurance represented by Z_1 pays only for failure in $(0,25]$, and the insurance represented by Z_2 pays only for failure in $(25,35]$. Therefore for all K_x one or the other of Z_1 and Z_2 must be zero, so $E[Z_1 \cdot Z_2] = 0$.

Therefore

$$\begin{aligned}Var(Z_1+Z_2) &= Var(Z_1) + Var(Z_2) - 2 \cdot E[Z_1] \cdot E[Z_2] \\ &= 5.76 + .10 - 2(2.80)(.12) = 5.188.\end{aligned}$$

5-9 Recall that $Var(Z) = 1000^2 ({}^2\!A_{x:\overline{n}|} - A_{x:\overline{n}|}{}^2)$.

Next recall that

$$\begin{aligned}{}^2\!A_{x:\overline{n}|} &= {}^2\!A^{\,1}_{x:\overline{n}|} + {}^2\!A_{x:\overline{n}|}^{1} \\ &= {}^2\!A_x - {}^2\!{}_n|A_x + {}^2\!A_{x:\overline{n}|}^{1} \\ &= {}^2\!A_x - {}^2\!A^{\,1}_{x:\overline{n}|} \cdot {}^2\!A_{x+n} + {}^2\!A_{x:\overline{n}|}^{1} \\ &= .2196 - (.5649)(.2836) + .5649 \\ &= .6243.\end{aligned}$$

Then

$$Var(Z) = 1000^2 (.6243 - (.7896)^2) = 831.84.$$

CHAPTER FIVE

5-10 We are given

$$Z_1 = 1000 \cdot {}_{10}E_x \cdot Z^1_{x:\overline{10|}} + 1000 \cdot Z^{}_{x:\overline{10|}},$$

so

$$E[Z_1] = 1000 \cdot {}_{10}E_x \cdot A^1_{x:\overline{10|}} + 1000 \cdot {}_{10}E_x.$$

Similarly,

$$E[Z_2] = 750 \cdot {}_{10}E_x \cdot A^1_{x:\overline{10|}} + 1000 \cdot {}_{10}E_x$$

and

$$E[Z_3] = 500 \cdot {}_{10}E_x \cdot A^1_{x:\overline{10|}} + 1000 \cdot {}_{10}E_x.$$

Then

$$\frac{E[Z_1]}{E[Z_2]} = \frac{1000 A^1_{x:\overline{10|}} + 1000}{750 A^1_{x:\overline{10|}} + 1000} = 1.005,$$

which solves for $A^1_{x:\overline{10|}} = \frac{5}{246.25} = .02030$. Next we find

$${}_{10}E_x = A_{x:\overline{10|}}^{1} = A_{x:\overline{10|}} - A^1_{x:\overline{10|}} = .5700 - .0203 = .5497.$$

Finally we have

$$E[Z_3] = (500)(.5497)(.0203) + (1000)(.5497) = 555.27.$$

5-11 From Equation (5.12) we have

$${}_n|A_x = \sum_{k=n+1}^{\infty} v^k \cdot {}_{k-1|}q_x = \sum_{k=n+1}^{\infty} v^k \cdot \frac{d_{x+k-1}}{\ell_x}.$$

Let $j = k-n$ so $k = j+n$. Then

$${}_n|A_x = \sum_{j=1}^{\infty} v^{j+n} \cdot \frac{d_{x+j+n-1}}{\ell_x} = v^n \cdot \frac{\ell_{x+n}}{\ell_x} \sum_{j=1}^{\infty} v^j \cdot \frac{d_{x+n+j-1}}{\ell_{x+n}}$$

$$= {}_nE_x \cdot A_{x+n}, \text{ as required.}$$

5-12 (a) From Equation (5.8), we have

$$A^1_{x:\overline{n}|} = \sum_{t=1}^{n} v^t \cdot {}_{t-1|}q_x$$

$$= \sum_{t=1}^{n} v^t \cdot \frac{d_{x+t-1}}{\ell_x}$$

$$= v \cdot \frac{d_x}{\ell_x} + v^2 \cdot \frac{d_{x+1}}{\ell_x} + \cdots + v^n \cdot \frac{d_{x+n-1}}{\ell_x},$$

which gives the NSP for a unit insurance with benefit paid at the end of the year of failure provided failure occurs *within* the first n years.

(b) From Equation (5.12),

$$_{n|}A_x = \sum_{t=n+1}^{\infty} v^t \cdot {}_{t-1|}q_x = v^{n+1} \cdot \frac{d_{x+n}}{\ell_x} + v^{n+2} \cdot \frac{d_{x+n+1}}{\ell_x} + \cdots,$$

the NSP for a unit insurance for failure occurring *after* the first n years.

(c) Here we have

$$A_{x:\overline{n}|} = A^1_{x:\overline{n}|} + {}_nE_x$$

$$= v \cdot \frac{d_x}{\ell_x} + v^2 \cdot \frac{d_{x+1}}{\ell_x} + \cdots + v^n \cdot \frac{d_{x+n-1}}{\ell_x} + v^n \cdot \frac{\ell_{x+n}}{\ell_x},$$

where the last term represents the present value of benefits paid to those who survive to age $x+n$.

5-13 Using the identity from Exercise 5-6 we have

$$A_{76} = v \cdot q_{76} + v \cdot p_{76} \cdot A_{77}$$
$$= v - v \cdot p_{76} + v \cdot p_{76} \cdot A_{77} = v - v \cdot p_{76}(1-A_{77}).$$

Substituting the given values we have

$$.800 = \frac{1}{1.03} - (.90)(1-A_{77}),$$

which solves for $A_{77} = .81014$.

5-14 We are given that

$$600 = 600 A^1_{x:\overline{n}|} + 1000 A_{x:\overline{n}|}^{1}$$
$$= 600\left(A_{x:\overline{n}|} - A_{x:\overline{n}|}^{1}\right) + 1000 A_{x:\overline{n}|}^{1}$$
$$= 600 A_{x:\overline{n}|} + 400 A_{x:\overline{n}|}^{1},$$

so

$$A_{x:\overline{n}|}^{1} = {}_nE_x = \frac{600(1-A_{x:\overline{n}|})}{400} = \frac{(600)(.20)}{400} = .30.$$

5-15 Using Equation (5.35) we have

$$APV = 50 \int_0^{100} v^t \cdot f(t)\, dt$$

$$= \frac{50}{5000} \int_0^{100} t \cdot \left. \frac{e^{-.10t}\, dt}{\frac{d}{dt}\, e^{-.10t}} \right|_{-.10}$$

$$= \frac{1}{100}\left[\left. \frac{t}{-.10} \cdot e^{-.10t} \right|_0^{100} + 10 \int_0^{100} e^{-.10t}\, dt \right]$$

$$= \frac{1}{100}\left[-1000 e^{-10} + \left. \frac{10}{-.10} \cdot e^{-.10t} \right|_0^{100} \right]$$

$$= \frac{1}{100}\left[-1000 e^{-10} + 100(1 - e^{-10}) \right]$$

$$= 1 - 11 e^{-10} = .99950.$$

5-16 (a) The random variable $\overline{Z}^1_{x:\overline{n}|}$ denotes the present value of a unit paid at the instant of failure, provided failure occurs in $(0,n]$. If failure occurs at time T_x, the present value is v^{T_x}, but only for $T_x \leq n$. If $T_x > n$, then the present value is zero.

(b) Since $\overline{Z}^1_{x:\overline{n}|}$ is a function of the continuous random variable T_x, its moments are found by integrating powers of $\overline{Z}^1_{x:\overline{n}|}$ times the PDF of T_x, which is given by ${}_t p_x \mu_{x+t}$.

5-17 (a) Payment is made at the moment of failure provided failure occurs after time n. Thus the present value is v^{T_x} for $T_x > n$. If $T_x \leq n$, then the present value is zero.

(b) Again the moments are found by integrating powers of $_n|\bar{Z}_x$ times the PDF of T_x, which is $_t p_x \mu_{x+t}$.

(c) From the definitions of $\bar{Z}^1_{x:\overline{n}|}$ and $_n|\bar{Z}_x$ given in Exercises 5-16(a) and 5-17(a), respectively, it is easy to see that

$$\bar{Z}_x = \bar{Z}^1_{x:\overline{n}|} + {_n|}\bar{Z}_x.$$

Taking the expectation on both sides produces the given relationship.

5-18 The random variable $_{20}|\bar{Z}_{40}$ takes on the discrete value zero whenever $T_{40} \leq 20$. Thus the discrete part of the distribution is $_{20}|\bar{Z}_{40} = 0$ with probability mass given by

$$Pr(T_{40} \leq 20) = \int_0^{20} (110-40)^{-1} dt = \frac{1}{70} t \Big|_0^{20} = \frac{2}{7}.$$

5-19 Recall that $\bar{Z}_{x:\overline{n}|} = \bar{Z}^1_{x:\overline{n}|} + \bar{Z}^{\ 1}_{x:\overline{n}|}$, so

$$Var(\bar{Z}_{x:\overline{n}|}) = Var(\bar{Z}^1_{x:\overline{n}|}) + Var(Z^{\ 1}_{x:\overline{n}|}) + 2 \cdot Cov(\bar{Z}^1_{x:\overline{n}|}, Z^{\ 1}_{x:\overline{n}|}).$$

First we find

$$\begin{aligned} Var(Z^{\ 1}_{x:\overline{n}|}) &= {^2A}^{\ 1}_{x:\overline{n}|} - (A^{\ 1}_{x:\overline{n}|})^2 \\ &= (v^n)^2 \cdot {_n p_x} - (v^n \cdot {_n p_x})^2 \\ &= (.20)^2(.50) - [(.20)(.50)]^2 = .01. \end{aligned}$$

From Equation (5.29) we have

$$\begin{aligned} Cov(\bar{Z}^1_{x:\overline{n}|} \cdot Z^{\ 1}_{x:\overline{n}|}) &= -\bar{A}^1_{x:\overline{n}|} \cdot A^{\ 1}_{x:\overline{n}|} \\ &= -(.23)(.20)(.50) = -.023. \end{aligned}$$

Then

$$Var(\bar{Z}_{x:\overline{n}|}) = .08 + .01 + 2(-.023) = .044.$$

CHAPTER FIVE

5-20 It follows from Equation (5.44) that

$$^2\bar{A}_x = E[\bar{Z}_x^2] = \frac{\lambda}{2\delta + \lambda}.$$

Then we have

$$Var(\bar{Z}_x) = \frac{\lambda}{2\delta + \lambda} - \left(\frac{\lambda}{\delta + \lambda}\right)^2.$$

5-21 For the deferred insurance we have

$$_n|\bar{A}_x = E[_n|\bar{Z}_x] = \int_n^\infty e^{-\delta t} \cdot e^{-\lambda t} \cdot \lambda\, dt$$

$$= \lambda \left(\frac{e^{-(\delta+\lambda)t}}{-(\delta+\lambda)}\right)\bigg|_n^\infty = \frac{\lambda}{\delta+\lambda} \cdot e^{-(\delta+\lambda)n}.$$

5-22 Since $\bar{Z}_{40} = v^{T_{40}}$, we have the transformation $z = v^t$ so $t = \dfrac{-\ln z}{\delta}$. The transformation is decreasing so we have

$$F_{Z_{40}}(z) = S_{T_{40}}\left[-\frac{\ln z}{\delta}\right].$$

But $S_{T_{40}}(t) = {}_t p_{40} = 1 - \dfrac{t}{\omega - 40} = 1 - \dfrac{t}{70}$ under a uniform distribution with $\omega = 110$. Therefore,

$$F_{Z_{40}}(z) = 1 - \frac{-\frac{\ln z}{\delta}}{70} = 1 + \frac{\ln z}{3.50},$$

since $\delta = .05$. Then

$$f_{Z_{40}}(z) = \frac{d}{dz} F_{Z_{40}}(z) = \frac{1}{3.50 z},$$

and finally

$$f_{Z_{40}}(.80) = \frac{1}{(3.50)(.80)} = .35714.$$

5-23 Recall (see Equation (2.13)) that the moment generating function is defined as $M_{T_x}(r) = E[e^{r \cdot T_x}]$. Then we have

$$M_{T_x}(-\delta) = E[e^{-\delta \cdot T_x}]$$
$$= \int_0^\infty e^{-\delta t} \cdot f_{T_x}(t)\, dt$$
$$= \int_0^\infty v^t \cdot {}_t p_x \mu_{x+t}\, dt,$$

which is $\bar{A}_x$ by Equation (5.35).

5-24 The expected value of $\bar{B}_x$ is

$$E[\bar{B}_x] = \int_0^{50} b_t \cdot v^t \cdot f(t)\, dt$$
$$= .02 \int_0^{50} (1+.10t) \cdot (1+.10t)^{-2}\, dt$$
$$= .02 \int_0^{50} (1+.10t)^{-1}\, dt = .02 \left[\frac{\ln(1+.10t)}{.10} \right]_0^{50}$$
$$= .02 \left[\frac{\ln 6}{.10} \right] = .358352.$$

The second moment is

$$E[\bar{B}_x^2] = \int_0^{50} (b_t \cdot v^t)^2 \cdot f(t)\, dt$$
$$= .02 \int_0^{50} (1+.10t)^{-2}\, dt$$
$$= .02 \left[\frac{(1+.10t)^{-1}}{-.10} \right]_0^{50}$$
$$= .02 \left[\frac{1 - 6^{-1}}{.10} \right] = .166667.$$

Then the variance is

$$Var(\bar{B}_x) = .166667 - (.358352)^2 = .03825.$$

CHAPTER FIVE

5-25 (a) From Equation (5.51) we have

$$(IA)_x = \sum_{k=1}^{\infty} k \cdot v^k \cdot {}_{k-1|}q_x = \sum_{k=1}^{\infty} v^k \cdot {}_{k-1|}q_x + \sum_{k=2}^{\infty} (k-1) \cdot v^k \cdot {}_{k-1|}q_x.$$

Let $r = k-1$ so $k = r+1$. Then

$$(IA)_x = A_x + \sum_{r=1}^{\infty} r \cdot v^{r+1} \cdot {}_{r|}q_x$$

$$= A_x + v \cdot p_x \sum_{r=1}^{\infty} r \cdot v^r \cdot {}_{r-1|}q_{x+1} = A_x + {}_1E_x \cdot (IA)_{x+1}.$$

(b) Note that $A_{35:\overline{1|}} = v = .9434$. Then

$${}_1E_{35} = v \cdot p_{35} = (.9434)(.9964) = .94000.$$

Using the result from part (a), we have

$$(IA)_{35} = A_{35} + {}_1E_{35} \cdot (IA)_{36}.$$

Then

$$(IA)_{36} = \frac{(IA)_{35} - A_{35}}{{}_1E_{35}} = \frac{3.711 - .130}{.940} = 3.80957.$$

5-26 First we need to find the parameters of the Pareto survival model. If $E[X] = 4$ and $Var(X) = 48$, then $E[X^2] = 48 + 16 = 64$. From Equation (12.3) we have $\frac{\theta}{\alpha - 1} = 4$, so $\theta = 4(\alpha - 1)$. From Equation (12.4) we have

$$\frac{2\theta^2}{(\alpha-1)(\alpha-2)} = \frac{2(16)(\alpha-1)^2}{(\alpha-1)(\alpha-2)} = \frac{32(\alpha-1)}{\alpha-2} = 64,$$

which solves for $\alpha = 3$ and therefore $\theta = 8$. Then we have

$$S(x) = \left(\frac{\theta}{x+\theta}\right)^\alpha = \left(\frac{8}{8+x}\right)^3, \text{ so } S(1) = \left(\frac{8}{9}\right)^3, S(2) = \left(\frac{8}{10}\right)^3, \text{ and}$$

$S(3) = \left(\frac{8}{11}\right)^3$. The warranty benefits are 1500, 1000, and 500, for failure in years 1, 2, 3, respectively. Then the APV is

$$APV = \frac{1500}{1.05}\left[1-\left(\frac{8}{9}\right)^3\right] + \frac{1000}{(1.05)^2}\left[\left(\frac{8}{9}\right)^3 - \left(\frac{8}{10}\right)^3\right]$$

$$+ \frac{500}{(1.05)^3}\left[\left(\frac{8}{10}\right)^3 - \left(\frac{8}{11}\right)^3\right]$$

$$= .425.24 + 172.64 + 54.99 = 652.87.$$

5-27 The rate of loan payment is

$$P = \frac{10,000}{\overline{a}_{\overline{20}|\delta=.08}} = \frac{10,000}{\frac{1-e^{-(.08)(20)}}{.08}} = 1002.38.$$

The outstanding balance at time t, which is the benefit under the contingent payment contract is

$$b_t = P \cdot \overline{a}_{\overline{20-t}|\delta=.08} = \frac{1002.38}{.08}(1-e^{-.08(20-t)})$$

$$= 12,529.70(1-e^{-1.6} \cdot e^{.08t}).$$

The APV is given by

$$APV = \int_0^{20} b_t \cdot v^t \cdot {}_tp_0 \cdot \mu_t \, dt$$

$$= (12,529.70)(.01)\int_0^{20}(1-e^{-1.6} \cdot e^{.08t}) \cdot e^{-.05t} \cdot e^{-.01t} \, dt$$

$$= 125.30\left[\int_0^{20} e^{-.06t} \, dt - e^{-1.6}\int_0^{20} e^{.02t} \, dt\right]$$

$$= 125.30\left[\frac{1-e^{-1.2}}{.06} - e^{-1.6}\left(\frac{e^{.40}-1}{.02}\right)\right] = 837.24.$$

5-28 The failure benefits are shown on the following diagram:

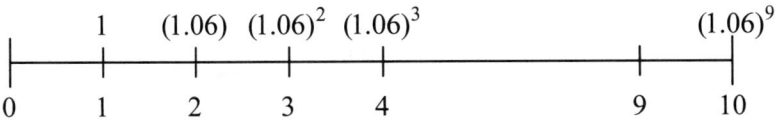

(a) $Z^* = b_k \cdot v^k = (1.06)^{-1}$ for all k, so $Z^* = (1.06)^{-1}$ if failure occurs during the 10-year period, the probability of which is
$$_{10}q_{30} = \frac{10}{\omega - 30} = \frac{10}{70}.$$

(b) The only other possible value for Z^* is v^{10}, which occurs upon survival to time 10, the probability of which is $_{10}p_{30} = \frac{6}{7}$. Then
$$E[Z^*] = \left(\frac{1}{1.06}\right)\left(\frac{1}{7}\right) + \left(\frac{1}{1.06}\right)^{10}\left(\frac{6}{7}\right) = .61339.$$

(c) Similarly,
$$E[Z^{*2}] = \left(\frac{1}{1.06}\right)^2\left(\frac{1}{7}\right) + \left(\frac{1}{1.06}\right)^{20}\left(\frac{6}{7}\right) = .39440.$$

Then
$$Var(Z^*) = .39440 - (.61339)^2 = .01816.$$

5-29 Recall that
$$\bar{A}_{35} = \bar{A}^1_{35:\overline{1}|} + v \cdot p_{35} \cdot \bar{A}_{36}.$$

Under UDD,
$$\bar{A}^1_{35:\overline{1}|} = \frac{i}{\delta} \cdot A^1_{35:\overline{1}|} = \frac{i}{\delta} \cdot v \cdot q_{35} = \left(\frac{.05}{\ln 1.05}\right)\left(\frac{1}{1.05}\right)(.01) = .00976.$$

Then
$$\bar{A}_{35} = .00976 + \left(\frac{.99}{1.05}\right)(.185) = .18419.$$

Finally, since $\bar{A}_{35} = \frac{i}{\delta} \cdot A_{35}$, then

$$A_{35} = \frac{\delta}{i} \cdot \bar{A}_{35} = \frac{\ln(1.05)}{.05}(.18419) = .17973.$$

5-30 From Equation (5.64b) we have

$$\bar{A}^1_{x:\overline{2}|} = \frac{i}{\delta} \cdot A^1_{x:\overline{2}|} = \frac{.10}{\ln 1.10}\left[\frac{.05}{1.10} + \frac{(.95)(.08)}{(1.10)^2}\right]$$
$$= 1.04921(.04545+.06281) = .11359.$$

5-31 The relationship given by Equation (5.64b) holds for the second moment functions using an interest rate based on 2δ. We have

$$^2\bar{A}^1_{x:\overline{2}|} = \frac{i'}{\delta'} \cdot {}^2A^1_{x:\overline{2}|} = \frac{(1.12)^2-1}{\ln(1.12)^2}\left[\frac{.10}{(1.12)^2} + \frac{(.90)(.20)}{(1.12)^4}\right]$$
$$= 1.12240(.07972+.11439) = .21787.$$

5-32 Consider the following diagram:

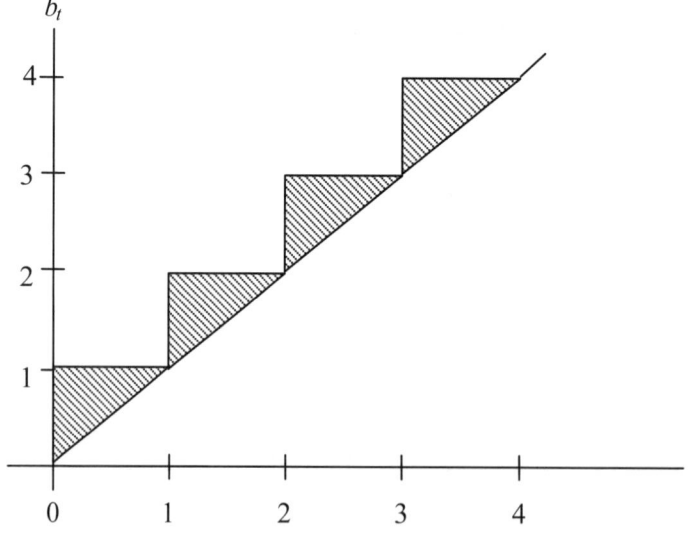

The benefit for which $(\bar{I}A)_x$ is the APV is 1 in the first year, 2 in the second year, and so on, as represented by the step graph in the diagram. The benefit for which $(\bar{I}\bar{A})_x$ is the APV is amount t at time t, as represented by the 45° line in the diagram. Then the difference $(\bar{I}A)_x - (\bar{I}\bar{A})_x$ is the APV of a benefit that decreases linearly from 1 to 0 *in each year*, as represented by the sequence of shaded triangles in the diagram. In the first year, this APV is

$$(\bar{D}\bar{A})^1_{x:\overline{1|}} = \int_0^1 (1-t) \cdot v^t \, {}_tp_x\mu_{x+t} \, dt.$$

To evaluate under UDD, we substitute q_x for ${}_tp_x\mu_{x+t}$ to obtain

$$\begin{aligned}(\bar{D}\bar{A})^1_{x:\overline{1|}} &= q_x \int_0^1 (v^t - t \cdot v^t) \, dt \\ &= q_x \left(\bar{a}_{\overline{1|}} - (\bar{I}\bar{a})_{\overline{1|}} \right) \\ &= q_x \left[\frac{d}{\delta} - \left(\frac{d}{\delta^2} - \frac{v}{\delta} \right) \right] \\ &= q_x \left(\frac{1}{\delta} - \frac{d}{\delta^2} \right).\end{aligned}$$

The sequence of one-year decreasing unit term insurance coverages then has APF given by

$$\begin{aligned}(\bar{I}A)_x - (\bar{I}\bar{A})_x &= \sum_{t=0}^{\infty} {}_tE_x \cdot (\bar{D}\bar{A})^1_{x+t:\overline{1|}} \\ &= \left(\frac{1}{\delta} - \frac{d}{\delta^2} \right) \cdot \sum_{t=0}^{\infty} {}_tE_x \cdot q_{x+t} \\ &= \left(\frac{1}{\delta} - \frac{d}{\delta^2} \right) \cdot \sum_{t=0}^{\infty} v^t \cdot {}_tp_x \cdot q_{x+t} \\ &= \left(\frac{1}{\delta} - \frac{d}{\delta^2} \right)(1+i) \cdot \sum_{t=0}^{\infty} v^{t+1} \cdot {}_t|q_x \\ &= \left(\frac{1}{\delta} - \frac{d}{\delta^2} \right)(1+i) \cdot A_x.\end{aligned}$$

Recall also that $\bar{A}_x = \frac{i}{\delta} \cdot A_x$ under UDD. Then the given expression becomes

$$\frac{(I\bar{A})_x - (I\bar{A}_x)}{\bar{A}_x} = \frac{\left(\frac{1}{\delta} - \frac{d}{\delta^2}\right)(1+i) \cdot A_x}{\frac{i}{\delta} \cdot A_x}$$

$$= \frac{(1+i)\left(1 - \frac{d}{\delta}\right)}{i}$$

$$= \frac{1}{d}\left(1 - \frac{d}{\delta}\right)$$

$$= \frac{1}{d} - \frac{1}{\delta},$$

as required.

CHAPTER SIX
CONTINGENT ANNUITY MODELS

6-1 Start with the identity derived in Example 6.2 and simply multiply both sides by $(1+i)$, obtaining

$$(1+i)A_x = 1 - i \cdot a_x,$$

and the desired relationship follows.

6-2 We begin with Equation (5.30), where $X = A_x$. Then we can write

$$A_{x+1} \cdot \ell_{x+1} = v \cdot d_{x+1} + v^2 \cdot d_{x+2} + v^3 \cdot d_{x+3} + \cdots,$$
$$A_{x+2} \cdot \ell_{x+2} = v \cdot d_{x+2} + v^2 \cdot d_{x+3} + v^3 \cdot d_{x+4} + \cdots,$$
$$A_{x+3} \cdot \ell_{x+3} = v \cdot d_{x+3} + v^2 \cdot d_{x+4} + v^3 \cdot d_{x+5} + \cdots,$$

and so on to the end of the survival model where $\ell_\omega = 0$. Summing this set of equations we have

$$\sum_{t=1}^{\infty} A_{x+t} \cdot \ell_{x+t} = v(d_{x+1} + d_{x+2} + \cdots) + v^2(d_{x+2} + d_{x+3} + \cdots)$$
$$+ v^3(d_{x+3} + d_{x+4} + \cdots) + \cdots$$
$$= v \cdot \ell_{x+1} + v^2 \cdot \ell_{x+2} + v^3 \cdot \ell_{x+3} + \cdots$$
$$= a_x \cdot \ell_x, \text{ by Equation (6.3).}$$

6-3   From Equation (6.4b) we have

$$a_x = v \cdot p_x + v^2 \cdot {}_2p_x + v^3 \cdot {}_3p_x + \cdots$$
$$= v \cdot p_x(1 + v \cdot p_{x+1} + v^2 \cdot {}_2p_{x+1} + \cdots)$$
$$= v \cdot p_x(1 + a_{x+1}).$$

6-4   From Equation (6.15) we have

$$Var(\ddot{Y}_x) = \frac{{}^2A_x - A_x^2}{d^2}.$$

We are given values of $\ddot{a}_x$ and ${}^2\ddot{a}_x$, so we use the relationship derived in Example 6.4 to write

$$Var(\ddot{Y}_x) = \frac{(1 - d' \cdot {}^2\ddot{a}_x) - (1 - d \cdot \ddot{a}_x)^2}{d^2}.$$

Here $i = \frac{1}{24}$ so $d = \frac{i}{1+i} = \frac{1/24}{25/24} = \frac{1}{25} = .04$. Furthermore, $i' = (1+i)^2 - 1 = \left(\frac{25}{24}\right)^2 - 1 = .08507$, so $d' = \frac{.08507}{1.08507} = .07840$. Then we have

$$Var(\ddot{Y}_x) = \frac{[1 - (.07840)(6)] - [1 - (.04)(10)]^2}{(.04)^2}$$
$$= \frac{.52960 - .36000}{.0016} = 106.$$

6-5.   Begin with the relationship found in Example 6.4 and substitute $d = 1 - v$ to obtain

$$A_x = 1 - (1-v) \cdot \ddot{a}_x = v \cdot \ddot{a}_x - (\ddot{a}_x - 1) = v \cdot \ddot{a}_x - a_x,$$

from Equation (6.10).

6-6 Recall that
$$a_x = v \cdot p_x + v^2 \cdot {}_2p_x + \cdots$$
$$= v \cdot p_x(1 + v \cdot p_{x+1} + v^2 \cdot {}_2p_{x+1} + \cdots) = v \cdot p_x \cdot \ddot{a}_{x+1}.$$

Then from Equation (6.10) we have
$$\ddot{a}_x = 1 + a_x = 1 + v \cdot p_x \cdot \ddot{a}_{x+1},$$
as required.

6-7 From Exercise 6-6 we have
$$\ddot{a}_x = 1 + v \cdot p_x \cdot \ddot{a}_{x+1}$$
$$= 1 + v \cdot p_x \left(1 + v \cdot p_{x+1} + v^2 \cdot {}_2p_{x+1} + \cdots\right)$$
$$= 1 + v \cdot p_x \left[1 + v \cdot p_{x+1}(1 + v \cdot p_{x+2} + \cdots)\right].$$

In the initial calculation $p_x = .99$ and $p_{x+1} = .95$, so we have
$$\ddot{a}_x = 1 + \frac{.99}{1.05}\left[1 + \frac{.95}{1.05} \cdot \ddot{a}_{x+2}\right].$$

But also we know that $\ddot{a}_{x+1} = 6.951$, so we can find
$$\ddot{a}_{x+2} = \frac{(6.951 - 1)(1.05)}{.95} = 6.57742.$$

Now using $p'_{x+1} = p_{x+1} + .03 = .98$ we find
$$\ddot{a}'_x = 1 + \frac{.99}{1.05}\left[1 + \frac{.98}{1.05} \cdot \ddot{a}_{x+2}\right],$$
so the increase is
$$\ddot{a}'_x - \ddot{a}_x = \frac{(.99)(.98)}{(1.05)^2} \cdot \ddot{a}_{x+2} - \frac{(.99)(.95)}{(1.05)^2} \cdot \ddot{a}_{x+2}$$
$$= \frac{6.57742}{(1.05)^2}\left((.99)(.98) - (.99)(.95)\right) = .17719.$$

6-8 If the death benefit is B, then the present value random variable for the new product is

$$W_x = 12{,}000\ddot{Y}_x + B \cdot Z_x$$
$$= 12{,}000\left(\frac{1-Z_x}{d}\right) + B \cdot Z_x$$
$$= \frac{12{,}000}{.08} + Z_x\left(B - \frac{12{,}000}{.08}\right)$$
$$= 150{,}000 + (B-150{,}000) \cdot Z_x.$$

Then

$$Var(W_x) = (B-150{,}000)^2 \cdot Var(Z_x),$$

which is minimized at $B = 150{,}000$.

6-9 We write Equation (6.14) as

$$E[\ddot{Y}_x] = \sum_{k=1}^{\infty}\left(\frac{1-v^k}{d}\right) \cdot {}_{k-1|}q_x$$
$$= \frac{1}{d}\left[\sum_{k=1}^{\infty} {}_{k-1|}q_x - \sum_{k=1}^{\infty} v^k \cdot {}_{k-1|}q_x\right]$$
$$= \frac{1}{d}[1 - A_x]$$
$$= \ddot{a}_x,$$

using the result of Example 6.4.

6-10 This is the continuous counterpart of the result of Example 6.4. Rearranging Equation (6.18) we have

$$\overline{Z}_x = 1 - \delta \cdot \overline{Y}_x,$$

and taking the expectation yields the desired relationship.

6-11 We use the definition of $\bar{a}_x$ given by Equation (6.17b), so we have

$$\frac{d}{dx}\bar{a}_x = \frac{d}{dx}\int_0^\infty v^t \cdot {}_tp_x\, dt$$
$$= \int_0^\infty v^t \cdot \left(\frac{d}{dx}{}_tp_x\right) dt$$
$$= \int_0^\infty v^t \cdot \left[{}_tp_x(\mu_x - \mu_{x+t})\right] dt,$$

using the result of Exercise 4-6(b). Then we have

$$\frac{d}{dx}\bar{a}_x = \mu_x \int_0^\infty v^t \cdot {}_tp_x\, dt - \int_0^\infty v^t \cdot {}_tp_x\mu_{x+t}\, dt$$
$$= \mu_x \cdot \bar{a}_x - \bar{A}_x$$
$$= \mu_x \cdot \bar{a}_x - (1 - \delta \cdot \bar{a}_x)$$
$$= \bar{a}_x(\mu_x + \delta) - 1,$$

as required.

6-12 Recall that $E[\bar{Y}_x] = \bar{a}_x$. We use the result of Exercise 6-10 to write

$$\bar{a}_x = \frac{1 - \bar{A}_x}{\delta}.$$

Then we use the result of Equation (5.49a), where $\bar{A}_x$ was derived under the uniform distribution, to write

$$E[\bar{Y}_x] = \bar{a}_x = \frac{1}{\delta}\left[1 - \frac{\bar{a}_{\overline{\omega-x|}}}{\omega-x}\right] = \frac{(\omega-x) - \bar{a}_{\overline{\omega-x|}}}{\delta(\omega-x)},$$

as required.

6-13   Recall that
$$Var(\bar{a}_{\overline{T_x|}}) = Var(\bar{Y}_x) = \frac{{}^2\bar{A}_x - \bar{A}_x^{\,2}}{\delta^2}.$$

We know that
$$\bar{A}_x = 1 - \delta \cdot \bar{a}_x = 1 - 10\delta$$
and
$$^2\bar{A}_x = 1 - 2\delta \cdot {}^2\bar{a}_x = 1 - 14.75\delta.$$
Then
$$Var(\bar{Y}_x) = \frac{(1-14.75\delta) - (1-10\delta)^2}{\delta^2} = \frac{5.25\delta - 100\delta^2}{\delta^2} = 50,$$

which solves for $\delta = .035$. Finally
$$\bar{A}_x = 1 - (.035)(10) = .65.$$

6-14   Since μ_{x+t} is constant, then T_x has an exponential distribution. From Example 6.5 we know that, in general, $\bar{a}_x = \frac{1}{\mu + \delta}$. Here we have $\mu = k$ and $\delta = 4k$, so

$$Var(\bar{a}_{\overline{T_x|}}) = \frac{{}^2\bar{A}_x - \bar{A}_x^{\,2}}{\delta^2}$$
$$= \frac{(1 - 2\delta \cdot {}^2\bar{a}_x) - (1 - \delta \cdot \bar{a}_x)^2}{\delta^2}$$
$$= \frac{\left[1 - 8k\left(\frac{1}{k+8k}\right)\right] - \left[1 - 4k\left(\frac{1}{k+4k}\right)\right]^2}{(4k)^2}$$
$$= \frac{\left(1 - \frac{8}{9}\right) - \left(1 - \frac{4}{5}\right)^2}{16k^2} = \frac{100}{9},$$

which solves for $k = .02$.

CHAPTER SIX

6-15 In general,
$$Pr(\bar{Y}_x > 20) = Pr\left(\frac{1-v^T}{\delta} > 20\right)$$
$$= Pr(1 - e^{-\delta T} > 20\delta)$$
$$= Pr(e^{-\delta T} < 1 - 20\delta)$$
$$= Pr[-\delta T < \ln(1-20\delta)]$$
$$= Pr\left[T > \frac{\ln(1-20\delta)}{-\delta}\right].$$

Here $\delta = .03$ so we have

$$Pr(T > 30.54302).$$

But T is exponential with parameter $\mu = .025$, so

$$Pr(T > 30.54302) = e^{-(.025)(30.54302)} = .46600.$$

6-16 We have
$$Cov(\bar{Y}_x, \bar{Z}_x) = E[\bar{Y}_x \cdot \bar{Z}_x] - E[\bar{Y}_x] \cdot E[\bar{Z}_x]$$
$$= E\left[\frac{1-\bar{Z}_x}{\delta} \cdot \bar{Z}_x\right] - E[\bar{Y}_x] \cdot E[\bar{Z}_x]$$
$$= \frac{1}{\delta} \cdot E[\bar{Z}_x - \bar{Z}_x^2] - E[\bar{Y}_x] \cdot E[\bar{Z}_x]$$
$$= \frac{1}{\delta}[\bar{A}_x - {}^2\bar{A}_x] - \bar{a}_x \cdot \bar{A}_x$$
$$= \frac{1}{\delta}[\bar{A}_x - {}^2\bar{A}_x] - \frac{1}{\delta}(1-\bar{A}_x) \cdot \bar{A}_x$$
$$= \frac{\bar{A}_x}{\delta} - \frac{{}^2\bar{A}_x}{\delta} - \frac{\bar{A}_x}{\delta} + \frac{\bar{A}_x^2}{\delta}$$
$$= \frac{\bar{A}_x^2 - {}^2\bar{A}_x}{\delta},$$

as required.

6-17 Recall that $_tp_x = e^{-\int_0^t \mu_{x+r}\, dr}$, so we can write $\bar{a}_x$ as

$$\bar{a}_x = \int_0^\infty v^t \cdot {_tp_x}\, dt = \int_0^\infty e^{-\delta t} \cdot e^{-\int_0^t \mu_{x+r}\, dr}\, dt.$$

Similarly,

$$\bar{a}_x^* = \int_0^\infty e^{-\delta^* t} \cdot e^{-\int_0^t \mu_{x+r}^*\, dr}\, dt$$

$$= \int_0^\infty e^{-3\delta t} \cdot e^{-\int_0^t \mu_{x+r}^*\, dr}\, dt.$$

But $\bar{a}_x = \bar{a}_x^*$, so we have

$$e^{-\delta t} \cdot e^{-\int_0^t \mu_{x+r}\, dr} = e^{-3\delta t} \cdot e^{-\int_0^t \mu_{x+r}^*\, dr}$$

$$= e^{-\delta t} \cdot e^{-2\delta t} \cdot e^{-\int_0^t \mu_{x+r}^*\, dr}$$

$$= e^{-\delta t} \cdot e^{-\int_0^t (\mu_{x+r}^* + 2\delta)\, dr},$$

which shows that $\mu_{x+r} = \mu_{x+r}^* + 2\delta$, as required.

6-18 Recall that $Var(\bar{Y}_x) = \dfrac{{}^2\bar{A}_x - \bar{A}_x^{\,2}}{\delta^2}$ and $E[\bar{Z}_x] = \bar{A}_x$. The unconditional first moment of $\bar{Z}_x$ is

$$(.50)\left(E[\bar{Z}_x^M] + E[\bar{Z}_x^F]\right) = (.50)(.09 + .15) = .1200.$$

We are given the values of $Var(\bar{Y}_x)$ for males and females separately, so we can find

$${}^2\bar{A}_x^M = (5.00)(.10)^2 + (.15)^2 = .0725$$

and

$${}^2\bar{A}_x^F = (4.00)(.10)^2 + (.09)^2 = .0481.$$

The unconditional second moment of $\bar{Z}_x$ is then

$$(.50)\left({}^2\bar{A}_x^M + {}^2\bar{A}_x^F\right) = (.50)(.0725 + .0481) = .0603.$$

Then the unconditional variance of $\bar{Y}_x$ is

$$\frac{.0603 - (.1200)^2}{(.10)^2} = 4.59.$$

Chapter Six

6-19 Taking the expectation of Equation (6.22b) we have

$$E[Y_{x:\overline{n}|}] = a_{x:\overline{n}|} = \frac{1}{i}[1 - E[U] - E[V]]$$
$$= \frac{1}{i}\left[1 - (1+i) \cdot A^1_{x:\overline{n}|} - A_{x:\overline{n}|}^{1}\right],$$

using Equations (5.7) and (5.20), respectively, to find $E[U]$ and $E[V]$. Then we have

$$i \cdot a_{x:\overline{n}|} = 1 - i \cdot A^1_{x:\overline{n}|} - A^1_{x:\overline{n}|} - A_{x:\overline{n}|}^{1} = 1 - i \cdot A^1_{x:\overline{n}|} - A_{x:\overline{n}|},$$

and the desired relationship follows.

6-20 As in Section 6.1.1, if X is paid by each of ℓ_x persons then the initial fund is $X \cdot \ell_x$ which we equate to the present value of all annuity payments. Then we have

$$X \cdot \ell_x = v \cdot \ell_{x+1} + v^2 \cdot \ell_{x+2} + \cdots + v^n \cdot \ell_{x+n}.$$

Dividing by ℓ_x produces

$$X = v \cdot \frac{\ell_{x+1}}{\ell_x} + v^2 \cdot \frac{\ell_{x+2}}{\ell_x} + \cdots + v^n \cdot \frac{\ell_{x+n}}{\ell_x}$$
$$= v \cdot p_x + v^2 \cdot {}_2p_x + \cdots + v^n \cdot {}_np_x,$$

which is $a_{x:\overline{n}|}$ by Equation (6.21).

6-21   From Equation (6.23) we have

$$E[Y_{x:\overline{n}|}] = \sum_{k=1}^{n}\left(\frac{1-v^{k-1}}{i}\right)\cdot {}_{k-1|}q_x + a_{\overline{n}|}\sum_{k=n+1}^{\infty} {}_{k-1|}q_x$$

$$= \frac{1}{i}\left[\sum_{k=1}^{n} {}_{k-1|}q_x - \sum_{k=1}^{n} v^{k-1}({}_{k-1}p_x - {}_k p_x)\right] + a_{\overline{n}|}\cdot {}_n p_x$$

$$= \frac{1}{i}\left[1 - {}_n p_x + (1-v^n)\cdot {}_n p_x - \sum_{k=1}^{n} v^{k-1}({}_{k-1}p_x - {}_k p_x)\right]$$

$$= \frac{1}{i}\left[1 - v^n\cdot {}_n p_x - \sum_{k=1}^{n} v^{k-1}\cdot {}_{k-1}p_x + \sum_{k=1}^{n} (1+i)\cdot v^k\cdot {}_k p_x\right]$$

$$= \frac{1}{i}\left[(1+i)\sum_{k=1}^{n} v^k\cdot {}_k p_x - \left(\sum_{k=1}^{n} v^{k-1}\cdot {}_{k-1}p_x - 1 + v^n\cdot {}_n p_x\right)\right]$$

$$= \frac{1}{i}\left[(1+i)\sum_{k=1}^{n} v^k\cdot {}_k p_x - \sum_{k=1}^{n} v^k\cdot {}_k p_x\right]$$

$$= \sum_{k=1}^{n} v^k\cdot {}_k p_x,$$

which is $a_{x:\overline{n}|}$ by Equation (6.21).

6-22   This time the present value of all annuity payments includes ℓ_x payments at age x but no payments at age $x+n$. We have

$$X\cdot \ell_x = \ell_x + v\cdot \ell_{x+1} + \cdots + v^{n-1}\ell_{x+n-1}.$$

Dividing by ℓ_x produces

$$X = 1 + v\cdot p_x + \cdots + v^{n-1}\cdot {}_{n-1}p_x,$$

which is $\ddot{a}_{x:\overline{n}|}$ by Equation (6.27).

6-23 This is similar to Exercise 6-21. We have

$$E\left[\ddot{Y}_{x:\overline{n}|}\right] = \sum_{k=1}^{n}\left(\frac{1-v^k}{d}\right) \cdot {}_{k-1|}q_x + \ddot{a}_{\overline{n}|} \sum_{k=n+1}^{\infty} {}_{k-1|}q_x$$

$$= \frac{1}{d}\left[\sum_{k=1}^{n} {}_{k-1|}q_x - \sum_{k=1}^{n} v^k ({}_{k-1}p_x - {}_{k}p_x)\right] + \ddot{a}_{\overline{n}|} \cdot {}_{n}p_x$$

$$= \frac{1}{d}\left[1 - {}_{n}p_x + (1-v^n) \cdot {}_{n}p_x - \sum_{k=1}^{n} v^k ({}_{k-1}p_x - {}_{k}p_x)\right]$$

$$= \frac{1}{d}\left[1 - v^n \cdot {}_{n}p_x + \sum_{k=1}^{n} v^k \cdot {}_{k}p_x - \sum_{k=1}^{n} v^k \cdot {}_{k-1}p_x\right]$$

$$= \frac{1}{d}\left[\sum_{k=0}^{n-1} v^k \cdot {}_{k}p_x - v\sum_{k=1}^{n} v^{k-1} \cdot {}_{k-1}p_x\right]$$

$$= \frac{1}{d}\left[\sum_{k=0}^{n-1} v^k \cdot {}_{k}p_x - (1-d)\sum_{k=0}^{n-1} v^k \cdot {}_{k}p_x\right] = \sum_{k=0}^{n-1} v^k \cdot {}_{k}p_x,$$

which is $\ddot{a}_{x:\overline{n}|}$ by Equation (6.27).

6-24 Beginning with Equation (6.24b), we first divide numerator and denominator by $(1+i)^2$ to obtain

$$Var(Y_{x:\overline{n}|}) = \frac{({}^2A^1_{x:\overline{n}|} - A^{1\,2}_{x:\overline{n}|}) + v^2({}^2A_{x:\overline{n}|}^{1} - A_{x:\overline{n}|}^{1\,2}) - 2v \cdot A^1_{x:\overline{n}|} \cdot A_{x:\overline{n}|}^{1}}{d^2}.$$

Then we rearrange terms in the numerator to obtain

$$Var(Y_{x:\overline{n}|}) = \frac{({}^2A^1_{x:\overline{n}|} + v^2 \cdot {}^2A_{x:\overline{n}|}^{1}) - (A^{1\,2}_{x:\overline{n}|} + 2v \cdot A^1_{x:\overline{n}|} \cdot A_{x:\overline{n}|}^{1} + v^2 \cdot A_{x:\overline{n}|}^{1\,2})}{d^2}$$

$$= \frac{({}^2A^1_{x:\overline{n}|} + v^2 \cdot {}^2A_{x:\overline{n}|}^{1}) - (A^1_{x:\overline{n}|} + v \cdot A_{x:\overline{n}|}^{1})^2}{d^2}.$$

Observe that the expression inside the parentheses of the squared term in the numerator can be written as

$$A^1_{x:\overline{n}|} + v \cdot A_{x:\overline{n}|}^{\;\;1} = v \cdot q_x + \cdots + v^n \cdot {}_{n-1|}q_x + v \cdot v^n \cdot {}_n p_x.$$

We add and subtract the term $v^{n+1} \cdot {}_{n+1}p_x$ to this expression, obtaining

$$v \cdot q_x + \cdots + v^n \cdot {}_{n-1|}q_x + v^{n+1} \cdot {}_n p_x - v^{n+1} \cdot {}_{n+1}p_x + v^{n+1} \cdot {}_{n+1}p_x$$

$$= v \cdot q_x + \cdots + v^n \cdot {}_{n-1|}q_x + v^{n+1} \cdot {}_{n|}q_x + {}_{n+1}E_x$$

$$= A^1_{x:\overline{n+1}|} + A_{x:\overline{n+1}|}^{\;\;\;\;1} = A_{x:\overline{n+1}|}.$$

The expression inside the first set of parentheses in the numerator is the same as that in the second set, except at interest rate $i' = (1+i)^2 - 1$ (or $\delta' = 2\delta$). Therefore the same steps as above will produce ${}^2A_{x:\overline{n+1}|}$ for this expression so we have

$$Var(Y_{x:\overline{n}|}) = \frac{{}^2A_{x:\overline{n+1}|} - A_{x:\overline{n+1}|}^{\;\;2}}{d^2},$$

which is Equation (6.34) with n replaced by $n+1$.

6-25 The process is the same as that shown on page 178, except here we have payment of ℓ_x at age x but no payment at age $x+n$. Then we have

$$X = \frac{\ell_x(1+i)^n + \ell_{x+1}(1+i)^{n-1} + \cdots + \ell_{x+n-1}(1+i)}{\ell_{x+n}}$$

$$= \frac{(1+i)^n \cdot \ell_x}{\ell_{x+n}} \left[\frac{\ell_x(1+i)^n + \ell_{x+1}(1+i)^{n-1} + \cdots + \ell_{x+n-1}(1+i)}{(1+i)^n \cdot \ell_x} \right]$$

$$= \frac{(1+i)^n \cdot \ell_x}{\ell_{x+n}} \left[\frac{\ell_x + v \cdot \ell_{x+1} + \cdots + v^{n-1} \cdot \ell_{x+n-1}}{\ell_x} \right]$$

$$= \frac{(1+i)^n \cdot \ell_x}{\ell_{x+n}} \left[1 + v \cdot p_x + \cdots + v^{n-1} \cdot {}_{n-1}p_x \right]$$

$$= \frac{(1+i)^n \cdot \ell_x}{\ell_{x+n}} \cdot \ddot{a}_{x:\overline{n}|},$$

which is Equation (6.35).

Chapter Six

6-26 From Equation (6.31) we have

$$\ddot{a}_{x:\overline{4}|} = E\left[\ddot{Y}_{x:\overline{4}|}\right]$$
$$= \ddot{a}_{\overline{1}|} \cdot q_x + \ddot{a}_{\overline{2}|} \cdot {}_{1|}q_x + \ddot{a}_{\overline{3}|} \cdot {}_{2|}q_x + \ddot{a}_{\overline{4}|} \cdot {}_{3|}q_x + \ddot{a}_{\overline{4}|} \cdot {}_4p_x.$$

Note that $\ddot{a}_{\overline{4}|}$ is the present value of payments if (x) fails in the fourth year or survives beyond the fourth year, so $\ddot{a}_{\overline{4}|}$ is the value if (x) survives beyond the third year, the probability of which is ${}_3p_x$. Then we have

$$\ddot{a}_{x:\overline{4}|} = (1.00)(.33) + (1.93)(.24)$$
$$+ (2.80)(.16) + (3.62)(1-.33-.24-.16)$$
$$= .3300 + .4632 + .4480 + .9774$$
$$= 2.2186.$$

6-27 We have

$$E\left[\ddot{Y}_{x:\overline{3}|}\right] = (1)(1-p_x) + (1.87)(p_x - {}_2p_x) + (2.62)({}_2p_x)$$
$$= (1)(.10) + (1.87)(.90-.81) + (2.62)(.81)$$
$$= .1000 + .1683 + 2.1222 = 2.3905$$

and

$$E\left[\ddot{Y}_{x:\overline{3}|}^2\right] = (1)^2(.10) + (1.87)^2(.90-.81) + (2.62)^2(.81)$$
$$= .10000 + .31472 + 5.56016 = 5.97488.$$

Then

$$Var\left(\ddot{Y}_{x:\overline{3}|}\right) = 5.97488 - (2.3905)^2 = .26039.$$

6-28 From Equation (6.40) we have

$$\begin{aligned}
Var\left(\bar{Y}_{x:\overline{n}|}\right) &= \frac{{}^2\bar{A}_{x:\overline{n}|} - \bar{A}_{x:\overline{n}|}^2}{\delta^2} \\
&= \frac{\left(1 - 2\delta \cdot {}^2\bar{a}_{x:\overline{n}|}\right) - \left(1 - \delta \cdot \bar{a}_{x:\overline{n}|}\right)^2}{\delta^2} \\
&= \frac{1 - 2\delta \cdot {}^2\bar{a}_{x:\overline{n}|} - 1 + 2\delta \cdot \bar{a}_{x:\overline{n}|} - \delta^2 \cdot \bar{a}_{x:\overline{n}|}^2}{\delta^2} \\
&= \frac{1}{\delta}\left(-2 \cdot {}^2\bar{a}_{x:\overline{n}|} + 2 \cdot \bar{a}_{x:\overline{n}|} - \delta \cdot \bar{a}_{x:\overline{n}|}^2\right) \\
&= \frac{2}{\delta}\left(\bar{a}_{x:\overline{n}|} - {}^2\bar{a}_{x:\overline{n}|}\right) - \bar{a}_{x:\overline{n}|}^2,
\end{aligned}$$

as required.

6-29 We have

$$\begin{aligned}
\int_0^n \bar{a}_{\overline{t}|} \cdot {}_tp_x \mu_{x+t}\, dt &= \frac{1}{\delta}\int_0^n (1-v^t) \cdot {}_tp_x \mu_{x+t}\, dt \\
&= \frac{1}{\delta}\left({}_nq_x - \bar{A}^1_{x:\overline{n}|}\right) \\
&= \frac{1}{\delta}\left[(1 - {}_np_x) - (1 - \delta \cdot \bar{a}_{x:\overline{n}|} - {}_nE_x)\right] \\
&= \frac{1}{\delta}\left(\delta \cdot \bar{a}_{x:\overline{n}|} - {}_np_x(1 - v^n)\right) \\
&= \bar{a}_{x:\overline{n}|} - {}_np_x \cdot \bar{a}_{\overline{n}|},
\end{aligned}$$

as required.

CHAPTER SIX

6-30 From Equation (6.47) we have

$$E[_n|Y_x] = \sum_{k=n+1}^{\infty} v^n \left(\frac{1-v^{k-n-1}}{i}\right) \cdot _{k-1}|q_x$$

$$= \frac{1}{i}\left[v^n \sum_{k=n+1}^{\infty} {_{k-1}}|q_x - \sum_{k=n+1}^{\infty} v^{k-1} \cdot {_{k-1}}|q_x\right]$$

$$= \frac{1}{i}\left[v^n \cdot {_n}p_x - \sum_{k=n+1}^{\infty} v^{k-1}({_{k-1}}p_x - {_k}p_x)\right]$$

$$= \frac{1}{i}\left[-\left(\sum_{k=n+1}^{\infty} v^{k-1} \cdot {_{k-1}}p_x - v^n \cdot {_n}p_x\right) + \sum_{k=n+1}^{\infty} v^{k-1} \cdot {_k}p_x\right]$$

$$= \frac{1}{i}\left[(1+i)\sum_{k=n+1}^{\infty} v^k \cdot {_k}p_x - \sum_{k=n+1}^{\infty} v^k \cdot {_k}p_x\right]$$

$$= \sum_{k=n+1}^{\infty} v^k \cdot {_k}p_x = \sum_{s=1}^{\infty} v^{s+n} \cdot {_{s+n}}p_x,$$

which is $_n|a_x$ by Equation (6.45).

6-31 This demonstration parallels that of Example 6.9. In this case,

$$_n|\ddot{Y}_x = \ddot{Y}_x - \ddot{Y}_{x:\overline{n}|},$$

so

$$_n|\ddot{Y}_x = \ddot{a}_{\overline{K_x|}} - \ddot{a}_{\overline{K_x|}} = 0$$

for $K_x \leq n$, and

$$_n|\ddot{Y}_x = \ddot{a}_{\overline{K_x|}} - \ddot{a}_{\overline{n|}} = v^n \cdot \ddot{a}_{\overline{K_x-n|}}$$

for $K_x > n$, as required. Then

$$E\left[_n|\ddot{Y}_x\right] = E\left[\ddot{Y}_x - \ddot{Y}_{x:\overline{n}|}\right] = \ddot{a}_x - \ddot{a}_{x:\overline{n}|} = {_n}E_x \cdot \ddot{a}_{x+n} = {_n}|\ddot{a}_x,$$

as required.

6-32 The force of mortality is constant, so $_tp_x = e^{-\mu t}$ for all t. Then we can calculate

$$\ddot{a}_x = 1 + v \cdot p_x + v^2 \cdot {}_2p_x + \cdots$$
$$= 1 + e^{-\delta} \cdot e^{-\mu} + e^{-2\delta} \cdot e^{-2\mu} + \cdots$$
$$= 1 + e^{-(\mu+\delta)} + (e^{-(\mu+\delta)})^2 + \cdots$$
$$= \frac{1}{1 - e^{-(\mu+\delta)}} = \frac{1}{1 - e^{-[.01 + \ln(1.04)]}} = 20.82075,$$

so

$$_5|\ddot{a}_x = \ddot{a}_x - \ddot{a}_{x:\overline{5}|} = 16.27875.$$

Then $S > {}_5|\ddot{a}_x$ if 17 payments are made, which occurs if (x) survives to age $x + 21$. This means that

$$Pr(S > {}_5|\ddot{a}_x) = {}_{21}p_x = e^{-(21)(.01)} = .81058.$$

6-33 The death benefit is a 30-year term insurance of the net single premium amount, so we have the equation value

$$NSP = NSP \cdot A^1_{35:\overline{30}|} + {}_{30}|\ddot{a}_{35} = NSP \cdot A^1_{35:\overline{30}|} + {}_{30}E_{35} \cdot \ddot{a}_{65}.$$

We find ${}_{30}E_{35}$ as

$$_{30}E_{35} = A_{35:\overline{30}|}^{1} = A_{35:\overline{30}|} - A^1_{35:\overline{30}|} = .14,$$

so

$$NSP = \frac{(.14)(9.90)}{1 - .07} = 1.49032.$$

6-34 From the definition of $\overline{Y}$ we have

$$E[\overline{Y}] = \int_0^n \overline{a_{\overline{n}|}} \cdot {}_t p_x \mu_{x+t}\, dt + \int_n^\infty \overline{a_{\overline{t}|}} \cdot {}_t p_x \mu_{x+t}\, dt$$

$$= \int_0^\infty \overline{a_{\overline{t}|}} \cdot {}_t p_x \mu_{x+t}\, dt - \int_0^n \overline{a_{\overline{t}|}} \cdot {}_t p_x \mu_{x+t}\, dt + \int_0^n \overline{a_{\overline{n}|}} \cdot {}_t p_x \mu_{x+t}\, dt$$

$$= \overline{a}_x - \left(\overline{a}_{x:\overline{n}|} - {}_n p_x \cdot \overline{a_{\overline{n}|}}\right) + \overline{a_{\overline{n}|}} \cdot {}_n q_x,$$

where we use the result of Exercise 6-29. This simplifies to

$$\overline{a}_x - \overline{a}_{x:\overline{n}|} + {}_n p_x \cdot \overline{a_{\overline{n}|}} + \overline{a_{\overline{n}|}} - {}_n p_x \cdot \overline{a_{\overline{n}|}} = {}_n| \overline{a}_x + \overline{a_{\overline{n}|}},$$

as required. The result is also intuitive. Payment is made for n years in any case, whether (x) survives or not, and then beyond $t = n$ if survival occurs. Thus the APV is $\overline{a_{\overline{n}|}} + {}_n| \overline{a}_x$.

6-35 (a) Equation (6.66): Start with Equation (6.61), and imitate the variable change that evolved Equation (6.44) into Equation (6.45).

(b) Equation (6.67): Start with Equation (6.64), and imitate the variable change that evolved Equation (6.48b) into Equation (6.51).

(c) Equation (6.68): Simply add the right sides of Equations (6.59) and (6.61) to obtain the right side of Equation (6.58).

(d) Equation (6.69): Simply add the right sides of Equations (6.63) and (6.64) to obtain the right side of Equation (6.62)

(e) Equation (6.70): Simply add $\frac{1}{m}$ to the right side of Equation (6.58), by including $t = 0$ in the summation, to obtain the right side of Equation (6.62).

6-36 (a) On the right side of Equation (6.59), add $\frac{1}{m}$ (by including $t=0$ in the summation) and subtract $\frac{1}{m} \cdot {}_nE_x$ (by deleting $t=mn$ in the summation) to reach the right side of Equation (6.63).

(b) On the right side of Equation (6.61), add $\frac{1}{m} \cdot {}_nE_x$ (by including $t=mn$ in the summation) to reach the right side of Equation (6.64).

6-37 Begin with the definition of $\ddot{Y}_x^{(m)}$ given by Equation (6.76). We have

$$\ddot{Y}_x^{(m)} = \frac{1}{m}\left(\frac{1-v^{J_x}}{d}\right),$$

where this d is the effective discount rate over $\frac{1}{m}$ of a year. Then $m \cdot d = d^{(m)}$, so we have

$$\ddot{Y}_x^{(m)} = \frac{1-v^{J_x}}{d^{(m)}} = \frac{1-Z_x^{(m)}}{d^{(m)}},$$

where $Z_x^{(m)}$ is defined by Equation (5.39). Taking expectations yields

$$\ddot{a}_x^{(m)} = E\left[\ddot{Y}_x^{(m)}\right] = \frac{1-E[Z_x^{(m)}]}{d^{(m)}} = \frac{1-A_x^{(m)}}{d^{(m)}},$$

and Equation (6.77) follows.

6-38 Let $\alpha(m) = \dfrac{id}{i^{(m)}d^{(m)}}$ and $\beta(m) = \dfrac{i-i^{(m)}}{i^{(m)}d^{(m)}}$.

(a) From Equation (6.67),

$$\begin{aligned}
{}_n|\ddot{a}_x^{(m)} &= {}_nE_x \cdot \ddot{a}_{x+n}^{(m)} \\
&= {}_nE_x\left[\alpha(m)\cdot \ddot{a}_{x+n} - \beta(m)\right] \\
&= \alpha(m)\cdot {}_n|\ddot{a}_x - \beta(m)\cdot {}_nE_x.
\end{aligned}$$

(b) From Equation (6.69),

$$\begin{aligned}
\ddot{a}_{x:\overline{n}|}^{(m)} &= \ddot{a}_x^{(m)} - {}_n|\ddot{a}_x^{(m)} \\
&= \left(\alpha(m)\cdot \ddot{a}_x - \beta(m)\right) - \left(\alpha(m)\cdot {}_n|\ddot{a}_x - \beta(m)\cdot {}_nE_x\right) \\
&= \alpha(m)\cdot(\ddot{a}_x - {}_n|\ddot{a}_x) - \beta(m)\cdot(1 - {}_nE_x) \\
&= \alpha(m)\cdot \ddot{a}_{x:\overline{n}|} - \beta(m)\cdot(1 - {}_nE_x).
\end{aligned}$$

(c) From Equation (6.65),

$$\begin{aligned}
\ddot{s}_{x:\overline{n}|}^{(m)} &= \frac{1}{{}_nE_x}\cdot \ddot{a}_{x:\overline{n}|}^{(m)} \\
&= \frac{1}{{}_nE_x}\left(\alpha(m)\cdot \ddot{a}_{x:\overline{n}|} - \beta(m)\cdot(1-{}_nE_x)\right) \\
&= \alpha(m)\cdot \ddot{s}_{x:\overline{n}|} - \beta(m)\cdot\left(\frac{1}{{}_nE_x} - 1\right).
\end{aligned}$$

6-39 (a) Begin with Equation (6.70), rewritten as
$$a_x^{(m)} = \ddot{a}_x^{(m)} - \frac{1}{m},$$
and substitute for $\ddot{a}_x^{(m)}$ from Equation (6.78). We have
$$a_x^{(m)} = \alpha(m) \cdot \ddot{a}_x - \beta(m) - \frac{1}{m}.$$
Then substitute $\ddot{a}_x = a_x + 1$, reaching
$$a_x^{(m)} = \alpha(m) \cdot a_x + \alpha(m) - \beta(m) - \frac{1}{m}$$
$$= \frac{id}{i^{(m)}d^{(m)}} \cdot a_x + \left(\frac{id}{i^{(m)}d^{(m)}} - \frac{i - i^{(m)}}{i^{(m)}d^{(m)}} - \frac{1}{m} \right)$$
$$= \frac{id}{i^{(m)}d^{(m)}} \cdot a_x + \frac{m(i-d) - m(i - i^{(m)}) - m(i^{(m)} - d^{(m)})}{m \cdot i^{(m)}d^{(m)}}$$
$$= \frac{id}{i^{(m)}d^{(m)}} \cdot a_x + \frac{d^{(m)} - d}{i^{(m)}d^{(m)}},$$
as required. Then with part (a) established, each of parts (b), (c), and (d) follow from part (a) in the same way Exercise 6-38, parts (a), (b), and (c) followed from Equation (6.78).

6-40 (a) The result follows immediately from
$$\delta = \lim_{m \to \infty} i^{(m)} = \lim_{m \to \infty} d^{(m)}.$$
(b) The result follows immediately for the same reason.
(c) Starting with the part (b) result we have
$$\bar{a}_x = \frac{id}{\delta^2}(\ddot{a}_x - 1) + \frac{\delta - d}{\delta^2} = \frac{id}{\delta^2} \cdot \ddot{a}_x - \frac{id}{\delta^2} + \frac{\delta - d}{\delta^2}$$
$$= \frac{id}{\delta^2} \cdot \ddot{a}_x - \left(\frac{id - \delta + d}{\delta^2} \right)$$
$$= \frac{id}{\delta^2} \cdot \ddot{a}_x - \left(\frac{i - d - \delta + d}{\delta^2} \right)$$
$$= \frac{id}{\delta^2} \cdot \ddot{a}_x - \frac{i - \delta}{\delta^2},$$
which is the part (a) result.

6-41 (a) $\displaystyle {}_n|\ddot{a}_x^{(m)} = {}_nE_x \cdot \ddot{a}_{x+n}^{(m)}$
$\displaystyle \approx {}_nE_x\left(\ddot{a}_{x+n} - \frac{m-1}{2m}\right) = {}_n|\ddot{a}_x - \frac{m-1}{2m}\cdot {}_nE_x$

(b) $\displaystyle \ddot{a}_{x:\overline{n}|}^{(m)} = \ddot{a}_x^{(m)} - {}_n|\ddot{a}_x^{(m)}$
$\displaystyle \approx \left(\ddot{a}_x - \frac{m-1}{2m}\right) - \left({}_n|\ddot{a}_x - \frac{m-1}{2m}\cdot {}_nE_x\right)$
$\displaystyle = \ddot{a}_{x:\overline{n}|} - \frac{m-1}{2m}(1 - {}_nE_x)$

(c) $\displaystyle \ddot{s}_{x:\overline{n}|}^{(m)} = \ddot{a}_{x:\overline{n}|}^{(m)}\cdot \frac{1}{{}_nE_x} \approx \left[\ddot{a}_{x:\overline{n}|} - \frac{m-1}{2m}(1 - {}_nE_x)\right]\cdot \frac{1}{{}_nE_x}$
$\displaystyle = \ddot{s}_{x:\overline{n}|} - \frac{m-1}{2m}\left(\frac{1}{{}_nE_x} - 1\right)$

(d) $\displaystyle a_x^{(m)} = \ddot{a}_x^{(m)} - \frac{1}{m}$
$\displaystyle \approx \ddot{a}_x - \frac{m-1}{2m} - \frac{1}{m}$
$\displaystyle = a_x + 1 - \frac{m-1}{2m} - \frac{1}{m}$
$\displaystyle = a_x + \frac{2m - m + 1 - 2}{2m} = a_x + \frac{m-1}{2m}$

(e) $\displaystyle {}_n|a_x^{(m)} = {}_nE_x \cdot a_{x+n}^{(m)} \approx {}_nE_x\left(a_{x+n} + \frac{m-1}{2m}\right)$
$\displaystyle = {}_n|a_x + \frac{m-1}{2m}\cdot {}_nE_x$

(f) $\displaystyle a_{x:\overline{n}|}^{(m)} = a_x^{(m)} - {}_n|a_x^{(m)} \approx \left(a_x + \frac{m-1}{2m}\right) - \left({}_n|a_x + \frac{m-1}{2m}\cdot {}_nE_x\right)$
$\displaystyle = a_{x:\overline{n}|} + \frac{m-1}{2m}(1 - {}_nE_x)$

(g) $\displaystyle s_{x:\overline{n}|}^{(m)} = a_{x:\overline{n}|}^{(m)}\cdot \frac{1}{{}_nE_x} \approx \left[a_{x:\overline{n}|} + \frac{m-1}{2m}(1 - {}_nE_x)\right]\cdot \frac{1}{{}_nE_x}$
$\displaystyle = s_{x:\overline{n}|} + \frac{m-1}{2m}\left(\frac{1}{{}_nE_x} - 1\right)$

6-42 By L'Hospital's Rule,

$$\lim_{m\to\infty} \frac{m-1}{2m} = \lim_{m\to\infty} \frac{1}{2} = \frac{1}{2},$$

so $\ddot{a}_x^{(m)}$ becomes

$$\bar{a}_x \approx \ddot{a}_x - \frac{1}{2}$$

and $a_x^{(m)}$ becomes

$$\bar{a}_x \approx a_x + \frac{1}{2}.$$

6-43 Recall that $\bar{A}_x = \frac{i}{\delta}\cdot A_x$, and $A_x = 1 - d\cdot \ddot{a}_x$, so we have

$$\begin{aligned}\bar{A}_x &= \frac{i}{\delta}(1-d\cdot\ddot{a}_x) \\ &= \frac{i}{\delta} - \frac{id}{\delta}\cdot\ddot{a}_x \\ &= \frac{i}{\delta} - \frac{i-d}{\delta}\cdot\ddot{a}_x.\end{aligned}$$

6-44 The APV of the contract is

$$\begin{aligned}APV &= 1 + 2\cdot v\cdot p_x + 3\cdot v^2\cdot {}_2p_x \\ &= 1 + (2)(.90)(.80) + (3)(.90)^2(.80)(.75) \\ &= 3.898.\end{aligned}$$

The present value of payments actually made is $1 + 2v = 2.80$ if only two payments are made, and $2.80 + 3v^2 = 5.23$ if all three payments are made. Then for the present value of payments actually made to exceed the APV, survival to time $t = 2$ is required, the probability of which is $(.80)(.75) = .60$.

CHAPTER SIX

6-45 The present value random variable Y is $y=2$ for failure in the first year (with probability .20), $y = 2+3v = 4.70$ for failure in the second year (with probability $(.80)(.25) = .20$), and $y = 4.70 + 4v^2 = 7.94$ for survival to the third year (with probability $(.80)(.75) = .60$). Then we have

$$E[Y] = (2)(.20) + (4.70)(.20) + (7.94)(.60) = 6.104$$

and

$$E[Y^2] = (2)^2(.20) + (4.70)^2(.20) + (7.94)^2(.60) = 43.04416,$$

so $Var(Y) = (43.04416) - (6.104)^2 = 5.78534$.

6-46 (a) Extending the result of Exercise 5-25(a), we have

$$\begin{aligned}(IA)_x &= A_x + {}_1E_x \cdot A_{x+1} + {}_2E_x \cdot A_{x+2} + \cdots \\ &= (1 - d \cdot \ddot{a}_x) + {}_1E_x(1 - d \cdot \ddot{a}_{x+1}) + {}_2E_x(1 - d \cdot \ddot{a}_{x+2}) + \cdots \\ &= (1 + {}_1E_x + {}_2E_x + \cdots) \\ &\quad - d(\ddot{a}_x + {}_1E_x \cdot \ddot{a}_{x+1} + {}_2E_x \cdot \ddot{a}_{x+2} + \cdots) \\ &= \ddot{a}_x - d \cdot (I\ddot{a})_x,\end{aligned}$$

as required.

(b) From Equation (5.55) we have

$$(\overline{I}\,\overline{A})_x = \int_0^\infty t \cdot v^t \cdot {}_tp_x \mu_{x+t}\, dt.$$

Using integration by parts we have

$$\begin{aligned}(\overline{I}\,\overline{A})_x &= \int_0^\infty \frac{t \cdot v^t}{-\delta \cdot t \cdot v^t + v^t} \bigg|\; \frac{{}_tp_x \mu_{x+t}\, dt}{-{}_tp_x} \\ &= -t \cdot v^t \cdot {}_tp_x \Big|_0^\infty - \int_0^\infty (\delta \cdot t \cdot v^t - v^t) \cdot {}_tp_x\, dt.\end{aligned}$$

The first term goes to zero at both limits, so we have

$$\begin{aligned}(\overline{I}\,\overline{A})_x &= \int_0^\infty v^t \cdot {}_tp_x\, dt - \delta \int_0^\infty t \cdot v^t \cdot {}_tp_x\, dt \\ &= \overline{a}_x - \delta \cdot (\overline{I}\,\overline{a})_x, \text{ as required.}\end{aligned}$$

CHAPTER SEVEN
FUNDING PLANS FOR CONTINGENT CONTRACTS

7-1 Starting with Equation (7.7a) we have

$$P_{x:\overline{n}|} = \frac{A_{x:\overline{n}|}}{\ddot{a}_{x:\overline{n}|}} = \frac{1-d\cdot\ddot{a}_{x:\overline{n}|}}{\ddot{a}_{x:\overline{n}|}},$$

by using Equation (6.33b) for $A_{x:\overline{n}|}$. Then the desired relationship follows directly.

7-2 We start with the idea that the APV at age x for n-year term insurance can be split into the APV for insurance over $(x, x+t)$ plus the APV (at age x) for insurance over $(x+t, x+n)$. Thus we have

$$A^1_{x:\overline{n}|} = A^1_{x:\overline{t}|} + {}_tE_x \cdot A^1_{x+t:\overline{n-t}|}.$$

Dividing both sides by $\ddot{a}_{x:\overline{t}|}$ produces the desired relationship.

7-3 If the net level annual premium is P, then the APV of all benefits is

$$APVB = 1000 A_{30} + P\cdot(IA)^1_{30:\overline{10}|} + 10P \cdot {}_{10|}A_{30}.$$

This means that the return-of-premium benefit during the first ten years is increasing, as each additional premium is paid, but is then level at $10P$ after the first ten years. This explains why the APV of the return-of-premium benefit is

$$P\cdot(IA)^1_{30:\overline{10}|} + 10P \cdot {}_{10|}A_{30}.$$

The APV of the premium stream is simply $P\cdot\ddot{a}_{30:\overline{10}|}$. Equating this to APVB and factoring out the terms involving P produces the desired relationship.

7-4 Equating the APV of benefits to the APV of net premiums, we have

$$1000 A_{75} = P_1 + P_2 \cdot vp_{75} + P_3 \cdot v^2 \,{}_2p_{75} + \cdots$$
$$= P_1 + P_1(1+i) \cdot vp_{75} + P_1(1+i)^2 \cdot v^2 \,{}_2p_{75} + \cdots$$
$$= P_1[1 + p_{75} + {}_2p_{75} + \cdots]$$
$$= P_1[1 + e_{75}].$$

Failure has a uniform distribution, so

$$_t p_{75} = 1 - \frac{t}{\omega - 75} = \frac{30 - t}{30},$$

so

$$1 + e_{75} = \frac{30}{30} + \frac{29}{30} + \frac{28}{30} + \cdots + \frac{1}{30} = \frac{(30)(31)}{(2)(30)} = 15.50.$$

Similarly,

$$_t|q_{75} = {}_tp_{75} - {}_{t+1}p_{75} = \frac{1}{30},$$

so

$$1000 A_{75} = 1000\left[v \cdot q_{75} + v^2 \cdot {}_1|q_{75} + \cdots\right]$$
$$= \frac{1000}{30}\left[v + v^2 + \cdots + v^{30}\right]$$
$$= \frac{100}{3} \cdot a_{\overline{30}|.05} = 512.41503.$$

Finally,

$$P_1 = \frac{1000 A_{75}}{1 + e_{75}} = \frac{512.41503}{15.50} = 33.06.$$

CHAPTER SEVEN

7-5 The annual mortgage payment is

$$P = \frac{100{,}000}{a_{\overline{25}|.05}} = 7095.25,$$

so the outstanding balance at the end of the kth year, but before the payment due then, is $7095.25\ddot{a}_{\overline{25-k+1}|}$. (We measure the OB in this way because this represents the death benefit for death in year k.) Then the APV of the benefit is

$$\begin{aligned}
APV &= 7095.25 \sum_{k=1}^{25} \ddot{a}_{\overline{25-k+1}|} \cdot v^k \cdot {}_{k-1|}q_{40} \\
&= \frac{7095.25}{\frac{.05}{1.05}} \sum_{k=1}^{25} (1 - v^{25-k+1}) \cdot v^k \cdot {}_{k-1|}q_{40} \\
&= 149{,}000 \left[A^1_{40:\overline{25}|} - v^{26} \cdot {}_{25}q_{40} \right] \\
&= 149{,}000 \left[1 - \frac{.05}{1.05} \cdot \ddot{a}_{40:\overline{25}|} - {}_{25}E_{40} - v^{26} \cdot {}_{25}q_{40} \right] \\
&= 149{,}000 \left[1 - \frac{.05}{1.05}(14) - \frac{.80}{(1.05)^{25}} - \frac{1-.80}{(1.05)^{26}} \right] \\
&= 149{,}000[1 - .66667 - .23624 - .05625] \\
&= 6085.94,
\end{aligned}$$

and the net level annual premium is

$$P = \frac{6085.94}{14} = 434.71.$$

7-6 We have

$$1000P(\bar{A}_{x:\overline{n}|}) = \frac{1000\bar{A}_{x:\overline{n}|}}{\ddot{a}_{x:\overline{n}|}} = \frac{(1000)(.804)}{\ddot{a}_{x:\overline{n}|}}.$$

We calculate $\ddot{a}_{x:\overline{n}|}$ from

$$\ddot{a}_{x:\overline{n}|} = \frac{1 - A_{x:\overline{n}|}}{d},$$

where, in turn, we find $A_{x:\overline{n}|}$ from

$$\bar{A}_{x:\overline{n}|} = \bar{A}^1_{x:\overline{n}|} + {}_nE_x$$

$$= \frac{i}{\delta} \cdot A^1_{x:\overline{n}|} + {}_nE_x = \frac{.05}{\ln(1.05)} \cdot A^1_{x:\overline{n}|} + .600 = 804,$$

which gives us $A^1_{x:\overline{n}|} = \frac{(.804 - .600) \cdot \ln(1.05)}{.05} = .200$. Then

$$A_{x:\overline{n}|} = A^1_{x:\overline{n}|} + {}_nE_x = .200 + .600 = .800,$$

so

$$\ddot{a}_{x:\overline{n}|} = \frac{1 - .800}{\frac{.04}{1.04}} = 5.20$$

and finally

$$1000P(\bar{A}_{x:\overline{n}|}) = \frac{(1000)(.804)}{5.20} = 154.62.$$

7-7 The return-of-premium benefit is a 10-year increasing insurance of amounts $P, 2P, \ldots, 10P$. Thus the equation of value is

$$P \cdot \ddot{a}_{55:\overline{10}|} = 10,000 \cdot {}_{10|}\ddot{a}_{55} + P \cdot (IA)^1_{55:\overline{10}|},$$

so we have

$$P = \frac{10,000 \cdot {}_{10|}\ddot{a}_{55}}{\ddot{a}_{55:\overline{10}|} - (IA)^1_{55:\overline{10}|}}$$

$$= \frac{(10,000)(\ddot{a}_{55} - \ddot{a}_{55:\overline{10}|})}{\ddot{a}_{55:\overline{10}|} - (IA)^1_{55:\overline{10}|}} = \frac{(10,000)(12 - 8)}{8 - 2.50} = 7272.73.$$

CHAPTER SEVEN

7-8 From Equation (6.35) we have

$$\ddot{s}_{x:\overline{n}|} = \frac{\ddot{a}_{x:\overline{n}|}}{_nE_x}.$$

Recall that $_nE_x = A_{x:\overline{n}|}^{1}$, so

$$P_{x:\overline{n}|}^{1} = \frac{A_{x:\overline{n}|}^{1}}{\ddot{a}_{x:\overline{n}|}} = \frac{_nE_x}{\ddot{a}_{x:\overline{n}|}},$$

and the desired relationship follows.

7-9 From Equation (7.17) we have

$$E[L_x^2] = E\left[\left(1+\frac{P_x}{d}\right)^2 \cdot Z_x^2 - 2\left(\frac{P_x}{d}\right)\left(1+\frac{P_x}{d}\right)\cdot Z_x + \left(\frac{P_x}{d}\right)^2\right]$$

$$= \left(1+\frac{P_x}{d}\right)^2 \cdot {}^2A_x - \left[2\left(\frac{P_x}{d}\right)\left(1+\frac{P_x}{d}\right)\cdot A_x - \left(\frac{P_x}{d}\right)^2\right].$$

Recall that

$$\frac{P_x}{d} = \frac{1}{d}\left(\frac{A_x}{\ddot{a}_x}\right) = \frac{A_x}{1-A_x},$$

so

$$1+\frac{P_x}{d} = 1+\frac{A_x}{1-A_x} = \frac{1}{1-A_x}.$$

Then the term in brackets in the second line of $E[L_x^2]$ above, in terms of A_x, is

$$2\left(\frac{A_x}{1-A_x}\right)\left(\frac{1}{1-A_x}\right)\cdot A_x - \left(\frac{A_x}{1-A_x}\right)^2 = \left(\frac{A_x}{1-A_x}\right)^2$$

$$= \left(1+\frac{P_x}{d}\right)^2 \cdot A_x^2,$$

which gives Equation (7.16b).

7-10 We know that
$$L_{49} = Z_{49} - P \cdot \ddot{Y}_{49}$$
$$= Z_{49} - P\left(\frac{1-Z_{49}}{d}\right)$$
$$= Z_{49}\left(1+\frac{P}{d}\right) - \frac{P}{d},$$

where P is not necessarily determined by the equivalence principle. Then
$$Var(L_{49}) = \left(1+\frac{P}{d}\right)^2 \cdot Var(Z_{49})$$
$$= \left(1+\frac{P}{d}\right)^2 \cdot \left(^2A_{49} - A_{49}^2\right)$$
$$= \left(1+\frac{P}{d}\right)^2 \cdot \left[.11723 - (.29224)^2\right]$$
$$= .03183\left(1+\frac{P}{d}\right)^2$$
$$= .10.$$

This can be solved for
$$\frac{P}{d} = \left[\left(\frac{.10}{.03183}\right)^{1/2} - 1\right] = .77248.$$

Then
$$E[L_{49}] = \left(1+\frac{P}{d}\right) \cdot E[Z_{49}] - \frac{P}{d}$$
$$= (1.77248)(.29224) - .77248$$
$$= -.25449.$$

7-11 The condition $E[L_x] = 0$ implies $P = P_x$. Then

$$\begin{aligned}Var(L_x) &= \left(1+\frac{P_x}{d}\right)^2 \cdot \left(^2A_x - A_x^2\right) \\ &= \left(\frac{1}{d \cdot \ddot{a}_x}\right)^2 \cdot \left(^2A_x - A_x^2\right) \\ &= .30,\end{aligned}$$

so

$$^2A_x - A_x^2 = (.30)(d \cdot \ddot{a}_x)^2.$$

Then observe that

$$\begin{aligned}E\left[L_x^*\right] &= A_x\left(1+\frac{P}{d}\right) - \frac{P}{d} \\ &= (1-d\cdot\ddot{a}_x)\left(1+\frac{P}{d}\right) - \frac{P}{d} \\ &= 1 - d\cdot\ddot{a}_x + \frac{P}{d} - P\cdot\ddot{a}_x - \frac{P}{d} = -.20,\end{aligned}$$

so $1 - (P_x + d)\ddot{a}_x = -.20$, or $P_x + d = \dfrac{1.20}{\ddot{a}_x}$.

Now observe that

$$\begin{aligned}Var(L_x^*) &= \left(1+\frac{P}{d}\right)^2 \cdot \left(^2A_x - A_x^2\right) \\ &= \left(\frac{P+d}{d}\right)^2 (.30)(d \cdot \ddot{a}_x)^2 \\ &= \left(\frac{1.20}{d \cdot \ddot{a}_x}\right)^2 (.30)(d \cdot \ddot{a}_x)^2 \\ &= (1.20)^2(.30) = .43200.\end{aligned}$$

7-12   We know that

$$L(\pi) = 10{,}000Z_{30} - \pi \cdot \ddot{Y}_{30}$$
$$= Z_{30}\left(10{,}000 + \frac{\pi}{d}\right) - \frac{\pi}{d} = v^{K_{30}}\left(10{,}000 + \frac{\pi}{d}\right) - \frac{\pi}{d}.$$

Now consider the condition $Pr[L(\pi) > 0] < .50$. We have

$$Pr\left[v^{K_{30}}\left(10{,}000 + \frac{\pi}{d}\right) - \frac{\pi}{d} > 0\right] < .50$$

or

$$Pr\left(v^{K_{30}} > \frac{\pi/d}{10{,}000 + \pi/d}\right) < .50$$

or

$$Pr\left[K_{30} > \frac{\ln\left(\frac{\pi/d}{10{,}000 + \pi/d}\right)}{\ln(1.06)^{-1}}\right] < .50.$$

The given life table values show us that $Pr(K_{30} > 48) = {}_{48}p_{30} = \frac{\ell_{78}}{\ell_{30}} = .47682$, so 48 is the first value of K_{30} at which the probability drops under .50. Then we solve for π by setting.

$$\frac{\ln\left(\frac{\pi/d}{10{,}000 + \pi/d}\right)}{\ln(1.06)^{-1}} = 48,$$

or

$$\ln\left(\frac{\pi/d}{10{,}000 + \pi/d}\right) = 48 \cdot \ln(1.06)^{-1} = -2.79691)$$

or

$$\frac{\pi/d}{10{,}000 + \pi/d} = .060998$$

or

$$\frac{\pi}{d} = 609.98 + .060998\frac{\pi}{d}$$

or

$$.939002\frac{\pi}{d} = 609.98$$

so

$$\pi = \left(\frac{609.98}{.939002}\right)\left(\frac{.06}{1.06}\right) = 36.77007.$$

CHAPTER SEVEN

7-13 First we calculate

$$A_x = \sum_{k=0}^{\infty} v^{k+1} \cdot {}_{k|}q_x$$

$$= \frac{1}{9}\sum_{k=0}^{\infty}(1.08)^{-(k+1)} \cdot (.90)^{k+1}$$

$$= \frac{1}{9}\sum_{k=0}^{\infty}\left(\frac{.90}{1.08}\right)^{k+1} = \left(\frac{1}{9}\right)\left(\frac{.90}{1.08}\right)\left[1+\left(\frac{.90}{1.08}\right)+\left(\frac{.90}{1.08}\right)^2+\cdots\right]$$

$$= \left(\frac{1}{9}\right)\left(\frac{.90}{1.08}\right)\left(\frac{1}{1-.90/1.08}\right) = \frac{5}{9}.$$

Then

$$P_x = \frac{A_x}{\ddot{a}_x} = \frac{A_x}{\frac{1-A_x}{d}} = \frac{\left(\frac{5}{9}\right)\left(\frac{.08}{1.08}\right)}{\frac{4}{9}} = .09259.$$

Next we recall from Example 7.5 that $\overline{P}(\overline{A}_x) = \mu$ under the exponential distribution. To find μ we note that

$$q_x = \frac{.90}{9} = .10,$$

so $p_x = .90$ and $\mu = -\ln p_x = -\ln(.90) = .10536$. Finally,

$$1000\left[\overline{P}(\overline{A}_x) - P_x\right] = 1000(.10536 - .09259) = 12.77.$$

7-14 The APV of benefit is

$$APVB = \int_0^\infty b_t \cdot v^t \cdot {}_tp_x\mu_{x+t}\, dt = 1,$$

since $b_t = (1+i)^t$ so $b_t \cdot v^t = 1$. The APV of premium is $P \cdot \overline{a}_x$. Equating we have $P = \frac{1}{\overline{a}_x}$. Then

$$L = \overline{L}(\overline{A}_x) = 1 - P \cdot \overline{a}_{\overline{T}|} = 1 - \frac{1}{\overline{a}_x}\left(\frac{1-v^T}{\delta}\right)$$

$$= 1 - \frac{1-v^T}{1-\overline{A}_x} = \frac{v^T - \overline{A}_x}{1-\overline{A}_x} = \frac{\overline{Z}_x - \overline{A}_x}{1-\overline{A}_x},$$

as required.

7-15   From Example 7.5 we know that

$$P = \bar{P}(\bar{A}_x) = \lambda,$$

and from earlier results we know that

$$\bar{A}_x = \frac{\lambda}{\lambda+\delta}$$

and

$$^2\bar{A}_x = \frac{\lambda}{\lambda+2\delta}.$$

Then from Equation (7.24a) we have

$$Var[\bar{L}(\bar{A}_x)] = \left(1+\frac{\lambda}{\delta}\right)^2 \cdot \left[\frac{\lambda}{\lambda+2\delta} - \left(\frac{\lambda}{\lambda+\delta}\right)^2\right]$$

$$= \left(\frac{\lambda+\delta}{\delta}\right)^2 \cdot \left[\frac{\lambda}{\lambda+2\delta} - \left(\frac{\lambda}{\lambda+\delta}\right)^2\right]$$

$$= \frac{\lambda(\lambda+\delta)^2}{\delta^2(\lambda+2\delta)} - \frac{\lambda^2}{\delta^2}$$

$$= \frac{\lambda(\lambda^2+2\lambda\delta+\delta^2) - \lambda^2(\lambda+2\delta)}{\delta^2(\lambda+2\delta)}$$

$$= \frac{\lambda^3+2\lambda^2\delta+\lambda\delta^2 - \lambda^3 - 2\lambda^2\delta}{\delta^2(\lambda+2\delta)}$$

$$= \frac{\lambda}{\lambda+2\delta}, \text{ as required.}$$

CHAPTER SEVEN

7-16 We know that
$$L = \bar{Z} - \bar{P}\left(\frac{1-\bar{Z}}{\delta}\right) = \bar{Z}\left(1+\frac{\bar{P}}{\delta}\right) - \frac{\bar{P}}{\delta},$$
where
$$\bar{P} = \frac{1}{\bar{a}_x} - \delta = .20 - .08 = .12.$$
Then
$$Var(L) = \left(1+\frac{\bar{P}}{\delta}\right)^2 \cdot Var(\bar{Z}) = \left(1+\frac{.12}{.08}\right)^2 \cdot Var(\bar{Z}) = .5652,$$
from which we find $Var(\bar{Z}) = .09043$. Similarly,
$$Var(L^*) = \left(1+\frac{(4/3)(.12)}{.08}\right)^2 (.09043) = .81387,$$
so
$$SD(L^*) = \sqrt{.81387} = .90215.$$
Furthermore,
$$E[L^*] = \bar{A}_x\left(1+\frac{(4/3)(.12)}{.08}\right) - \frac{(4/3)(.12)}{.08}$$
$$= [1-(.08)(5)]\left[1+\frac{.16}{.08}\right] - \frac{.16}{.08} = -.20,$$
so
$$E[L^*] + SD(L^*) = -.20 + .90215 = .70215.$$

7-17 We have
$$L = 2\cdot\bar{Z}_x - .09\cdot\bar{Y}_x = 2\cdot\bar{Z}_x - .09\left(\frac{1-\bar{Z}_x}{\delta}\right)$$
$$= \left(2+\frac{.09}{.06}\right)\bar{Z}_x - \frac{.09}{.06} = 3.50\bar{Z}_x - 1.50.$$
Then
$$Var(L) = (3.50)^2 \cdot Var(\bar{Z}_x) = 12.25\left(^2\bar{A}_x - \bar{A}_x^2\right)$$
$$= 12.25\left[\frac{.04}{.16} - \left(\frac{.04}{.10}\right)^2\right] = 1.1025.$$

7-18 We are given

$$\frac{Var(\bar{Z}_x)}{Var(L)} = \frac{\left(^2\bar{A}_x - \bar{A}_x^2\right)}{\left(1 + \frac{\bar{P}(\bar{A}_x)}{\delta}\right)^2 \left(^2\bar{A}_x - \bar{A}_x^2\right)} = \frac{1}{\left(1 + \frac{\bar{P}(\bar{A}_x)}{\delta}\right)^2} = .36.$$

Then

$$\frac{1}{1 + \frac{\bar{P}(\bar{A}_x)}{\delta}} = .60,$$

so

$$1 + \frac{\bar{P}(\bar{A}_x)}{\delta} = \frac{10}{6}$$

and

$$\bar{P}(\bar{A}_x) = \left(\frac{10}{6} - 1\right)\delta = \frac{4\delta}{6}.$$

But we also know that

$$\bar{P}(\bar{A}_x) = \frac{1}{\bar{a}_x} - \delta = \frac{1}{10} - \delta,$$

so

$$\frac{1 - 10\delta}{10} = \frac{4\delta}{6},$$

which solves for $\delta = .06$ and therefore

$$\bar{P}(\bar{A}_x) = \frac{(4)(.06)}{6} = .04.$$

CHAPTER SEVEN

7-19 For a fully continuous contract, from Equation (7.24a), we have

$$Var(L) = \left(\frac{1}{\delta \cdot \bar{a}_{40}}\right)^2 \left(^2\bar{A}_{40} - \bar{A}_{40}^2\right).$$

For this uniform survival model, $_tp_{40} = 1 - \frac{t}{60}$ so

$$_tp_{40}\mu_{40+t} = -\frac{d}{dt}\,_tp_{40} = \frac{1}{60}.$$

Then we have

$$\bar{A}_{40} = \int_0^{60} v^t \cdot {}_tp_{40}\mu_{40+t}\, dt = \frac{1}{60}\int_0^{60} e^{-.02t}\, dt$$

$$= \frac{1-e^{-(.02)(60)}}{(60)(.02)} = .58234.$$

Similarly,

$$^2\bar{A}_{40} = \frac{1}{60}\int_0^{60} e^{-.04t}\, dt = \frac{1-e^{-(.04)(60)}}{(60)(.04)} = .37887.$$

Note also that

$$\bar{a}_{40} = \frac{1-\bar{A}_{40}}{\delta} = \frac{1-.58234}{.02} = 20.883.$$

Then

$$Var(L) = \left(\frac{1}{(.02)(20.883)}\right)^2 \left(.37887 - (.58234)^2\right)$$

$$= (5.73263)(.03975) = .22787.$$

7-20 From Equation (7.21b) we have

$$\bar{P}(\bar{A}_x) = \frac{\bar{A}_x}{\bar{a}_x}.$$

Substituting for $\bar{a}_x$ using the result of Exercise 6-10 we directly have

$$\bar{P}(\bar{A}_x) = \frac{\bar{A}_x}{(1-\bar{A}_x)/\delta} = \frac{\delta \cdot \bar{A}_x}{1-\bar{A}_x},$$

as required.

7-21 We have

$$10{,}000 P^{1\,(12)}_{30:\overline{10|}} = \frac{10{,}000 A^1_{30:\overline{10|}}}{\ddot{a}^{(12)}_{30:\overline{10|}}} = \frac{150}{\ddot{a}^{(12)}_{30:\overline{10|}}}$$

and

$$10{,}000 P^{1\,(2)}_{30:\overline{10|}} = \frac{10{,}000 A^1_{30:\overline{10|}}}{\ddot{a}^{(2)}_{30:\overline{10|}}} = \frac{150}{\ddot{a}^{(2)}_{30:\overline{10|}}}.$$

Recall from Section 6.4 that

$$\ddot{a}^{(m)}_{x:\overline{n|}} = \frac{id}{i^{(m)}d^{(m)}} \cdot \ddot{a}_{x:\overline{n|}} - \frac{i - i^{(m)}}{i^{(m)}d^{(m)}}(1 - {}_nE_x)$$

under the UDD assumption. Here $\ddot{a}_{30:\overline{10|}} = 8$ and ${}_{10}E_{30} = .604$ so we have

$$\ddot{a}^{(m)}_{x:\overline{n|}} = 8\left(\frac{id}{i^{(m)}d^{(m)}}\right) - .396\left(\frac{i - i^{(m)}}{i^{(m)}d^{(m)}}\right).$$

We have

$$i^{(2)} = 2[(1.05)^{1/2} - 1] = .049390,$$

$$d^{(2)} = 2\left[\frac{.024695}{1.024695}\right] = .048200,$$

$$i^{(12)} = 12[(1.05)^{1/12} - 1] = .048889,$$

$$d^{(12)} = 12\left[\frac{.004074}{1.004074}\right] = .048691.$$

Then

$$\ddot{a}^{(2)}_{30:\overline{10}|} = 8\left[\frac{(.05)(.05/1.05)}{(.049390)(.048200)}\right] - .396\left[\frac{.05-.049390}{(.049390)(.048200)}\right]$$
$$= 8(1.000149) - .396(.256238) = 7.899722.$$

Similarly,

$$\ddot{a}^{(12)}_{30:\overline{10}|} = 8\left[\frac{(.05)(.05/1.05)}{(.048889)(.048691)}\right] - .396\left[\frac{.05-.048889}{(.048889)(.048691)}\right]$$
$$= 8(1.000209) - .396(.466718) = 7.816852.$$

Finally,

$$10,000 P^{1\,(12)}_{30:\overline{10}|} = \frac{150}{7.816852} = 19.18931$$

and

$$10,000 P^{1\,(2)}_{30:\overline{10}|} = \frac{150}{7.899722} = 18.98801$$

so the difference is

$$19.18931 - 18.98801 = .20130.$$

7-22 If the net level annual premium is P, then the gross premium is $1.20P$ and the equation of value is

$$P \cdot \ddot{a}_{25:\overline{40}|} = 150{,}000 \cdot {}_{40}E_{25} + \sum_{k=1}^{40} 1.20P \cdot \ddot{s}_{\overline{k}|} \cdot v^k \cdot {}_{k-1|}q_{25}$$
$$= 150{,}000 \cdot {}_{40}E_{25} + \frac{1.20P}{d}\sum_{k=1}^{40}\left[(1+i)^k - 1\right]\cdot v^k \cdot {}_{k-1|}q_{25}$$
$$= 150{,}000 \cdot {}_{40}E_{25} + \frac{1.20P}{d}\left[{}_{40}q_{25} - A^1_{25:\overline{40}|}\right].$$

To find $A^1_{25:\overline{40}|}$ we first recall that

$$\ddot{a}_{25:\overline{40}|} = \frac{1}{P_{25:\overline{40}|} + d}$$

$$= \frac{1}{.008 + \frac{.06}{1.06}} = 15.47897,$$

and then

$$A_{25:\overline{40}|} = 1 - d \cdot \ddot{a}_{25:\overline{40}|}$$

$$= 1 - \left(\frac{.06}{1.06}\right)(15.47897) = .12383.$$

Then

$$A^1_{25:\overline{40}|} = A_{25:\overline{40}|} - {}_{40}E_{25}$$

$$= .12383 - (1.06)^{-40}(.80) = .04605.$$

Finally,

$$15.47897 P = (150,000)(1.06)^{-40}(.80) + \frac{1.20 P}{\frac{.06}{1.06}}[.20 - .04605],$$

so

$$P = \frac{(150,000)(1.06)^{-40}(.80)}{15.47897 - \frac{1.20}{.06/1.06}(.15395)}$$

$$= \frac{11,666.66}{15.47897 - 3.26374} = 955.07.$$

7-23   The expense-augmented equation of value is

$$G \cdot \ddot{a}_{x:\overline{20}|} = A_x + .05 + .02 \ddot{a}_x + .03 G \cdot \ddot{a}_{x:\overline{20}|}.$$

Then

$$G = \frac{A_x + .05 + .02 \ddot{a}_x}{(1 - .03)\ddot{a}_{x:\overline{20}|}}$$

$$= \frac{1 - (.04)(20) + .05 + (.02)(20)}{(.97)(10)}$$

$$= .06701.$$

CHAPTER EIGHT
CONTINGENT CONTRACT RESERVES

8-1 (a) For $t < h$, the contract is still within the premium-paying period, with $h - t$ premiums remaining. For $t \geq h$, there are no future premiums.

(b) Same reasoning as in part (a), and the textbook answer follows.

8-2 Here we have three cases. For $t < h$, the contract is still within the premium-paying period, with $h - t$ premiums remaining; note that the APV of benefit is still a deferred insurance. For $h \leq t < n$, the contract is paid up (i.e., premium-paying is completed), but the APV of benefit is still deferred. For $t \geq n$, the reserve is simply the APV of benefit which is no longer deferred.

8-3 The retrospective approach is suggested by the presence of the $P^1_{45:\overline{20|}}$ value. We have

$$_{20}V_{45} = P_{45} \cdot \ddot{s}_{45:\overline{20|}} - _{20}k_{45}$$

$$= P_{45} \left(\frac{\ddot{a}_{45:\overline{20|}}}{_{20}E_{45}} \right) - \frac{A^1_{45:\overline{20|}}}{_{20}E_{45}}$$

$$= P_{45} \left(\frac{\ddot{a}_{45:\overline{20|}}}{_{20}E_{45}} \right) - \frac{P^1_{45:\overline{20|}} \cdot \ddot{a}_{45:\overline{20|}}}{_{20}E_{45}}$$

$$= P_{45} \left(\frac{1}{P^{\ 1}_{45:\overline{20|}}} \right) - \frac{P_{45:\overline{20|}} - P^{\ 1}_{45:\overline{20|}}}{P^{\ 1}_{45:\overline{20|}}}$$

$$= \frac{.014}{.022} - \frac{.030 - .022}{.022} = .27273.$$

8-4 (a) The result follows directly from definition.

(b) The result follows directly from definition.

(c) The result follows directly from definition, but note that there is no past cost of insurance for the pure endowment contract prior to age $x+t$.

(d) Since $t>h$, the premium is accumulated to age $x+h$ by the $\ddot{s}_{x:\overline{h}|}$ term, and then accumulated on to age $x+t$ before deducting the actuarial accumulated value of the benefit.

8-5 Note that these derivations parallel those given in Section 8.1.3 for the whole life contract.

(a) Starting with the basic prospective expression we have
$$\begin{aligned}{}_t V_{x:\overline{n}|} &= A_{x+t:\overline{n-t}|} - P_{x:\overline{n}|} \cdot \ddot{a}_{x+t:\overline{n-t}|} \\ &= (1 - d \cdot \ddot{a}_{x+t:\overline{n-t}|}) - P_{x:\overline{n}|} \cdot \ddot{a}_{x+t:\overline{n-t}|} \\ &= 1 - (P_{x:\overline{n}|} + d) \cdot \ddot{a}_{x+t:\overline{n-t}|}.\end{aligned}$$

(b) From Equation (7.7a) we find
$$P_{x:\overline{n}|} = \frac{1 - d \cdot \ddot{a}_{x:\overline{n}|}}{\ddot{a}_{x:\overline{n}|}} = \frac{1}{\ddot{a}_{x:\overline{n}|}} - d,$$
so $P_{x:\overline{n}|} + d = \frac{1}{\ddot{a}_{x:\overline{n}|}}$ and
$${}_t V_{x:\overline{n}|} = 1 - \frac{\ddot{a}_{x+t:\overline{n-t}|}}{\ddot{a}_{x:\overline{n}|}}$$
follows from part (a).

(c) From part (b) we then have
$$\begin{aligned}{}_t V_{x:\overline{n}|} &= 1 - \left(\frac{1}{\ddot{a}_{x:\overline{n}|}}\right) \cdot \ddot{a}_{x+t:\overline{n-t}|} \\ &= 1 - (P_{x:\overline{n}|} + d)\left(\frac{1}{P_{x+t:\overline{n-t}|} + d}\right) = \frac{P_{x+t:\overline{n-t}|} - P_{x:\overline{n}|}}{P_{x+t:\overline{n-t}|} + d}.\end{aligned}$$

CHAPTER EIGHT

(d) Substituting for the two $\ddot{a}$ terms in part (b) in terms of A terms, we have

$$_tV_{x:\overline{n}|} = 1 - \frac{(1-A_{x+t:\overline{n-t}|})/d}{(1-A_{x:\overline{n}|})/d} = \frac{A_{x+t:\overline{n-t}|} - A_{x:\overline{n}|}}{1 - A_{x:\overline{n}|}}.$$

(e) Substituting $P_{x+t:\overline{n-t}|} \cdot \ddot{a}_{x+t:\overline{n-t}|}$ for the $A_{x+t:\overline{n-t}|}$ term in the original prospective expression and factoring out the $\ddot{a}_{x+t:\overline{n-t}|}$ term we have

$$_tV_{x:\overline{n}|} = \left(P_{x+t:\overline{n-t}|} - P_{x:\overline{n}|}\right) \cdot \ddot{a}_{x+t:\overline{n-t}|}.$$

(f) Conversely, substituting $\frac{A_{x+t:\overline{n-t}|}}{P_{x+t:\overline{n-t}|}}$ for the $\ddot{a}_{x+t:\overline{n-t}|}$ term in the original prospective expression and factoring out the $A_{x+t:\overline{n-t}|}$ term we have

$$_tV_{x:\overline{n}|} = A_{x+t:\overline{n-t}|}\left(1 - \frac{P_{x:\overline{n}|}}{P_{x+t:\overline{n-t}|}}\right).$$

8-6 The value of $1000\ _1V_{x:\overline{3}|}$ is best calculated retrospectively as

$$1000\ _1V_{x:\overline{3}|} = 1000\left(P_{x:\overline{3}|} \cdot \frac{1}{_1E_x} - v \cdot q_x \cdot \frac{1}{_1E_x}\right)$$

$$= 1000\left(\frac{.33251}{(1.06)^{-1}(.90)} - \frac{.10}{.90}\right) = 280.51.$$

The value of $1000\ _2V_{x:\overline{3}|}$ is best calculated prospectively as

$$1000\ _2V_{x:\overline{3}|} = 1000\left(A_{x+2:\overline{1}|} - P_{x:\overline{3}|}\right)$$

$$= 1000\left((1.06)^{-1} - .33251\right) = 610.89.$$

Then the difference is

$$610.89 - 280.51 = 330.38.$$

8-7 The reserve is
$$_{10}V = 5000 A_{x+10} - P \cdot \ddot{a}_{x+10}.$$

We find P using the equivalence principle. Because there is no benefit in the first year, we have

$$P \cdot \ddot{a}_x = 5000(v \cdot p_x \cdot A_{x+1}).$$

Recall also that
$$A_x = v \cdot q_x + v \cdot p_x \cdot A_{x+1}.$$

Here we have
$$A_x = 1 - d \cdot \ddot{a}_x = 1 - (.10)(5) = .50,$$

so
$$v \cdot p_x \cdot A_{x+1} = .50 - (.90)(.05) = .455,$$

and therefore
$$P = \frac{(5000)(.455)}{5} = 455.00.$$

Next recall that
$$_{10}V_x = 1 - \frac{\ddot{a}_{x+10}}{\ddot{a}_x} = 1 - \frac{\ddot{a}_{x+10}}{5} = .20,$$

from which we find $\ddot{a}_{x+10} = 4$ and therefore
$$A_{x+10} = 1 - (.10)(4) = .60.$$

Finally,
$$_{10}V = (5000)(.60) - (455.00)(4) = 1180.00.$$

8-8 (a) The development here parallels that for the whole life contract in Section 8.1.4. We let $Z_{x+t:\overline{n-t|}}$ denote the present value of loss random variable, given alive at age $x+t$, and we let $\ddot{Y}_{x+t:\overline{n-t|}}$ denote the present value random variable for future benefit premiums. If the interval of failure K_x occurs within the n-year duration of the contract, then the two present value random variables are v^{K_x-t} and $\ddot{a}_{\overline{K_x-t|}}$, respectively. If $K_x > n$, then the endowment benefit is paid at time n and the premiums are paid to time n, so the two present value random variables are v^{n-t} and $\ddot{a}_{\overline{n-t|}}$, respectively.

(b) This result follows directly from part (a) by taking the expectation.

(c) Here we have

$$_tL_{x:\overline{n|}} = Z_{x+t:\overline{n-t|}} - P_{x:\overline{n|}}\left(\frac{1-Z_{x+t:\overline{n-t|}}}{d}\right)$$

$$= \left(1+\frac{P_{x:\overline{n|}}}{d}\right)\cdot Z_{x+t:\overline{n-t|}} - \frac{P_{x:\overline{n|}}}{d},$$

so

$$Var(_tL_{x:\overline{n|}}) = \left(1+\frac{P_{x:\overline{n|}}}{d}\right)^2 \cdot \left(^2A_{x+t:\overline{n-t|}} - A_{x+t:\overline{n-t|}}^2\right).$$

8-9 The loss at issue, denoted L, will be

$$L = \frac{400}{1.10} - (400)(.185825) = 289.31$$

if failure occurs in the first year, which happens with probability q_x. The loss will be

$$L = \frac{400}{(1.10)^2} - 74.33 - \frac{74.33}{1.10} = 188.68$$

if failure occurs in the second year, which happens with probability $p_x \cdot q_{x+1}$. Certainly the loss will be less than 190 if (x) survives to age $x+2$, so we can conclude that the loss is less than 190 with probability p_x.

To find p_x we first use

$$_1V^1_{x:\overline{2}|} = v \cdot q_{x+1} - .185825 = .04145,$$

which solves for $q_{x+1} = .25$. Then we use

$$P^1_{x:\overline{2}|} = \frac{\frac{q_x}{1.10} + \frac{p_x \cdot q_{x+1}}{(1.10)^2}}{1 + \frac{p_x}{1.10}} = \frac{\frac{1-p_x}{1.10} + \frac{.25 p_x}{(1.10)^2}}{1 + \frac{p_x}{1.10}}$$

$$= \frac{(1.10)(1-p_x) + .25 p_x}{(1.10)^2 + 1.10 p_x} = .185825,$$

which solves for $p_x = .83$.

8-10 Starting with Equation (8.27) we have

$$_t\overline{k}_x = \overline{A}^1_{x:\overline{t}|} \cdot \frac{1}{_tE_x} = \frac{i}{\delta} \cdot A^1_{x:\overline{t}|} \cdot \frac{1}{_tE_x},$$

using Equation (5.64b), and then

$$_t\overline{k}_x = \frac{i}{\delta} \cdot {_tk_x}$$

by Equation (8.12).

CHAPTER EIGHT

8-11 Starting with the basic prospective formula

$$_tV(\overline{A}_x) = \overline{A}_{x+t} - P(\overline{A}_x) \cdot \ddot{a}_{x+t},$$

we then substitute $P(\overline{A}_{x+t}) \cdot \ddot{a}_{x+t}$ for $\overline{A}_{x+t}$ obtaining

$$_tV(\overline{A}_x) = \left[P(\overline{A}_{x+t}) - P(\overline{A}_x) \right] \cdot \ddot{a}_{x+t},$$

as required.

8-12 The determination of $Var(_5L)$ is conditional on survival to time 5, or age 85 in this case. There is no further premium, so the present value of loss at time 5 is

$$_5L = \begin{cases} \overline{a}_{\overline{T}|} & \text{for } T \leq 5 \\ \overline{a}_{\overline{5}|} & \text{for } T > 5, \end{cases}$$

where T denotes the future lifetime of (85). The survival model is uniform, so we have

$$f_T(t) = {}_tp_{85}\mu_{85+t} = \frac{1}{15}$$

and $_5p_{85} = \frac{10}{15}$. Then

$$E[_5L] = \int_0^5 \overline{a}_{\overline{t}|} \cdot {}_tp_{85}\mu_{85+t}\, dt + \overline{a}_{\overline{5}|} \cdot {}_5p_{85}$$

$$= \frac{1}{\delta}\left[\frac{1}{15}\int_0^5 (1-v^t)\, dt + \frac{10}{15}(1-v^5) \right] = 5 - \overline{a}_{\overline{5}|} + 10(1-v^5),$$

since $\frac{1}{\delta} = 15$. This evaluates to

$$E[_5L] = 5 - \frac{1-e^{-1/3}}{\frac{1}{15}} + 10(1-e^{-1/3})$$

$$= 5 - 4.25203 + 10(.28346) = 3.58266.$$

Similarly,

$$\begin{aligned}E[_5L^2] &= \int_0^5 (\bar{a}_{\overline{t}|})^2 \cdot {}_tp_{85}\mu_{85+t}\, dt + (\bar{a}_{\overline{5}|})^2 \cdot {}_5p_{85}\\ &= \frac{1}{\delta^2}\left[\frac{1}{15}\int_0^5 (1-v^t)^2\, dt + \frac{10}{15}(1-v^5)^2\right]\\ &= 15\left[5 - 2\bar{a}_{\overline{5}|} + {}^2\bar{a}_{\overline{5}|} + 10(1-2v^5+v^{10})\right]\\ &= 15\left[5 - 2\left(\frac{1-e^{-1/3}}{1/15}\right)+\left(\frac{1-e^{-2/3}}{2/15}\right)\right.\\ &\qquad\left. + 10 - 20e^{-1/3} + 10e^{-2/3}\right]\\ &= 15[5 - 2(4.25203) + 3.64937\\ &\qquad + 10 - 14.33063 + 5.13417]\\ &= 14.23275.\end{aligned}$$

Finally,

$$Var(_5L) = 14.23275 - (3.58266)^2 = 1.39730.$$

8-13 The given information suggests the recursion formula

$$_{10}V = (_9V+P)(1+i) - q_{44}(B-{}_{10}V),$$

so we have

$$500 = (500)(1.10) - q_{44}(2000)$$

which easily solves for $q_{44} = .025$.

CHAPTER EIGHT

8-14 The contract is 20-pay whole life, and the given information is at durations beyond the premium-paying period. Thus we have the recursive relationship

$$_{24}^{20}V_{15} = {}_{23}^{20}V_{15}(1+i) - q_{38}\left(1 - {}_{24}^{20}V_{15}\right)$$

or

$$.600 = (.585)(1.04) - q_{38}(.400),$$

which solves for $q_{38} = .021$ and hence $p_{38} = .979$.

8-15 Using the recursive relationship

$$(_9V+P)(1+i) = 1000q_{x+9} + {}_{10}V \cdot p_{x+9},$$

we have

$$(322.87+32.88)(1.06) = 12.62 + {}_{10}V(.98738),$$

which solves for $_{10}V = 369.13$. At duration 10 the contract is paid up, so the reserve prospectively is $1000 A_{x+10} = 369.13$. Then

$$P_{x+10} = \frac{A_{x+10}}{\ddot{a}_{x+10}} = \frac{.36913}{\frac{1-.36913}{.06/1.06}} = .03312.$$

8-16 Since it is a single premium contract, the reserve recursion formula is

$$_9V(1+i) = q_{x+9}\left[P(1+i)^{10}\right] + p_{x+9} \cdot {}_{10}V,$$

where P denotes the new single premium. We know from Example 8.5 that the reserve is the same as the failure benefit under this model, so

$$_9V = P(1+i)^9 = 15.238,$$

which solves for $P = \dfrac{15.238}{(1.05)^9} = 9.82254$.

8-17   From Example 8.5 we know that the 20th reserve is the same as the failure benefit, which is $P(1+i)^{20}$, where P is the net single premium. Similarly the 25th reserve is $P(1+i)^{25}$, but is also $\ddot{a}_{65}$ prospectively. Under the uniform survival model we have

$$\ddot{a}_{65} = \sum_{t=0}^{34} v^t \left(1 - \frac{t}{35}\right)$$

$$= \ddot{a}_{\overline{35}|} - \frac{1}{35}(I a)_{\overline{34}|}$$

$$= 17.19291 - \frac{1}{35}(210.60978) = 11.17549,$$

so

$$P = \frac{11.17549}{(1.05)^{25}} = 3.30016$$

and finally

$$_{20}V = P(1.05)^{20} = 8.75630.$$

8-18   Given alive at age $x+t$, the probability of the event $K_x = j$ is $_{j-t-1}p_{x+t} \cdot q_{x+j-1}$ and the probability of the event $K_x > j$ is $_{j-t-1}p_{x+t} \cdot p_{x+j-1}$. Taking Equation (8.37) as the definition of Λ_j, we then find

$$E[\Lambda_j \mid K_x > t] = (v - {}_{j-1}V - P) \cdot {}_{j-t-1}p_{x+t} \cdot q_{x+j-1}$$
$$+ (v \cdot {}_jV - {}_{j-1}V - P) \cdot {}_{j-t-1}p_{x+t} \cdot p_{x+j-1}$$
$$= {}_{j-t-1}p_{x+t}[v \cdot q_{x+j-1} + v \cdot {}_jV \cdot p_{x+j-1} - ({}_{j-1}V + P)].$$

But we know from Equation (8.30c) that

$$_{j-1}V + P = v \cdot q_{x+j-1} + v \cdot {}_jV \cdot p_{x+j-1},$$

which shows that $E[\Lambda_j \mid K_x > t] = 0$, as required.

CHAPTER EIGHT

8-19 Since the conditional first moment of Λ_j is zero, from Exercise 8-18, then the conditional variance is the same as the conditional second moment. We have

$$Var(\Lambda_j \mid K_x > t) = E[\Lambda_j^2 \mid K_x > t]$$
$$= (v - {}_{j-1}V - P)^2 \cdot {}_{j-t-1}p_{x+t} \cdot q_{x+j-1}$$
$$+ (v \cdot {}_jV - {}_{j-1}V - P)^2 \cdot {}_{j-t-1}p_{x+t} \cdot p_{x+j-1}.$$

From Equation (8.30e), with t replaced by $j - 1$, we have

$$({}_{j-1}V + P)(1 + i) = {}_jV + q_{x+j-1}(1 - {}_jV),$$

so we can write

$$(v - {}_{j-1}V - P) = v - v \cdot {}_jV - v \cdot q_{x+j-1}(1 - {}_jV) = v(1 - {}_jV) \cdot p_{x+j-1}$$

and

$$(v \cdot {}_jV - {}_{j-1}V - P) = -v \cdot q_{x+j-1}(1 - {}_jV).$$

Substituting in the expression for $Var(\Lambda_j \mid K_x > t)$ we have

$$Var(\Lambda_j \mid K_x > t)$$
$$= \left[v(1 - {}_jV) \cdot p_{x+j-1}\right]^2 \cdot {}_{j-t-1}p_{x+t} \cdot q_{x+j-1}$$
$$+ \left[-v \cdot q_{x+j-1}(1 - {}_jV)\right]^2 \cdot {}_{j-t-1}p_{x+t} \cdot p_{x+j-1}$$
$$= v^2(1 - {}_jV)^2 \cdot p_{x+j-1}^2 \cdot {}_{j-t-1}p_{x+t} \cdot q_{x+j-1}$$
$$+ v^2(1 - {}_jV)^2 \cdot q_{x+j-1}^2 \cdot {}_{j-t-1}p_{x+t} \cdot p_{x+j-1}$$
$$= v^2(1 - {}_jV)^2 \cdot {}_{j-t-1}p_{x+t} \cdot p_{x+j-1} \cdot q_{x+j-1}\left[p_{x+j-1} + q_{x+j-1}\right]$$
$$= v^2(1 - {}_jV)^2 \cdot {}_{j-t-1}p_{x+t} \cdot p_{x+j-1} \cdot q_{x+j-1},$$

as required.

8-20 From Equation (8.39) we have
$$Var(\Lambda_{11}\,|\,K_{40}>10) = v^2(1-{}_{11}V)^2\cdot q_{50}\cdot p_{50}.$$
Here we have
$$_{11}V = 1000\cdot{}_{11}V_{40} = 1000\left(1-\frac{\ddot{a}_{51}}{\ddot{a}_{40}}\right) = 117.19.$$
To find p_{50} we use $\ddot{a}_{50} = 1+v\cdot p_{50}\cdot\ddot{a}_{51}$, so
$$p_{50} = \frac{(\ddot{a}_{50}-1)(1+i)}{\ddot{a}_{51}} = \frac{(12.2669)(1.06)}{13.0803} = .99408.$$
Then
$$Var(\Lambda_{11}\,|\,K_{40}>10) = (1.06)^{-2}(1000-117.19)^2(.99408)(.00592)$$
$$= 4081.93.$$

8-21 (a) Starting with Equation (8.55), we substitute
$$\bar{a}_{x+t} = \frac{1-\bar{A}_{x+t}}{\delta}$$
and
$$\bar{a}_x = \frac{1-\bar{A}_x}{\delta},$$
producing
$$_t\bar{V}(\bar{A}_x) = 1-\frac{(1-\bar{A}_{x+t})/\delta}{(1-\bar{A}_x)/\delta} = \frac{\bar{A}_{x+t}-\bar{A}_x}{1-\bar{A}_x},$$
as required.

(b) Starting with Equation (8.52), we substitute
$$\bar{a}_{x+t} = \frac{\bar{A}_{x+t}}{\bar{P}(\bar{A}_{x+t})},$$
producing
$$_t\bar{V}(\bar{A}_x) = \bar{A}_{x+t} - \bar{P}(\bar{A}_x)\cdot\frac{\bar{A}_{x+t}}{\bar{P}(\bar{A}_{x+t})} = \left(1-\frac{\bar{P}(\bar{A}_x)}{\bar{P}(\bar{A}_{x+t})}\right)\cdot\bar{A}_{x+t},$$
as required.

8-22 Let L denote $_0\overline{L}(\overline{A}_x)$. Recall that

$$Var(L) = \left(\frac{1}{\delta \cdot \overline{a}_x}\right)^2 \cdot (^2\overline{A}_x - \overline{A}_x^2)$$

$$= \left(\frac{1}{1-\overline{A}_x}\right)^2 \cdot (.30 - \overline{A}_x^2) = .20,$$

so

$$(.30 - \overline{A}_x^2) = .20(1 - 2\overline{A}_x + \overline{A}_x^2)$$

or

$$1.20\overline{A}_x^2 - .40\overline{A}_x - .10 = 0,$$

which solves for $\overline{A}_x = .50$. Then

$$_{20}\overline{V}(\overline{A}_x) = 1 - \frac{\overline{a}_{x+20}}{\overline{a}_x} = 1 - \frac{1-\overline{A}_{x+20}}{1-\overline{A}_x} = 1 - \frac{.30}{.50} = .40.$$

8-23 Using the basic prospective expression we have

$$_t\overline{V}(\overline{A}_x) = \overline{A}_{x+t} - \overline{P}(\overline{A}_x) \cdot \overline{a}_{x+t}$$
$$= 1 - (.03)\overline{a}_{x+t} - (.0105)\overline{a}_{x+t} = 1 - (.0405)\overline{a}_{x+t} = .1000,$$

which solves for $\overline{a}_{x+t} = \frac{.9000}{.0405} = 22.22.$

8-24 Recall that $_{10}\overline{V}(\overline{A}_{40}) = 1 - \frac{\overline{a}_{50}}{\overline{a}_{40}}$. Using the result of Exercise 6-12 we find

$$\overline{a}_{40} = \frac{60 - \overline{a}_{\overline{60}|}}{60\delta} = \frac{60 - \frac{1-(1.05)^{-60}}{\ln(1.05)}}{60 \cdot \ln(1.05)} = 13.86939$$

and

$$\overline{a}_{50} = \frac{50 - \overline{a}_{\overline{50}|}}{50\delta} = \frac{50 - \frac{1-(1.05)^{-50}}{\ln(1.05)}}{50 \cdot \ln(1.05)} = 12.82694.$$

Then

$$_{10}\overline{V}(\overline{A}_{40}) = 1 - \frac{12.82694}{13.86939} = .07516.$$

8-25 Recall from earlier results that the exponential survival model implies

$$\bar{a}_x = \frac{1}{\lambda + \delta},$$

for all x. Then, clearly,

$$_t\bar{V}(\bar{A}_x) = 1 - \frac{\bar{a}_{x+t}}{\bar{a}_x} = 0,$$

since $\bar{a}_{x+t} = \bar{a}_x$. Recall also that

$$\bar{A}_x = \frac{\lambda}{\lambda + \delta},$$

so

$$\bar{P}(\bar{A}_x) = \frac{\bar{A}_x}{\bar{a}_x} = \lambda.$$

Then at any duration t the APV of future benefit is $\bar{A}_{x+t} = \frac{\lambda}{\lambda + \delta}$, and the APV of future premium is $\lambda \cdot \bar{a}_{x+t} = \frac{\lambda}{\lambda + \delta}$.

Since the future premiums will provide the future benefit, then no reserve is ever needed.

8-26 Differentiate the left side of Equation (8.57) using the product rule to obtain

$$\ell_{x+t} \cdot \frac{d}{dt}\, _t\bar{V}(\bar{A}_x) + {_t\bar{V}(\bar{A}_x)} \cdot -\ell_{x+t}\mu_{x+t}.$$

Equate this to the right side, divide both sides by ℓ_{x+t}, and transpose the second term above to the right side to obtain

$$\frac{d}{dt}\, _t\bar{V}(\bar{A}_x) = \bar{P}(\bar{A}_x) + \delta \cdot {_t\bar{V}(\bar{A}_x)} - \mu_{x+t} + {_t\bar{V}(\bar{A}_x)} \cdot \mu_{x+t}$$
$$= \bar{P}(\bar{A}_x) + \delta \cdot {_t\bar{V}(\bar{A}_x)} - \mu_{x+t}\left(1 - {_t\bar{V}(\bar{A}_x)}\right),$$

as required.

8-27 Begin with Equation (8.68) from Example 8.8, using

$$\beta(4) = \frac{i - i^{(4)}}{i^{(4)} d^{(4)}}.$$

We have

$$1000({}_5V_{35}^{(4)} - {}_5V_{35}) = 1000 \cdot \beta(4) \cdot P_{35}^{(4)} \cdot {}_5V_{35}.$$

At $i = .05$ we find $\beta(4) = .38657$ and

$$\alpha(4) = \frac{id}{i^{(4)} d^{(4)}} = 1.00045.$$

Then

$$\ddot{a}_{35} = \frac{1 - A_{35}}{d} = \frac{1 - .17092}{.05/1.05} = 17.41068$$

and

$$\ddot{a}_{35}^{(4)} = \alpha(4) \cdot \ddot{a}_{35} - \beta(4) = 17.03195,$$

so

$$P_{35}^{(4)} = \frac{A_{35}}{\ddot{a}_{35}^{(4)}} = \frac{.17092}{17.03195} = .01004.$$

Finally we find

$$1000\left({}_5V_{35}^{(4)} - {}_5V_{35}\right) = 1000 \cdot \beta(4) \cdot P_{35}^{(4)} \cdot {}_5V_{35}$$

$$= (1000)(.38657)(.01004)(.04471)$$

$$= .17353.$$

8-28 First recall that

$$_4V_x = 1 - \frac{\ddot{a}_{x+4}}{\ddot{a}_x} = 1 - \frac{\ddot{a}_{x+4}}{20} = .06,$$

from which we find $\ddot{a}_{x+4} = 18.80$. Then from Exercise 6-41 we find

$$\ddot{a}_x^{(2)} \approx \ddot{a}_x - \frac{1}{4} = 19.75$$

and

$$\ddot{a}_{x+4}^{(2)} \approx \ddot{a}_{x+4} - \frac{1}{4} = 18.55.$$

Then

$$_4V_x^{(2)} = A_{x+4} - P_x^{(2)} \cdot \ddot{a}_{x+4}^{(2)}$$
$$= (1 - d \cdot \ddot{a}_{x+4}) - \frac{A_x}{\ddot{a}_x^{(2)}} \cdot \ddot{a}_{x+4}^{(2)}$$
$$= 1 - (.026)(18.80) - \left(\frac{1 - (.026)(20)}{19.75}\right)(18.55)$$
$$= 1 - .4888 - (.02430)(18.55) = .06036.$$

8-29 (a) At duration 10 there are still 10 premiums to be paid. Prospectively we have

$$_{10}V^E = A_{x+10} + .02\ddot{a}_{x+10} + .03G \cdot \ddot{a}_{x+10:\overline{10}|} - G \cdot \ddot{a}_{x+10:\overline{10}|}$$
$$= 1 - (.04)(16.5) + (.02)(16.5) - (.97)(.06701)(7)$$
$$= .21500,$$

where $G = .06701$ was found in Exercise 7-22.

(b) At duration 20 the policy is paid up, so the prospective reserve is

$$_{20}V^E = A_{x+20} + .02\ddot{a}_{x+20}$$
$$= 1 - (.04)(12.5) + (.02)(12.5) = .75000.$$

8-30 From Equation (8.73) we have

$$r = \frac{{}_{s|1-s}q_{x+t}}{q_{x+t}}$$
$$= \frac{(1-s)\cdot q_{x+t}}{q_{x+t}}$$
$$= 1-s,$$

using the important result developed in Example 4.8.

8-31 Recall that the mean reserve is given by Equation (8.76) with $s = \frac{1}{2}$. Here we seek an expression for ${}_{t-1/2}V$, so the interpolation in Equation (8.76) is between ${}_{t-1}V$ and ${}_tV$. We have

$$_{t-1/2}V = \frac{1}{2}\cdot {}_{t-1}V + \frac{1}{2}\cdot {}_tV + \frac{1}{2}\cdot P.$$

Next recall the basic recursive relationship

$$({}_{t-1}V+P)(1+i) = q_{x+t-1} + p_{x+t-1}\cdot {}_tV,$$

which can be written as

$$_{t-1}V = v\cdot q_{x+t-1} + v\cdot p_{x+t-1}\cdot {}_tV - P.$$

We substitute this for ${}_{t-1}V$ in the expression for ${}_{t-1/2}V$, obtaining

$$_{t-1/2}V = \frac{1}{2}(v\cdot q_{x+t-1} + v\cdot p_{x+t-1}\cdot {}_tV - P) + \frac{1}{2}\cdot {}_tV + \frac{1}{2}\cdot P$$
$$= \frac{1}{2}\cdot v\cdot q_{x+t-1} + \frac{1}{2}(1+v\cdot p_{x+t-1})\cdot {}_tV,$$

as required.

8-32 The past premium stream is $P_1, P_2, \ldots, P_t$, with accumulated value of age $x+t$ given by

$$P_1 \cdot \frac{1}{{}_tE_x} + P_2 \cdot \frac{1}{{}_{t-1}E_{x+1}} + \cdots + P_t \cdot \frac{1}{{}_1E_{x+t-1}} = \sum_{k=0}^{t-1} P_{k+1} \cdot \frac{1}{{}_{t-k}E_{x+k}}.$$

The past costs of insurance, valued at age x, are

$$b_1 \cdot v \cdot q_x, \; b_2 \cdot v^2 \cdot {}_{1|}q_x, \ldots, \; b_t \cdot v^t \cdot {}_{t-1|}q_x.$$

The accumulated cost of insurance at age $x+t$ is therefore

$$\left(\sum_{k=1}^{t} b_k \cdot v^k \cdot {}_{k-1|}q_x\right) \cdot \frac{1}{{}_tE_x} = \sum_{k=1}^{t} b_k \cdot \frac{v^{k-t} \cdot {}_{k-1|}q_x}{{}_tp_x},$$

which is deducted from the accumulated premiums to give the retrospective reserve.

8-33 The level benefit premium is found as

$$P = \frac{200 \cdot v \cdot q_x + 150 \cdot v^2 \cdot p_x \cdot q_{x+1} + 100 \cdot v^3 \cdot {}_2p_x \cdot q_{x+2}}{1 + v \cdot p_x + v^2 \cdot {}_2p_x}$$

$$= \frac{(200)(.03)(1.06)^{-1} + (150)(.97)(.06)(1.06)^{-2} + (100)(.97)(.94)(.09)(1.06)^{-3}}{1 + (.97)(1.06)^{-1} + (.97)(.94)(1.06)^{-2}}$$

$$= \frac{20.32013}{2.72659} = 7.45258.$$

Then the first terminal reserve is

$$_1V = \frac{(7.45258)(1.06) - (200)(.03)}{.97} = 1.95848,$$

and the second initial reserve is

$$_1V + P = 1.95848 + 7.45258 = 9.41107.$$

8-34 When the failure benefit is a fixed amount plus the benefit reserve, we use the recursive relationship approach. For the first year, where $_0V = 0$, we have

$$P(1+i) = q_x(1000+{_1V}) + p_x \cdot {_1V} = 1000q_x + {_1V},$$

so

$$_1V = P(1+i) - 1000q_x = P(1.10) - 100.$$

For the second year we have

$$({_1V}+P)(1+i) = q_{x+1}(1000+{_2V}) + p_{x+1} \cdot {_2V},$$

so

$$\begin{aligned}{_2V} &= ({_1V}+P)(1+i) - 1000q_{x+1} \\ &= [P(1.10)-100+P](1.10) - 110 = P \cdot \ddot{s}_{\overline{2}|.10} - 220.\end{aligned}$$

But, prospectively, $_2V = 1000$, as we have

$$P = \frac{1000 + 220}{\ddot{a}_{\overline{2}|.10}} = 528.14.$$

8-35 Again the recursive relationship is suggested. We have

$$_{11}V = \frac{({_{10}V}+P)(1+i) - b_{11} \cdot q_{50}}{p_{50}},$$

where $_{10}V$, $_{11}V$, and P are equal to $_{10}V_{20}$, $_{11}V_{20}$, and P_{20}, respectively. Next we use the recursive relationship

$$\begin{aligned}({_{10}V_{20}}+P_{20})(1+i) &= q_{30} + p_{30} \cdot {_{11}V_{20}} \\ &= .008427 + (.991573)(.08154) = .089280.\end{aligned}$$

Returning to the first recursive relationship we have

$$\begin{aligned}{_{11}V} = .08154 &= \frac{({_{10}V_{20}}+P_{20})(1+i) - b_{11}(q_{30}+.01)}{1-(q_{30}+.01)} \\ &= \frac{.089280 - b_{11}(.018427)}{.981573},\end{aligned}$$

so

$$b_{11} = \frac{.089280 - (.08154)(.981573)}{.018427} = .50158.$$

8-36 At duration 10 the APV of future premium is

$$\bar{P}\cdot \bar{a}_{50:\overline{15}|} = (200)\left(\frac{1-.60}{\ln(1.05)}\right) = 1639.67.$$

The APV of future benefit is

$$\begin{aligned}APVB &= \int_0^{15} b_{s+10}\cdot v^s \cdot {}_sp_{50}\mu_{50+s}\, ds \\ &= 1000\int_0^{15} \bar{a}_{\overline{15-s}|}\cdot v^s \cdot {}_sp_{50}\mu_{50+s}\, ds \\ &= \frac{1000}{\ln(1.05)}\int_0^{15}(1-v^{15-s})\cdot v^s \cdot {}_sp_{50}\mu_{50+s}\, ds \\ &= 20{,}495.93\left[\bar{A}^{\,1}_{50:\overline{15}|} - v^{15}\cdot {}_{15}q_{50}\right] \\ &= 20{,}495.93\left[\bar{A}^{\,1}_{50:\overline{15}|} - v^{15} + v^{15}\cdot {}_{15}p_{50}\right] \\ &= 20{,}495.93\left[\bar{A}_{50:\overline{15}|} - v^{15}\right] \\ &= 20{,}495.93\left[.60-(1.05)^{-15}\right] = 2438.67.\end{aligned}$$

Then the reserve is

$$_{10}\bar{V} = 2438.67-1639.67 = 799.00.$$

8-37 Multiply both sides of Equation (8.85) by v^t and transpose the term involving δ to reach

$$v^t\cdot \frac{d}{dt}\bigl(\ell_{x+t}\cdot {}_t\bar{V}\bigr) - \delta\cdot v^t\bigl(\ell_{x+t}\cdot {}_t\bar{V}\bigr) = v^t\cdot \ell_{x+t}\bigl(\bar{P}(t)-b_t\cdot \mu_{x+t}\bigr),$$

which is the same as

$$\frac{d}{dt}\bigl(v^t\cdot \ell_{x+t}\cdot {}_t\bar{V}\bigr) = v^t\cdot \ell_{x+t}\bigl(\bar{P}(t)-b_t\cdot \mu_{x+t}\bigr).$$

Then integrate both sides of this equation to reach

$$\int_0^n d\left(v^t \cdot \ell_{x+t} \cdot {}_t\overline{V}\right) = \int_0^n v^t \cdot \ell_{x+t} \left(\overline{P}(t) - b_t \cdot \mu_{x+t}\right) dt$$

or

$$v^n \cdot \ell_{x+n} \cdot {}_n\overline{V} = \int_0^n v^t \cdot \ell_{x+t} \left(\overline{P}(t) - b_t \cdot \mu_{x+t}\right) dt,$$

since ${}_0\overline{V} = 0$. Then divide both sides by $v^n \cdot \ell_{x+n}$, and split the right side into two integrals, to obtain

$$\begin{aligned}
{}_n\overline{V} &= \int_0^n \overline{P}(t) \cdot v^{t-n} \cdot \frac{\ell_{x+t}}{\ell_{x+n}} dt - \int_0^n b_t \cdot \mu_{x+t} \cdot v^{t-n} \cdot \frac{\ell_{x+t}}{\ell_{x+n}} dt \\
&= \int_0^n \overline{P}(t) \cdot \frac{1}{v^{n-t} \cdot \frac{\ell_{x+n}}{\ell_{x+t}}} dt - \int_0^n b_t \cdot \mu_{x+t} \cdot \frac{1}{v^{n-t} \cdot \frac{\ell_{x+n}}{\ell_{x+t}}} dt \\
&= \int_0^n \overline{P}(t) \cdot \frac{1}{{}_{n-t}E_{x+t}} dt - \int_0^n b_t \cdot \mu_{x+t} \cdot \frac{1}{{}_{n-t}E_{x+t}} dt,
\end{aligned}$$

which is Equation (8.84) with r replaced by t and t replaced by n.

CHAPTER NINE
MODELS DEPENDENT ON MULTIPLE SURVIVALS

9-1 From Equation (9.5b), with $t=1$, we have
$$q_{xy} = q_x + q_y - q_x \cdot q_y = q_x + q_y(1-q_x) = q_x + p_x \cdot q_y,$$
as required.

9-2 The SDF of T_{xy} is
$$_tp_{xy} = {_tp_x} \cdot {_tp_y} = (1-.080t^2)(1-.004t^2)$$
$$= 1-.084t^2 + .00032t^4,$$
for $0 \le t \le 1$. Then the PDF is given by
$$-\frac{d}{dt}{_tp_{xy}} = 2(.084)t - .00128t^3,$$
and the PDF at $t=.50$ is
$$(2)(.084)(.50) - (.00128)(.50)^3 = .08384.$$

9-3 We seek the value of
$$_{1|3}q_{2:\overline{2}|} = p_{2:\overline{2}|} - {_4}p_{2:\overline{2}|}.$$
Type I has an exponential survival model with
$$_tp_2 = e^{-t \cdot \ln 1.25} = (1.25)^{-t} = (.80)^t,$$
and Type II has a uniform survival model with $\omega = 9$, so
$$_tp_2 = \frac{7-t}{7}.$$
Then due to the independence we have
$$_{1|3}q_{2:\overline{2}|} = (.80)\left(\frac{6}{7}\right) - (.80)^4\left(\frac{3}{7}\right) = .51017.$$

9-4 For nonsmokers we have

$$_tp_{65}^N = 1 - \frac{t}{10},$$

for $0 \le t \le 10$, and $\mu_{65+t}^N = \frac{1}{10-t}$. For a nonsmoker age 55 we have $\mu_{55+t}^N = \frac{1}{20-t}$, so the force of mortality for a smoker age 55 is $\mu_{55+t}^S = \frac{2}{20-t}$, and the SDF for this smoker is

$$_tp_{55}^S = \exp\left[-\int_0^t \frac{2}{20-r}\,dr\right] = \left(1 - \frac{t}{20}\right)^2,$$

for $0 \le t \le 20$. Since T_{65}^N and T_{55}^S are independent, then

$$_tp_{65:55} = {_tp_{65}^N} \cdot {_tp_{65}^S} = \left(1 - \frac{t}{10}\right)\left(1 - \frac{t}{20}\right)^2,$$

for $0 \le t \le 10$, and therefore

$$\begin{aligned}
\overset{o}{e}_{65:55} &= \int_0^{10}\left(1 - \frac{t}{10}\right)\left(1 - \frac{t}{20}\right)^2 dt \\
&= \int_0^{10}\left(1 - \frac{2t}{10} + \frac{5t^2}{400} - \frac{t^3}{4000}\right) dt \\
&= \left. t - \frac{t^2}{10} + \frac{5t^3}{1200} - \frac{t^4}{16,000} \right|_0^{10} \\
&= 10 - 10 + \frac{5000}{1200} - \frac{10,000}{16,000} = 3.54167.
\end{aligned}$$

9-5 As shown in Example 9.3, if T_x and T_y are independent with exponential distributions, then T_{xy} is also exponential with hazard rate $\lambda = \lambda_x + \lambda_y$. Here $\lambda_x = \lambda_y = .05$, so T_{xy} is exponential with hazard rate $\lambda = .10$. It is known (see Equation (2.52)) that

$$Var(T_{xy}) = \frac{1}{\lambda^2} = \frac{1}{.01} = 100.$$

CHAPTER NINE

9-6 We seek the value of

$$\begin{aligned}
{}_5q_{\overline{80:85}} &= 1 - {}_5p_{\overline{80:85}} \\
&= 1 - {}_5p_{80} - {}_5p_{85} + {}_5p_{80:85} \\
&= 1 - \left(1 - \frac{5}{20}\right) - \left(1 - \frac{5}{15}\right) + \left(1 - \frac{5}{20}\right)\left(1 - \frac{5}{15}\right) \\
&= 1 - \frac{15}{20} - \frac{10}{15} + \left(\frac{15}{20}\right)\left(\frac{10}{15}\right) = \frac{1}{12}.
\end{aligned}$$

Alternatively,

$$ {}_5q_{\overline{80:85}} = {}_5q_{80} \cdot {}_5q_{85} = \frac{5}{20} \cdot \frac{5}{15} = \frac{1}{12}.$$

9-7 (a) We have

$$ {}_tq_{\overline{xy}} = 1 - {}_tp_{\overline{xy}} = 1 - ({}_tp_x + {}_tp_y - {}_tp_{xy}),$$

from Equation (9.20b). Recall that this relationship does *not* require independence. Then we have

$$\begin{aligned}
{}_tq_{\overline{xy}} &= 1 - (1 - {}_tq_x) - (1 - {}_tq_y) + (1 - {}_tq_{xy}) \\
&= {}_tq_x + {}_tq_y - {}_tq_{xy},
\end{aligned}$$

as required, without requiring independence.

(b) We begin with Equation (9.21), which gives $f_{T_{\overline{xy}}}(t)$ as

$$f_{T_{\overline{xy}}}(t) = {}_tp_x\mu_{x+t} + {}_tp_y\mu_{y+t} - {}_tp_{xy}\mu_{x+t:y+t},$$

which has not yet required independence to this point. However when we now substitute ${}_tp_{xy} = {}_tp_x \cdot {}_tp_y$ and $\mu_{x+t:y+t} = \mu_{x+t} + \mu_{y+t}$, we are assuming independence. We now have

$$\begin{aligned}
f_{T_{\overline{xy}}}(t) &= {}_tp_x\mu_{x+t} + {}_tp_y\mu_{y+t} - {}_tp_x \cdot {}_tp_y(\mu_{x+t} + \mu_{y+t}) \\
&= \mu_{x+t}({}_tp_x - {}_tp_x \cdot {}_tp_y) + \mu_{y+t}({}_tp_y - {}_tp_x \cdot {}_tp_y) \\
&= \mu_{x+t} \cdot {}_tp_x \cdot {}_tq_y + \mu_{y+t} \cdot {}_tp_y \cdot {}_tq_x,
\end{aligned}$$

as required, but only by assuming independence.

(c) Here we have

$$\begin{aligned}
{}_n|q_{\overline{xy}} &= {}_nP_{\overline{xy}} - {}_{n+1}P_{\overline{xy}} \\
&= \left({}_nP_x + {}_nP_y - {}_nP_{xy}\right) - \left({}_{n+1}P_x + {}_{n+1}P_y - {}_{n+1}P_{xy}\right) \\
&= {}_n|q_x + {}_n|q_y - {}_n|q_{xy} \\
&= {}_n|q_x + {}_n|q_y - {}_nP_{xy} \cdot q_{x+n:y+n},
\end{aligned}$$

without yet having assumed independence.

Then we assume independence when we write

$$\begin{aligned}
{}_n|q_{\overline{xy}} &= {}_n|q_x + {}_n|q_y - {}_nP_x \cdot {}_nP_y \left[1-(1-q_{x+n})(1-q_{y+n})\right] \\
&= {}_n|q_x + {}_n|q_y - {}_nP_x \cdot {}_nP_y \left[q_{x+n}+q_{y+n}-q_{x+n}\cdot q_{y+n}\right] \\
&= {}_n|q_x + {}_n|q_y - {}_nP_y \cdot {}_n|q_x - {}_nP_x \cdot {}_n|q_y + {}_n|q_x \cdot {}_n|q_y \\
&= {}_n|q_x(1- {}_nP_y) + {}_n|q_y(1- {}_nP_x) + {}_n|q_x \cdot {}_n|q_y,
\end{aligned}$$

as required by assuming independence.

9-8 From Example 9.1 we know that

$$_t q_{xy} = t \cdot q_x + t \cdot q_y - t^2 \cdot q_x \cdot q_y,$$

so here we have

$$\begin{aligned}
18({}_{1/3}q_{xy}) &- 12({}_{1/2}q_{xy}) \\
&= 18\left(\frac{1}{3} \cdot q_x + \frac{1}{3} \cdot q_y - \frac{1}{9} \cdot q_x \cdot q_y\right) \\
&\quad -12\left(\frac{1}{2} \cdot q_x + \frac{1}{2} \cdot q_y - \frac{1}{4} \cdot q_x \cdot q_y\right) \\
&= 6 \cdot q_x + 6 \cdot q_y - 2 \cdot q_x \cdot q_y - 6 \cdot q_x - 6 \cdot q_y + 3 \cdot q_x \cdot q_y \\
&= q_x \cdot q_y = q_{\overline{xy}},
\end{aligned}$$

as required.

Chapter Nine

9-9 Since the force of failure is constant, then

$$_{.75}p_{x+.25} = (p_x)^{.75} = (.92)^{.75} = .93938.$$

Similarly,

$$_{.75}p_{y+.25} = (p_y)^{.75} = (.94)^{.75} = .95465.$$

Then

$$_{.75}p_{\overline{x+.25:y+.25}} = .93938 + .95465 - (.93938)(.95465)$$
$$= .99725.$$

9-10 Since T_x and T_y are both exponential, and are independent, then T_{xy} is also exponential. From Exercise 9-5 we have

$$\overset{o}{e}_x = \frac{1}{\lambda_x} = 20,$$

$$\overset{o}{e}_y = \frac{1}{\lambda_y} = 20,$$

and

$$\overset{o}{e}_{xy} = \frac{1}{\lambda} = 10.$$

Then from Equation (9.31) we have

$$Cov(T_{xy}, T_{\overline{xy}}) = (20-10)(20-10) = 100.$$

9-11 Each machine is age 0, and we seek the value of $Pr(T_I < T_{II})$. For Machine I,

$$S_I(x) = \exp\left[-\int_0^x \frac{1.80}{9-y}\,dy\right]$$
$$= \exp\{-[-1.80\ln(9-y)]_0^x\}$$
$$= \left(\frac{9-x}{9}\right)^{1.80}.$$

Similarly, for Machine II,

$$S_{II}(x) = \left(\frac{9-x}{9}\right)^{1.50}.$$

Then

$$Pr(T_I < T_{II}) = \int_0^9 f_I(x)\cdot S_{II}(x)\,dx$$
$$= \int_0^9 \left(\frac{9-x}{9}\right)^{1.80}\left(\frac{1.80}{9-x}\right)\left(\frac{9-x}{9}\right)^{1.50}dx$$
$$= \frac{1.80}{9^{3.3}}\int_0^9 (9-x)^{2.3}\,dx$$
$$= \frac{1.80}{9^{3.3}}\left[-\frac{(9-x)^{3.3}}{3.3}\right]_0^9$$
$$= \frac{1.80}{9^{3.3}}\left(\frac{9^{3.3}}{3.3}\right) = .54545.$$

9-12 We are given

$$Z = Z_{xy} + Z_{\overline{xy}},$$

so

$$E[Z] = A_{xy} + A_{\overline{xy}} = A_x + A_y$$
$$= 1 - \frac{.04}{1.04}(10) + 1 - \frac{.04}{1.04}(14) = 1.07692.$$

9-13   Payment is made at time t, for $0 \leq t \leq 14$, if either of (x) or (y) survives, the probability of which is ${}_t p_{\overline{xy}}$. Payment is also made at time t, for $15 \leq t < \infty$, if exactly one survives, the probability of which is ${}_t p_{\overline{xy}} - {}_t p_{xy}$. Then the APV of payments is given by

$$E[Y] = \sum_{t=0}^{14} v^t \cdot {}_t p_{\overline{xy}} + \sum_{t=15}^{\infty} v^t ({}_t p_{\overline{xy}} - {}_t p_{xy})$$

$$= \sum_{t=0}^{\infty} v^t \cdot {}_t p_{\overline{xy}} - \sum_{t=15}^{\infty} v^t \cdot {}_t p_{xy}$$

$$= \ddot{a}_{\overline{xy}} - {}_{15|}\ddot{a}_{xy} = \ddot{a}_x + \ddot{a}_y - \ddot{a}_{xy} - {}_{15|}\ddot{a}_{xy}$$

$$= 9.80 + 11.60 - 7.60 - 3.70 = 10.10.$$

(Note that independence of T_x and T_y need not be assumed.)

9-14   Extending the results from Section 6.1.2 in the single life case, we let $\ddot{Y}_{xy} = \ddot{a}_{\overline{K_{xy}|}}$. Then

$$Var(\ddot{Y}_{xy}) = \frac{{}^2A_{xy} - A_{xy}^2}{d^2}.$$

Here we have
$$A_{xy} = 1 - d \cdot \ddot{a}_{xy} = 1 - 10d$$

and
$${}^2A_{xy} = 1 - d' \cdot {}^2\ddot{a}_{xy} = 1 - 7d',$$

where
$$d' = 1 - v' = 1 - v^2 = 1 - (1-d)^2 = 2d - d^2.$$

Then we have

$$Var(\ddot{Y}_{xy}) = \frac{1 - 7(2d - d^2) - (1 - 10d)^2}{d^2}$$

$$= \frac{1 - 14d + 7d^2 - 1 + 20d - 100d^2}{d^2}$$

$$= \frac{6d - 93d^2}{d^2} = 27,$$

which solves for $d = .05$.

9-15 Recall that

$$P_{\overline{xy}} = \frac{A_{\overline{xy}}}{\ddot{a}_{\overline{xy}}} = \frac{A_x + A_y - A_{xy}}{\ddot{a}_x + \ddot{a}_y - \ddot{a}_{xy}}.$$

We find $\ddot{a}_x$ and $\ddot{a}_y$ from

$$\ddot{a}_y = \ddot{a}_x = \frac{1}{P_x + d} = \frac{1}{.16} = 6.25,$$

and then we find A_x and A_y from

$$A_y = A_x = 1 - d \cdot \ddot{a}_x = 1 - (.06)(6.25) = .625.$$

Then we have

$$P_{\overline{xy}} = \frac{.625 + .625 - 1 + .06\ddot{a}_{xy}}{6.25 + 6.25 - \ddot{a}_{xy}} = .06,$$

or

$$.25 + .06\ddot{a}_{xy} = .75 - .06\ddot{a}_{xy},$$

which solves for $\ddot{a}_{xy} = \frac{50}{12}$ and therefore $A_{xy} = 1 - (.06)\left(\frac{50}{12}\right) = .75$. Then

$$P_{\overline{xy}} = \frac{A_{\overline{xy}}}{\ddot{a}_{\overline{xy}}} = \frac{.75}{\frac{50}{12}} = .18.$$

9-16 The APV of the benefit is $A_{\overline{xx}} = A_x + A_x - A_{xx}$. The APV of the premium stream is

$$P \cdot \ddot{a}_{xx} + .75P(\ddot{a}_{\overline{xx}} - \ddot{a}_{xx}) = P \cdot \ddot{a}_{xx} + .75P(2\ddot{a}_x - 2\ddot{a}_{xx})$$
$$= P(1.50\ddot{a}_x - .50\ddot{a}_{xx}).$$

We use the given values of A_x and $\ddot{a}_x$ to find d, from

$$A_x = .40 = 1 - d \cdot \ddot{a}_x = 1 - 10d,$$

so $d = .06$, and then to find $\ddot{a}_{xx}$ from

$$\ddot{a}_{xx} = \frac{1 - A_{xx}}{d} = \frac{.45}{.06} = 7.50.$$

Then

$$P = \frac{2A_x - A_{xx}}{1.50\ddot{a}_x - .50\ddot{a}_{xx}}$$
$$= \frac{(2)(.40) - .55}{(1.50)(10.00) - (.50)(7.50)}$$
$$= .02222.$$

9-17 We are given

$$1180 = 100\overline{a}_{xy} + 70\overline{a}_{y|x} + 50\overline{a}_{x|y}$$
$$= 100\overline{a}_{xy} + 70(\overline{a}_x - \overline{a}_{xy}) + 50(\overline{a}_y - \overline{a}_{xy})$$
$$= 70\overline{a}_x + 50\overline{a}_y - 20\overline{a}_{xy}$$
$$= (70)(12) + (50)(10) - 20\overline{a}_{xy},$$

from which we find $\overline{a}_{xy} = 8$. Then

$$\overline{a}_{\overline{xy}} = \overline{a}_x + \overline{a}_y - \overline{a}_{xy}$$
$$= 12 + 10 - 8 = 14.$$

9-18 First we find the marginal density of T_x as

$$f_{T_x}(t_x) = 4\int_0^\infty (1+t_x+2t_y)^{-3}\, dt_y$$

$$= \left. \frac{4(1+t_x+2t_y)^{-2}}{(-2)(2)} \right|_0^\infty$$

$$= (1+t_x)^{-2},$$

and the marginal density of T_y as

$$f_{T_y}(t_y) = 4\int_0^\infty (1+t_x+2t_y)^{-3}\, dt_x$$

$$= \left. \frac{4(1+t_x+2t_y)^{-2}}{-2} \right|_0^\infty$$

$$= 2(1+2t_y)^{-2}.$$

The lack of independence is shown by the fact that

$$f_{T_x}(t_x)\cdot f_{T_y}(t_y) \neq f_{T_x,T_y}(t_x,t_y).$$

9-19 The SDF of T_x is found as

$$S_{T_x}(t) = \int_t^\infty f_{T_x}(t_x)\, dt_x$$

$$= \int_t^\infty (1+t_x)^{-2}\, dt_x$$

$$= \left. -(1+t_x)^{-1} \right|_t^\infty$$

$$= \frac{1}{1+t}.$$

CHAPTER NINE

9-20 This value of joint CDF is found as

$$F_{T_x,T_y}(1,2) = 4\int_0^1 \int_0^2 (1+t_x+2t_y)^{-3} \, dt_y \, dt_x$$

$$= \int_0^1 \left. \frac{4(1+t_x+2t_y)^{-2}}{(-2)(2)} \right|_0^2 dt_x$$

$$= \int_0^1 \left[(1+t_x)^{-2} - (5+t_x)^{-2}\right] dt_x$$

$$= \left. -(1+t_x)^{-1} + (5+t_x)^{-1} \right|_0^1$$

$$= -(2)^{-1} + (6)^{-1} + (1)^{-1} - (5)^{-1}$$

$$= 1 + \frac{1}{6} - \frac{1}{2} - \frac{1}{5} = .46667.$$

9-21 This value of the joint SDF is found as

$$S_{T_x,T_y}(1,2) = 4\int_1^\infty \int_2^\infty (1+t_x+2t_y)^{-3} \, dt_y \, dt_x$$

$$= \int_1^\infty \left. \frac{4(1+t_x+2t_y)^{-2}}{(-2)(2)} \right|_2^\infty dt_x$$

$$= \int_1^\infty (5+t_x)^{-2} \, dt_x$$

$$= \left. -(5+t_x)^{-1} \right|_1^\infty = 6^{-1} = .16667.$$

9-22 Recall that $_n p_{xy} = S_{T_x,T_y}(n,n)$, so we have

$$_n p_{xy} = 4\int_n^\infty \int_n^\infty (1+t_x+2t_y)^{-3} \, dt_y \, dt_x$$

$$= \int_n^\infty \left. \frac{4(1+t_x+2t_y)^{-2}}{(-2)(2)} \right|_n^\infty dt_x$$

$$= \int_n^\infty (1+2n+t_x)^{-2} \, dt_x$$

$$= \left. -(1+2n+t_x)^{-1} \right|_n^\infty = (1+2n+n)^{-1} = \frac{1}{1+3n}.$$

9-23 Recall that $_nq_{\overline{xy}} = F_{T_x,T_y}(n,n)$, so we have

$$_nq_{\overline{xy}} = 4\int_0^n \int_0^n (1+t_x+2t_y)^{-3}\, dt_y\, dt_x$$

$$= \int_0^n \left. \frac{4(1+t_x+2t_y)^{-2}}{(-2)(2)} \right|_0^n dt_x$$

$$= \int_0^n \left[(1+t_x)^{-2} - (1+2n+t_x)^{-2}\right] dt_x$$

$$= \left. -(1+t_x)^{-1} + (1+2n+t_x)^{-1} \right|_0^n$$

$$= -(1+n)^{-1} + (1+3n)^{-1} + 1 - (1+2n)^{-1}$$

$$= \frac{1}{1+3n} - \frac{1}{1+n} - \frac{1}{1+2n} + 1$$

$$= \frac{(1+3n)(1+n)(1+2n) + (1+n)(1+2n) - (1+3n)(1+2n) - (1+3n)(1+n)}{(1+3n)(1+n)(1+2n)}$$

$$= \frac{(1+6n+11n^2+6n^3) + (1+3n+2n^2) - (1+5n+6n^2) - (1+4n+3n^2)}{(1+3n)(1+n)(1+2n)}$$

$$= \frac{4n^2+6n^3}{(1+3n)(1+n)(1+2n)} = \frac{2n^2(2+3n)}{(1+3n)(1+n)(1+2n)}.$$

9-24 Under the assumption of independence, the APV is

$$\overline{A}_{\overline{xy}} = \overline{A}_x + \overline{A}_y - \overline{A}_{xy} = \frac{.06}{.11} + \frac{.06}{.11} - \frac{.12}{.17} = .38503.$$

Recognition of the common shock hazard means that $\mu_x = \mu_y = .06$ as before, but the joint hazard rate is now

$$\mu_{xy} = \mu_x^* + \mu_y^* + \lambda = .04 + .04 + .02 = .10.$$

Now the APV is

$$\overline{A}_{\overline{xy}} = \frac{.06}{.11} + \frac{.06}{.11} - \frac{.10}{.15} = .42424,$$

so the difference is

$$.42424 - .38503 = .03921.$$

9-25 Recall that

$$p_x = p_x^* \cdot e^{-\lambda} = e^{-\mu_x^*} \cdot e^{-\lambda},$$

since T_x^* is exponential. With $\lambda = .01$ we have

$$p_x = .96 = p_x^* \cdot e^{-.01},$$

so $p_x^* = .96e^{.01}$. In similar manner we find $p_y^* = .97e^{.01}$. Since T_x^* and T_y^* are exponential, then

$$_5p_x^* = (p_x^*)^5 = (.96e^{.01})^5$$

and

$$_5p_y^* = (p_y^*)^5 = (.97e^{.01})^5.$$

Then

$$\begin{aligned}_5p_{xy} &= {_5p_x^*} \cdot {_5p_y^*} \cdot e^{-5\lambda} \\ &= (.96e^{.01})^5 (.97e^{.01})^5 \cdot e^{-.05} \\ &= (.96)^5 (.97)^5 e^{.05} = .73609.\end{aligned}$$

CHAPTER TEN
MULTIPLE CONTINGENCIES

10-1   The probability of completing Year 1 is $1-.40-.20=.40$, so if (arbitrarily) 1000 begin Year 1, then 400 begin Year 2. The partial table shows that 70% who begin Year 2 either fail or complete the year, and we are told that the number of failures (F) is 40% of the number who complete (C). Then we have the equations

$$F + C = (.70)(400) = 280$$

and

$$F = .40C,$$

so $.40C+C=280$, giving us $C=200$.

In Year 3, $(.60)(200)=120$ complete the year, and 20 fail, so 60 withdraw.

Then the total number of withdrawals is

$$(1000)(.20) + (400)(.30) + 60 = 380$$

of the original 1000, so the probability of withdrawal is $\frac{380}{1000} = .380$.

10-2   First we observe that

$$p_{40}^{(\tau)} = 1 - q_{40}^{(\tau)} = 1 - \left(q_{40}^{(1)} + q_{40}^{(2)}\right) = .66,$$

so

$$\ell_{41}^{(\tau)} = (2000)(.66) = 1320.$$

Next we find

so
$$p_{40}^{(\tau)} = p_{40}^{\prime(1)} \cdot p_{40}^{\prime(2)} = .75(1-y) = .66,$$

$$y = 1 - \frac{.66}{.75} = .12.$$

Then we have

$$p_{41}^{(\tau)} = p_{41}^{\prime(1)} \cdot p_{41}^{\prime(2)} = .80(1-2y) = .608.$$

Finally,

$$\ell_{42}^{(\tau)} = \ell_{41}^{(\tau)} \cdot p_{41}^{(\tau)} = (1320)(.608) = 802.56.$$

10-3 We seek the value of $_5p_{50}^{(\tau)} - _{10}p_{50}^{(\tau)}$. We have

$$_5p_{50}^{(\tau)} = {_5p_{50}^{\prime(1)}} \cdot {_5p_{50}^{\prime(2)}} = \left(1 - \frac{5}{50}\right)\left(e^{-(.05)(5)}\right) = .70092,$$

and

$$_{10}p_{50}^{(\tau)} = \left(1 - \frac{10}{50}\right)\left(e^{-(.05)(10)}\right) = .48522,$$

so

$$_5p_{50}^{(\tau)} - _{10}p_{50}^{(\tau)} = .70092 - .48522 = .21570.$$

10-4 (a) From the definition of conditional density we have

$$f_{J|T}(j|t) = \frac{f_{T,J}(t,j)}{f_T(t)} = \frac{_tp_x^{(\tau)} \cdot \mu_{x+t}^{(j)}}{_tp_x^{(\tau)} \cdot \mu_{x+t}^{(\tau)}} = \frac{\mu_{x+t}^{(j)}}{\mu_{x+t}^{(\tau)}},$$

as required.

(b) Recall that $\mu_{x+t}^{(\tau)} = \mu_{x+t}^{(1)} + \mu_{x+t}^{(2)} + \mu_{x+t}^{(3)}$. Here we have

$$f_{J|T}(1,t) = \frac{\mu_{x+t}^{(1)}}{\mu_{x+t}^{(\tau)}} = \frac{.03}{.03 + .03t + .03t^2} = \frac{1}{1 + t + t^2}.$$

CHAPTER TEN

10-5 (a) To find ${}_tp'^{(1)}_x$ analytically, we have

$$
\begin{aligned}
{}_tp'^{(1)}_x &= \exp\left[-\int_0^t \mu^{(1)}_{x+r}\, dr\right] \\
&= \exp\left[-\int_0^t \frac{1}{75-r}\, dr\right] \\
&= \exp\left[\ln(75-r)\Big|_0^t\right] \\
&= \exp\left[\ln(75-t) - \ln 75\right] \\
&= \exp\left[\ln\left(\frac{75-t}{75}\right)\right] = \frac{75-t}{75}, \quad 0 \le t < 75.
\end{aligned}
$$

However we should reorganize that the given HRF tells us that the random variable $T^{(1)}_x$ is uniform with $\omega = 75$, so the form of ${}_tp'^{(x)}_x$ is known. Similarly,

$$
\begin{aligned}
{}_tp'^{(2)}_x &= \exp\left[-\int_0^t \frac{2}{50-r}\, dr\right] \\
&= \exp\left[2\cdot\ln(50-r)\Big|_0^t\right] \\
&= \exp\left[\ln(50-t)^2 - \ln(50)^2\right] \\
&= \exp\left[\ln\left(\frac{50-t}{50}\right)^2\right] = \left(\frac{50-t}{50}\right)^2, \quad 0 \le t < 50.
\end{aligned}
$$

Then

$$
{}_tp^{(\tau)}_x = {}_tp'^{(1)}_x \cdot {}_tp'^{(2)}_x = \left(\frac{75-t}{75}\right)\left(\frac{50-t}{50}\right)^2, \text{ for } 0 \le t < 50.
$$

(Note that ${}_tp^{(\tau)}_x = 0$ for $t > 50$ because ${}_tp'^{(2)}_x = 0$.)

(b) Recall that the density function for the time-to-failure random variable due to Cause (j) is ${}_tp^{(\tau)}_x \mu^{(j)}_{x+t}$. Here we have

$$
f_{T,J}(t,1) = {}_tp^{(\tau)}_x \mu^{(1)}_{x+t} = \frac{1}{75}\left(\frac{50-t}{50}\right)^2
$$

and

$$
f_{T,J}(t,2) = {}_tp^{(\tau)}_x \mu^{(2)}_{x+t} = (2)\left(\frac{75-t}{75}\right)\left(\frac{50-t}{2500}\right).
$$

In both cases the domain is $0 \le t < 50$, because ${}_tp^{(\tau)}_x$ becomes zero at $t = 50$.

(c) $q_x^{(1)} = \int_0^1 {}_tp_x^{(\tau)} \mu_{x+t}^{(1)} \, dt = \int_0^1 \frac{(50-t)^2}{(75)(50)^2} \, dt$

$$= \frac{-(50-t)^3}{(3)(75)(50)^2} \bigg|_0^1$$

$$= .22222 - .20915 = .01307$$

$q_x^{(2)} = \int_0^1 {}_tp_x^{(\tau)} \mu_{x+t}^{(2)} \, dt = \int_0^1 \frac{2(75-t)(50-t)}{(75)(50)^2} \, dt$

$$= \frac{2}{(75)(50)^2} \left[(75)(50)t - \frac{125}{2}t^2 + \frac{1}{3}t^3 \right]_0^1$$

$$= \frac{2}{(75)(50)^2} \left[(75)(50) - \frac{125}{2} + \frac{1}{3} \right]$$

$$= .03934$$

Then $q_x^{(\tau)} = q_x^{(1)} + q_x^{(2)} = .05241$.

(d) $q_x'^{(1)} = 1 - p_x'^{(1)} = 1 - \frac{75-1}{75} = .01333$

$q_x'^{(2)} = 1 - p_x'^{(2)} = 1 - \left(\frac{50-1}{50}\right)^2 = .03960$

(e) $f_J(1) = \int_0^{50} f_{T|J}(t,1) \, dt$

$$= \int_0^{50} \frac{(50-t)^2}{(75)(50)^2} \, dt$$

$$= \frac{-(50-t)^3}{(3)(75)(50)^2} \bigg|_0^{50} = \frac{(50)^3}{(3)(75)(50)^2} = \frac{2}{9}$$

$f_J(2) = \int_0^{50} f_{T|J}(t,2) \, dt$

$$= \int_0^{50} \frac{2(75-t)(50-t)}{(75)(50)^2} \, dt$$

$$= \frac{2}{(75)(50)^2} \left[(75)(50)t - \frac{125}{2}t^2 + \frac{1}{3}t^3 \right]_0^{50}$$

$$= \frac{2}{(75)(50)^2} \left[(75)(50)(50) - \frac{125}{2}(50)^2 + \frac{1}{3}(50)^3 \right]$$

$$= 2 - \frac{125}{75} + \frac{2(50)}{3(75)} = \frac{175}{225} = \frac{7}{9}$$

(f) From Exercise 10-4(a) we have

$$f_{J|T}(j|t) = \frac{\mu_{x+t}^{(j)}}{\mu_{x+t}^{(\tau)}},$$

so

$$f_{J|T}(1|1) = \frac{\mu_{x+1}^{(1)}}{\mu_{x+1}^{(\tau)}} = \frac{1/74}{1/74 + 2/49} = .24873$$

and

$$f_{J|T}(2|1) = \frac{\mu_{x+1}^{(2)}}{\mu_{x+1}^{(\tau)}} = \frac{2/49}{1/74 + 2/49} = .75127.$$

10-6 The total force of decrement is $\mu^{(\tau)} = .04 + \mu$, so the total survival probability is $e^{-(.04+\mu)}$. Then the expected number of survivors in the first year is

$$1000 \cdot e^{-(.04+\mu)} = 952,$$

so the annual survival probability is .952. This means we expect

$$1000(.952)^3 = 862.80$$

survivors at the start of the fourth year. The annual force of failure is

$$\mu^{(1)} = -\ln.952 - .04 = .009,$$

so the annual probability of failure is

$$q^{(1)} = 1 - e^{-.009}.$$

Finally, the expected number of failures in the fourth year is

$$(862.80)(1 - e^{-.009}) = 7.73036.$$

10-7 Since ${}_tp_x^{(\tau)} = 1 - {}_tq_x^{(\tau)}$, then Equation (10.13a) can be written as

$$\mu_{x+t}^{(\tau)} = \frac{-\frac{d}{dt}(1 - {}_tq_x^{(\tau)})}{{}_tp_x^{(\tau)}} = \frac{\frac{d}{dt}{}_tq_x^{(\tau)}}{{}_tp_x^{(\tau)}}.$$

Substituting for ${}_tq_x^{(\tau)}$ from Equation (10.5b) we have

$$\mu_{x+t}^{(\tau)} = \frac{\frac{d}{dt}(_tq_x^{(1)} + _tq_x^{(2)} + \cdots)}{_tp_x^{(\tau)}}$$

$$= \frac{\frac{d}{dt}\,_tq_x^{(1)}}{_tp_x^{(\tau)}} + \frac{\frac{d}{dt}\,_tq_x^{(2)}}{_tp_x^{(\tau)}} + \cdots$$

$$= \mu_{x+t}^{(1)} + \mu_{x+t}^{(2)} + \cdots,$$

from Equation (10.19), which establishes Equation (10.17). Then using Equation (10.13b) we have

$$_tp_x^{(\tau)} = \exp\left(-\int_0^t \left(\mu_{x+t}^{(1)} + \mu_{x+t}^{(2)} + \cdots\right) dt\right),$$

$$= \exp\left(-\int_0^t \mu_{x+t}^{(1)} \, dt\right) \cdot \exp\left(-\int_0^t \mu_{x+t}^{(2)} \, dt\right) \cdot \cdots,$$

which, by use of Equation (10.12b), establishes Equation (10.16) without the assumption of independence of causes.

10-8   Recall that

$$p_x^{(\tau)} = p_x'^{(1)} \cdot p_x'^{(2)} = (.80)(.90) = .72,$$

so $q_x^{(\tau)} = 1 - .72 = .28$. From Equation (10.26) we have

$$p_x'^{(j)} = (p_x^{(\tau)})^{q_x^{(j)}/q_x^{(\tau)}},$$

so

$$.80 = (.72)^{q_x^{(1)}/.28}$$

and

$$.90 = (.72)^{q_x^{(2)}/.28}.$$

Then

$$\frac{q_x^{(1)}}{.28} \cdot \ln(.72) = \ln(.80)$$

so

$$q_x^{(1)} = (.28)\left(\frac{\ln(.80)}{\ln(.72)}\right) = .19020.$$

10-9 The following diagram will support the solution:

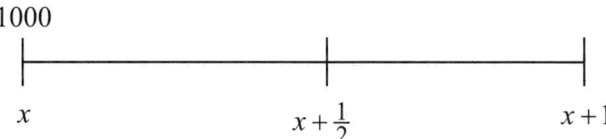

During the first half year, retirements cannot occur so deaths are occurring in a single-decrement environment. Therefore the probability of death is $\frac{1}{2} \cdot q_x'^{(1)} = .0075$, so there are 7.50 deaths and therefore $1000 - 7.50 = 992.50$ survivors at mid-year. Then retirements occur at this point of time, which also has no competing cause because of the instantaneous interval. Therefore there are

$$(.030)(992.50) = 29.775$$

retirements, so there are $992.50 - 29.775 = 962.725$ persons moving into the second half year. Death is again in a single-decrement environment in the second half, with probability

$$_{1/2}q_{x+1/2} = \frac{(.50)(.015)}{1-(.50)(.015)} = .0075568,$$

so there are $(962.725)(.0075568) = 7.275$ expected deaths in the second half. Then the total expected deaths is $7.50 + 7.275 = 14.775$.

10-10 Recall that

$$q_x^{(\tau)} = q_x^{(1)} + q_x^{(2)} + q_x^{(3)} = .96,$$

so $p_x^{(\tau)} = .04$. Then from Equation (10.26),

$$p_x'^{(1)} = (p_x^{(\tau)})^{q_x^{(1)}/q_x^{(\tau)}} = (.04)^{.48/.96} = .20.$$

10-11 Parallel to the derivation of Equation (10.29) we have

$$q_x^{(1)} = \int_0^1 {}_tp_x^{(\tau)} \mu_{x+t}^{(1)} \, dt$$
$$= \int_0^1 {}_tp_x'^{(1)} \mu_{x+t}^{(1)} \cdot {}_tp_x'^{(2)} \cdot {}_tp_x'^{(3)} \, dt$$
$$= \int_0^1 q_x'^{(1)} (1 - t \cdot q_x'^{(2)})(1 - t \cdot q_x'^{(3)}) \, dt$$
$$= q_x'^{(1)} \int_0^1 \left(1 - t \cdot q_x'^{(2)} - t \cdot q_x'^{(3)} + t^2 \cdot q_x'^{(2)} \cdot q_x'^{(3)}\right) dt$$
$$= q_x'^{(1)} \left(1 - \frac{1}{2} \cdot q_x'^{(2)} - \frac{1}{2} \cdot q_x'^{(3)} + \frac{1}{3} \cdot q_x'^{(2)} \cdot q_x'^{(3)}\right),$$

as required.

10-12 From Equations (10.29a) and (10.29b), we have

$$q_x^{(1)} = q_x'^{(1)} \left(1 - \frac{1}{2} \cdot q_x'^{(2)}\right) = .02$$

and

$$q_x^{(2)} = q_x'^{(2)} \left(1 - \frac{1}{2} \cdot q_x'^{(1)}\right) = .06.$$

From the second equation we have

$$q_x'^{(2)} = \frac{.06}{1 - \frac{1}{2} \cdot q_x'^{(1)}}.$$

Substituting into the first equation we have

$$q_x'^{(1)} \left(1 - \frac{(.50)(.06)}{1 - \frac{1}{2} \cdot q_x'^{(1)}}\right) = .02,$$

or

$$q_x'^{(1)} \left(1 - \frac{1}{2} \cdot q_x'^{(1)} - .03\right) = .02 - .01 \cdot q_x'^{(1)},$$

or

$$.97 q_x'^{(1)} - .50 (q_x'^{(1)})^2 + .01 q_x'^{(1)} = .02,$$

or

$$.50 (q_x'^{(1)})^2 - .98 q_x'^{(1)} + .02 = 0,$$

so

Chapter Ten

$$q_x'^{(1)} = \frac{.98 \pm \sqrt{(.98)^2 - (4)(.50)(.02)}}{(2)(.50)} = .020625,$$

so $1000 q_x'^{(1)} = 20.625$.

10-13 The decrements are uniformly distributed in the associated single-decrement tables. Therefore

$$q_0^{(1)} = .10[1 - (.50)(.25)] = .0875,$$

$$q_0^{(2)} = .25[1 - (.50)(.10)] = .2375,$$

$$q_1^{(1)} = .20[1 - (.50)(.20)] = .1800,$$

$$q_1^{(2)} = .20[1 - (.50)(.20)] = .1800,$$

$$q_2^{(1)} = .20[1 - (.50)(.10)] = .1900,$$

and

$$q_2^{(2)} = .10[1 - (.50)(.20)] = .0900.$$

10-14 To evaluate the marginal probabilities, it will be useful to constrict the double-decrement table from the probabilities found in Exercise 10-13. We choose an arbitrary radix of 10,000.

x	$\ell_x^{(\tau)}$	$d_x^{(1)}$	$d_x^{(2)}$
0	10,000.0	875.0	2,375.0
1	6,750.0	1,215.0	1,215.0
2	4,320.0	820.8	388.8
3	3,110.4		

(a) Then

$$p_{J_0}(1) = \frac{875.0 + 1215.0 + 820.8}{10,000} = .29108$$

and

$$p_{J_0}(2) = \frac{2375.0 + 1215.0 + 388.8}{10,000} = .39788.$$

(b) Similarly,

$$p_{K_0}(1) = \frac{875+2375}{10,000} = .32500,$$

$$p_{K_0}(2) = \frac{1215+1215}{10,000} = .24300,$$

and

$$p_{K_0}(3) = \frac{820.8+388.8}{10,000} = .12096.$$

Note: The probability of graduation (which can be viewed as a third decrement, all occurring at the start of Year 4) is .31104. Then we have

$$p_{J_0}(3) = p_{K_0}(4) = .31104,$$

which is needed to make both sets of marginal probabilities sum to 1.

10-15 (a) Given that decrement in the third year occurs, the probability that it is failure is

$$\frac{d_2^{(1)}}{d_2^{(\tau)}} = \frac{820.8}{820.8+388.8} = .67857.$$

(b) Given that a student enters Year 2, the probability of eventual failure is

$$\frac{d_1^{(1)}+d_2^{(1)}}{\ell_1^{(\tau)}} = \frac{1215.0+820.8}{6750} = .30160.$$

10-16 Since withdrawal occurs only at year-end, then the total probability of surviving the year is

$$p_x^{(\tau)} = p_x'^{(1)} \cdot p_x'^{(2)} = (.99)(.95) = .9405.$$

CHAPTER TEN

Then if $\ell_x^{(\tau)} = 10,000$ we would have 9405 survivors at year-end, of which $(.10)(9405) = 940.50$ withdraw. Then the probability of withdrawal is

$$q_x^{(3)} = \frac{940.50}{10,000} = .09405.$$

10-17 In the sub-interval $(x, x+.70)$, Decrement 2 cannot occur, so Decrement 1 is operating in a single-decrement environment and is uniformly distributed. Therefore $_{.70}q_x'^{(1)} = (.70)(.100) = .070$. If we assume an arbitrary radix of $\ell_x^{(\tau)} = 1000$, then we have 70 decrements in the interval so we have 930 survivors at age $x+.70$. Then there are $(930)(.125) = 116.25$ occurrences of Decrement 2 at age $x+.70$, and therefore in $(x, x+1]$, so the probability is

$$q_x^{(2)} = \frac{116.25}{1000} = .11625.$$

10-18 (a) Retirees will have $65-25 = 40$ years of service, so the annual retirement benefit rate is $(40)(500) = 20,000$. The APV of this benefit at age 25 is

$$20,000 \,_{40|}\bar{a}_{25} = 20,000(v^{40} \cdot \,_{40}p_{25}^{(\tau)} \cdot \bar{a}_{65}).$$

(b) The APV of the death benefit is
$$200,000 \int_0^{40} v^t \cdot \,_t p_{25}^{(\tau)} \mu_{25+t}^{(1)} \, dt.$$

(c) If resignation is at time t, so that t years of employment occurred, then the benefit rate at age 65 is $400t$. The value of the eventual benefit is

$$400t \cdot \,_{40-t|}\bar{a}_{25+t}$$

at time of resignation, so its APV is

$$400 \int_0^{40} t \cdot v^t \cdot \,_t p_{25}^{(\tau)} \cdot \mu_{25+t}^{(2)} \cdot \,_{40-t|}\bar{a}_{25+t} \, dt.$$

10-19 To show the desired relationship, we start with Equation (10.33b). We multiply both sides by $p_{x+k-1}^{(\tau)}$, and substitute

$$p_{x+k-1}^{(\tau)} = 1 - q_{x+k-1}^{(1)} - q_{x+k-1}^{(2)}.$$

Then move the two terms $_kAS \cdot q_{x+k-1}^{(1)}$ and $_kAS \cdot q_{x+k-1}^{(2)}$ to the right side of the equation and group the terms $q_{x+k-1}^{(1)}\left(b_k^{(1)} - {}_kAS\right)$ and $q_{x+k-1}^{(2)}\left(b_k^{(2)} - {}_kAS\right)$.

10-20 The matrix of transition probabilities among transient states only is

$$\mathbf{S} = \begin{vmatrix} .65 & .32 \\ .25 & .72 \end{vmatrix}.$$

We need the fundamental matrix

$$\mathbf{Q} = (\mathbf{I} - \mathbf{S})^{-1} = \begin{vmatrix} .35 & -.32 \\ -.25 & .28 \end{vmatrix}^{-1}.$$

The inverse matrix (via computer software or "by hand") is

$$\mathbf{Q} = \begin{vmatrix} \frac{140}{9} & \frac{160}{9} \\ \frac{125}{9} & \frac{175}{9} \end{vmatrix}.$$

The requested probability is given by Equation (A.17a) as

$$r_{12} = \frac{q_{12}}{q_{22}} = \frac{160/9}{175/9} = .91429.$$

10-21 The expected number of years for a new subscriber to be a subscriber is given directly by $q_{11} = \frac{140}{9}$.

CHAPTER TEN

10-22 Since recovery means never again entering the acutely ill state, then it is an absorbing state for the process. The matrix of transition probabilities is

$$\mathbf{P} = \begin{vmatrix} .60 & .30 & .10 \\ .20 & .50 & .30 \\ 0 & 0 & 1 \end{vmatrix}.$$

To find the expected years in each state, we form the fundamental matrix

$$\mathbf{Q} = (\mathbf{I} - \mathbf{S})^{-1} = \begin{vmatrix} .40 & -.30 \\ -.20 & .50 \end{vmatrix}^{-1} = \begin{vmatrix} \frac{25}{7} & \frac{15}{7} \\ \frac{10}{7} & \frac{20}{7} \end{vmatrix}.$$

Then for a person currently acutely ill, the expected (nondiscounted) total treatment cost is

$$\left(\frac{25}{7}\right)(10) + \left(\frac{15}{7}\right)(1) = \frac{265}{7} = 37.85714.$$

10-23 (a) The employee never becomes disabled, so the benefit is paid at the end of the first year with probability p_{13}, at the end of the second year with probability $p_{11} \cdot p_{13}$, at the end of the third year with probability $p_{11}^2 \cdot p_{13}$, and so on. The APV is

$$APV = 20,000 \left[v \cdot p_{13} + v^2 \cdot p_{11} \cdot p_{13} + v^3 \cdot p_{11}^2 \cdot p_{13} + \cdots \right]$$
$$= 20,000 \left[v \cdot p_{13} \left(1 + v \cdot p_{11} + v^2 \cdot p_{11}^2 + \cdots \right) \right]$$
$$= 20,000 \left(\frac{v \cdot p_{13}}{1 - v \cdot p_{11}} \right)$$
$$= \frac{20,000 \left(\frac{.005}{1.05} \right)}{1 - \frac{.993}{1.05}} = 1754.39.$$

(b) The employee is currently disabled and never moves back to the active state. Then the benefit is paid at the end of the first year with probability p_{23}, at the end of the second year with probability $p_{22} \cdot p_{23}$, at the end of the third year with probability $p_{22}^2 \cdot p_{23}$, and so on. The APV is

$$APV = 10,000\left[v \cdot p_{23} + v^2 \cdot p_{22} \cdot p_{23} + v^3 \cdot p_{22}^2 \cdot p_{23} + \cdots\right]$$

$$= 10,000\left[v \cdot p_{23}\left(1 + v \cdot p_{22} + v^2 \cdot p_{22}^2 + \cdots\right)\right]$$

$$= 10,000\left(\frac{v \cdot p_{23}}{1 - v \cdot p_{22}}\right)$$

$$= \frac{10,000\left(\frac{.050}{1.05}\right)}{1 - \frac{.949}{1.05}} = 4950.50.$$

(c) In this case we must consider all possible times of transitioning from active to disabled, as well as all possible times of death once disabled. (Note that recovery back to the active state does not occur.) Suppose disability occurs in the first year, which happens with probability p_{12}. Then as of time $t = 1$ the APV is

$$X = 10,000\left(\frac{v \cdot p_{23}}{1 - v \cdot p_{22}}\right),$$

from part (b) above. Suppose disability occurs in the second year, which happens with probability $p_{11} \cdot p_{12}$. Then as of time $t = 2$ the APV is again X. Similarly, the APV is X as of time $t = 3$ if disability occurs in the third year, which happens with probability $p_{11}^2 \cdot p_{12}$, and so on. Then the overall APV is

$$APV = X\left[v \cdot p_{12} + v^2 \cdot p_{11} \cdot p_{12} + v^3 \cdot p_{11}^2 \cdot p_{12} + \cdots\right]$$

$$= 10,000\left(\frac{v \cdot p_{23}}{1 - v \cdot p_{22}}\right)\left(\frac{v \cdot p_{12}}{1 - v \cdot p_{11}}\right)$$

$$= \frac{10,000\left(\frac{.050}{1.05}\right)\left(\frac{.002}{1.05}\right)}{\left(1 - \frac{.949}{1.05}\right)\left(1 - \frac{.993}{1.05}\right)} = 173.70.$$

CHAPTER TEN 139

10-24 (a) The APV is given by

$$APV = 20,000\left[v \cdot p_{13}^{(1)} + v^2 \cdot p_{11}^{(1)} \cdot p_{13}^{(2)} + v^3 \cdot p_{11}^{(1)} \cdot p_{11}^{(2)} \cdot p_{13}^{(3)}\right]$$

$$= 20,000\left[\frac{.005}{1.05} + \frac{(.993)(.0055)}{(1.05)^2} + \frac{(.993)(.9923)(.00605)}{(1.05)^3}\right]$$

$$= 20,000(.00476 + .00495 + .00515) = 297.20.$$

(b) The benefit would be paid at age 64 (if disability occurs in the first year and death while disabled occurs in the second year), or at age 65 (if disability occurs in the first year and death while disabled occurs in the third year), or at age 65 (if disability occurs in the second year and death while disabled occurs in the third year). The APV is given by

$$APV = 10,000\left[v^2 \cdot p_{12}^{(1)} \cdot p_{23}^{(2)} + v^3 \cdot p_{12}^{(1)} \cdot p_{22}^{(2)} \cdot p_{23}^{(3)}\right.$$

$$\left. + v^3 \cdot p_{11}^{(1)} \cdot p_{12}^{(2)} \cdot p_{23}^{(3)}\right]$$

$$= 10,000\left[\frac{(.002)(.055)}{(1.05)^2} + \frac{(.002)(.944)(.0605)}{(1.05)^3}\right.$$

$$\left. + \frac{(.993)(.0022)(.0605)}{(1.05)^3}\right]$$

$$= 10,000(.0000998 + .0000987 + .0001142) = 3.13.$$

10-25 Note that in this model the state transition probabilities are not the same each year, which is a more realistic model than the standard (homogeneous) Markov model.

(a) The probability of being in the Active State at the start of the second year, which is represented by $x=1$, is

$$p_0^{(11)} = 1 - p_0^{(12)} - p_0^{(13)} = .97$$

and the probability of being in the Disabled State is $p_0^{(12)} = .01$, so the numbers in each state at $x=1$ is

$$\ell_1^{(a)} = \ell_0^{(a)} \cdot p_0^{(11)} = 970$$

and
$$\ell_1^{(d)} = \ell_0^{(a)} \cdot p_0^{(12)} = 10.$$

(The other 20 policyholders died before $x=1$.)

The number of actives at $x=2$ is made up of the
$$\ell_1^{(a)} \cdot p_1^{(11)} = (970)(.94) = 911.80$$

who were active at $x=1$ and remained active, plus the
$$\ell_1^{(d)} \cdot p_1^{(21)} = (10)(.50) = 5$$

who were disabled at $x=1$ and recovered to the Active State at $x=2$, for a total of 916.80.

The number of disableds at $x=2$ is found in the opposite way, as the
$$\ell_1^{(d)} \cdot p_1^{(22)} = (10)(1-.50-.10) = 4$$

who were disabled at $x=1$ and remained disabled, plus the
$$\ell_1^{(a)} \cdot p_1^{(12)} = (970)(.02) = 19.40$$

who were active at $x=1$ but became disabled at $x=2$, for a total of 23.40.

Similarly, the actives at $x=3$ is found as
$$\ell_3^{(a)} = \ell_2^{(a)} \cdot p_2^{(11)} + \ell_2^{(d)} \cdot p_2^{(21)} = 873.49,$$

and the disables at $x=3$ is found as
$$\ell_3^{(d)} = \ell_2^{(d)} \cdot p_2^{(22)} + \ell_2^{(a)} \cdot p_2^{(12)} = 27.70.$$

Continuing in this manner the values shown in the answer to the exercise on text page 590 are obtained.

Chapter Ten

(b) The single benefit premium per policy is found by dividing the total present value of benefit by the 1000 policyholders in the initial group, as described in the section on the group deterministic approach on text pages 164-165. Here we have

$$NSP = \frac{10,000}{\ell_0^{(a)}} \sum_{x=1}^{10} v^x \cdot \ell_x^{(d)},$$

at interest rate $i = .06$. We have

$$NSP = \frac{10,000}{1,000} \left[\frac{10}{1.06} + \frac{23.40}{(1.06)^2} + \frac{27.70}{(1.06)^3} + \cdots + \frac{44.57}{(1.06)^{10}} \right],$$

which evaluates to 2,451.40.

(c) The initial aggregate benefit reserve fund is the total of all NSP's, which is $_0V = (1000)(2,451.40) = 2,451,400$. This grows with interest at 6% to time 1, at which point $(10)(10,000) = 100,000$ is paid in benefit, so the reserve is

$$_1V = (2,451,400)(1.06) - 100,000 = 2,498,484.$$

This fund again grows at $i = .06$ to time 2, at which point $(23.40)(10,000) = 234,000$ is paid in benefit, so the fund is

$$_2V = (2,498,484)(1.06) - 234,000 = 2,414,393.$$

Continuing in this way the answers shown on text page 590 are obtained.

CHAPTER ELEVEN
CLAIM FREQUENCY MODELS

11-1   Binomial: From Equation (11.1a) we have

$$p(x) = \left(\frac{n-x+1}{x} \cdot \frac{p}{1-p}\right) \cdot p(x-1)$$

$$= \left[\frac{p}{1-p}\left(\frac{n+1}{x} - 1\right)\right] \cdot p(x-1)$$

$$= \left[-\frac{p}{1-p} + \left(\frac{p(n+1)}{1-p}\right) \cdot \frac{1}{x}\right] \cdot p(x-1),$$

so $\alpha = -\frac{p}{1-p}$ and $\beta = \frac{p(n+1)}{1-p}$.

Poisson: From Equation (11.3b) we have

$$p(x) = \frac{\lambda}{x} \cdot p(x-1),$$

which directly shows that $\alpha = 0$ and $\beta = \lambda$.

Negative binomial: From Equation (11.19b) we have

$$p(x) = \left[\frac{x+r-1}{x}(1-p)\right] \cdot p(x-1)$$

$$= \left[(1-p)\left(1 + \frac{r-1}{x}\right)\right] \cdot p(x-1)$$

$$= \left[(1-p) + \frac{(r-1)(1-p)}{x}\right] \cdot p(x-1),$$

so $\alpha = 1-p$ and $\beta = (r-1)(1-p)$.

Geometric: Letting $r = 1$ in the negative binomial, we directly have $\alpha = 1-p$ and $\beta = 0$.

11-2 We recognize $p(x) = \frac{2}{k} \cdot p(x-1)$ as the Poisson distribution with $\lambda = 2$ (see Equation (11.3b)), so $p(4) = \frac{e^{-2} 2^4}{4!} = .09022$.

11-3 Because the distribution satisfies Equation (11.22), we can write
$$\frac{p(1)}{p(0)} = \alpha + \frac{\beta}{1} = \frac{.2500}{.2500} = 1,$$
and
$$\frac{p(2)}{p(1)} = \alpha + \frac{\beta}{2} = \frac{.1875}{.2500} = .75.$$
These two equations are easily solved for $\alpha = \beta = .50$. Then
$$p(3) = \left(\alpha + \frac{\beta}{3}\right) \cdot p(2) = \left(.50 + \frac{.50}{3}\right)(.1875) = .125.$$

11-4 From Equation (11.22) we can see that $\alpha = \beta = c$ for the given distribution. Referring to Table 11.1 we observe that $\alpha = 0$ for Poisson, $\beta = 0$ for geometric, and $\alpha < 0$ for binomial. The only $(\alpha, \beta, 0)$ distribution that allows for $\alpha = \beta$ is the negative binomial with $r = 2$. (In that case we then have $\alpha = \beta = 1-p$.) Under negative binomial, $p(0) = p^r = p^2 = .50$ in this case, so $p = \sqrt{.50}$. Finally we have
$$c = \alpha = \beta = 1 - p = 1 - \sqrt{.50} = .29289.$$

11-5 The total number of claims is Poisson with $\lambda = 50$. By the decomposition property, the number of large claims is also Poisson with $\lambda = (50)(.10) = 5$. Then
$$Pr(N_L > 3) = 1 - Pr(N_L \leq 3)$$
$$= 1 - e^{-5}\left[1 + \frac{5}{1} + \frac{5^2}{2!} + \frac{5^3}{3!}\right] = .73497.$$

CHAPTER ELEVEN

11-6 For the Poisson distribution, $P_X(s) = e^{\lambda(s-1)}$. Then the successive derivatives are

$$P'_X(s) = \lambda \cdot e^{\lambda(s-1)},$$

$$P''_X(s) = \lambda^2 \cdot e^{\lambda(s-1)},$$

and

$$P'''_X(s) = \lambda^3 \cdot e^{\lambda(s-1)},$$

so

$$\frac{P'''_X(0)}{3!} = \frac{e^{-\lambda} \cdot \lambda^3}{3!} = p(3),$$

as required.

11-7 (a) We use the result from Example 11.6, namely that

$$P_X(s) = M_X(t)|_{t=\ln s},$$

with the binomial distribution MGF given by Equation (2.29). Then we have

$$P_X(s) = (q + pe^t)^n |_{t=\ln s} = (q + ps)^n.$$

Further, since $q = 1 - p$, we can write this as

$$P_X(s) = (1 - p + ps)^n = [1 + p(s-1)]^n.$$

(b) Similarly, for the negative binomial distribution, with MGF given by Equation (2.33), we have

$$P_X(s) = \left(\frac{p}{1-qe^t}\right)^r \bigg|_{t=\ln s} = \left(\frac{p}{1-qs}\right)^r = \left(\frac{p}{1-(1-p)s}\right)^r.$$

(c) The geometric distribution is the negative binomial distribution with $r = 1$, so we have

$$P_X(s) = \frac{p}{1-qs} = \frac{p}{1-(1-p)s}.$$

11-8 Using Equation (2.67) for the MGF of a compound distribution, we have
$$M_S(t) = M_N[\ln M_X(t)].$$
Since X is Poisson with parameter λ_2, then
$$M_X(t) = e^{\lambda_2(e^t-1)}$$
and
$$\ln M_X(t) = \lambda_2(e^t-1).$$
Similarly, the MGF of N is
$$M_N(t) = e^{\lambda_1(e^t-1)},$$
so
$$M_S(t) = e^{\lambda_1\left[e^{\lambda_2(e^t-1)}-1\right]}.$$

11-9 Since N is Poisson, then $\alpha = 0$ and $\beta = \lambda$ so the denominator of Equation (11.25) is 1. The term $\left(\alpha + \frac{\beta k}{s}\right)$ becomes $\frac{\lambda k}{s}$. Factor out the $\frac{\lambda}{s}$ to reach
$$p_S(s) = \frac{\lambda}{s}\sum_{k=1}^{s} k \cdot p_X(k) \cdot p_S(s-k).$$

11-10 Using Equation (11.26) we have
$$p_S(0) = M_N[\ln p_X(0)]$$
$$= e^{\lambda(e^t-1)}\Big|_{t=\ln p_X(0)}$$
$$= e^{\lambda[p_X(0)-1]}$$
$$= e^{-\lambda[1-p_X(0)]}.$$

11-11 From Equation (2.67) we know the MGF of the compound distribution satisfies
$$M_S(t) = M_N[\ln M_X(t)].$$
Then
$$M_S(t)|_{t=\ln s} = M_N[\ln M_X(t)]|_{t=\ln s},$$
and using the result of Example 11.6 we have

CHAPTER ELEVEN

$$P_S(s) = M_N[\ln P_X(s)] = P_N[P_X(s)],$$

as required.

11-12 The PGF of the Poisson secondary distribution is $P_X(s) = e^{\lambda(s-1)}$ and the PGF of the negative binomial primary distribution is

$$P_N(s) = \left(\frac{p}{1-(1-p)s}\right)^r = \left(\frac{.25}{1-.75s}\right)^2$$

in this case. Then using the result developed in Exercise 11-11 we find the PGF of the compound distribution to be

$$P_S(s) = P_N[P_X(s)] = \left(\frac{.25}{1-.75e^{\lambda(s-1)}}\right)^2.$$

But we also know that

$$\Pr(S=0) = P_S(0) = \left(\frac{.25}{1-.75e^{-\lambda}}\right)^2 = .067,$$

so

$$.25 = \sqrt{.067}\,(1-.75e^{-\lambda})$$

which solves for $\lambda = 3.08885$.

11-13 (a) N is negative binomial, so we have

$$M_N(t) = \left(\frac{p}{1-q\cdot e^t}\right)^r.$$

X is Poisson, so we have

$$\ln M_X(t) = \ln\left[e^{\lambda(e^t-1)}\right] = \lambda(e^t-1).$$

Then

$$M_S(t) = M_N[\ln M_x(t)] = \left(\frac{p}{1-q\cdot e^{\lambda(e^t-1)}}\right)^r.$$

(b) Let S denote the random variable of the (unconditional) mixture distribution, and let Λ denote the random variable of the negative binomial mixing distribution. Then the PF of S is given by

$$p_S(s) = Pr(S=s) = \sum_{\lambda=0}^{\infty} Pr(S=s \mid \Lambda=\lambda) \cdot p_\Lambda(\lambda),$$

since Λ has a counting distribution with domain $\lambda = 0, 1, 2, \ldots$. Then the MGF of S is

$$M_S(t) = E[e^{St}] = \sum_{s=0}^{\infty} e^{st} \cdot Pr(S=s)$$

$$= \sum_{s=0}^{\infty} e^{st} \sum_{\lambda=0}^{\infty} Pr(S=s \mid \Lambda=\lambda) \cdot p_\Lambda(\lambda)$$

$$= \sum_{\lambda=0}^{\infty} p_\Lambda(\lambda) \sum_{s=0}^{\infty} e^{st} \cdot Pr(S=s \mid \Lambda=\lambda),$$

by reversing the order of summation. Since $Pr(S=s \mid \Lambda=\lambda)$ is Poisson, then the inside summation gives the MGF of a Poisson random variable, which is $e^{\lambda(e^t-1)}$. This reduces the expression for $M_S(t)$ to

$$M_S(t) = \sum_{\lambda=0}^{\infty} e^{\lambda(e^t-1)} \cdot p_\Lambda(\lambda).$$

By substituting $z = e^t - 1$, we have

$$M_S(t) = \sum_{\lambda=0}^{\infty} e^{\lambda z} \cdot p_\Lambda(\lambda),$$

which is the MGF of the negative binomial random variable Λ. Thus we have

$$M_S(t) = \left(\frac{p}{1-q \cdot e^z}\right)^r = \left(\frac{p}{1-q \cdot e^{(e^t-1)}}\right)^r.$$

11-14 From Equation (11.27b) we have

$$Pr(N=n) = \int_0^5 Pr(N=n|\Lambda=\lambda)\cdot f_\Lambda(\lambda)\,d\lambda$$
$$= \int_0^5 \frac{e^{-\lambda}\lambda^n}{n!}\cdot\frac{1}{5}\,d\lambda.$$

Then
$$Pr(N=0) = \frac{1}{5}\int_0^5 e^{-\lambda}\,d\lambda = \frac{1}{5}(1-e^{-5}) = .19865$$
and
$$Pr(N=1) = \frac{1}{5}\int_0^5 \lambda\cdot e^{-\lambda}\,d\lambda$$
$$= \frac{1}{5}\left[\lambda\cdot -e^{-\lambda}\Big|_0^5 + \int_0^5 e^{-\lambda}\,d\lambda\right]$$
$$= \frac{1}{5}[-5e^{-5}+1-e^{-5}] = .19191.$$

Finally,
$$Pr(N\geq 2) = 1-Pr(N=0)-Pr(N=1)$$
$$= 1-.19865-.19191 = .60944.$$

11-15 Recall that the negative binomial distribution results from a Poisson-gamma mixture. For the negative binomial distribution we are given $E[N]=\frac{rq}{p}=.20$ and $Var(N)=\frac{rq}{p^2}=.40$, which we solve to find $p=q=.50$ and $r=.20$. From the derivation in Section 11.2.2 we know that $r=\alpha$ and $q=\frac{1}{1+\beta}$, so $\beta=\frac{p}{q}$ (see text page 402). Thus we have $\alpha=r=.20$ and $\beta=\frac{p}{q}=1$, so the variance of the gamma mixing distribution is

$$Var(X) = \frac{\alpha}{\beta^2} = .20.$$

11-16 For the gamma distribution (see Section 2.3.4), the mean is $\frac{\alpha}{\beta}=3$ and the variance is $\frac{\alpha}{\beta^2}=3$, so $\beta=1$ and $\alpha=3$. Then the mixture distribution is negative binomial with $r = \alpha = 3$ and $q = \frac{1}{1+\beta} = .50$, so $p = .50$ as well. Then

$$Pr(N \leq 1) = p(0) + p(1) = (.50)^3 + 3(.50)^3(.50) = .3125.$$

11-17 The payment random variable W has a Poisson mixture distribution with a uniform mixing distribution with PDF $g_\Lambda(\lambda) = .25$. Since $W = 2^N$, then we have

$$\begin{aligned}E[W] &= E[2^N]\\ &= \sum_{n=0}^{\infty} 2^n \cdot Pr(N=n)\\ &= \sum_{n=0}^{\infty} 2^n \cdot \int_0^4 Pr(N=n \mid \Lambda=\lambda) \cdot g_\Lambda(\lambda)\, d\lambda\\ &= \sum_{n=0}^{\infty} 2^n \cdot \int_0^4 .25\left(\frac{e^{-\lambda}\lambda^n}{n!}\right) d\lambda,\end{aligned}$$

since N is Poisson, given $\Lambda = \lambda$. This can be written as

$$E[W] = .25 \sum_{n=0}^{\infty} \int_0^4 \left(\frac{e^{-\lambda}(2\lambda)^n}{n!}\right) d\lambda,$$

since $2n$ is constant with respect to λ. Reversing the order of summation and integration we have

$$\begin{aligned}E[W] &= .25 \int_0^4 e^{-\lambda} \left[1 + 2\lambda + \frac{(2\lambda)^2}{2!} + \frac{(2\lambda)^3}{3!} + \cdots\right] d\lambda\\ &= .25 \int_0^4 e^{-\lambda} \cdot e^{2\lambda}\, d\lambda\\ &= .25 \int_0^4 e^{\lambda}\, d\lambda = 13.39954.\end{aligned}$$

11-18 (a) Let S denote the random variable with the binomial-beta mixture distribution. Its PF is given by

$$Pr(S = x) = \int_0^1 Pr(S = x \mid P = p) \cdot f_P(p)\, dp$$

$$= \int_0^1 \binom{n}{x} \cdot p^x (1-p)^{n-x} \cdot \frac{\Gamma(a+b)}{\Gamma(a) \cdot \Gamma(b)} p^{a-1} (1-p)^{b-1}\, dp$$

$$= \binom{n}{x} \cdot \frac{\Gamma(a+b)}{\Gamma(a) \cdot \Gamma(b)} \int_0^1 p^{x+a-1} (1-p)^{n-x+b-1}\, dp.$$

By the definition of the beta function, the integral evaluates to $\frac{\Gamma(x+a)\cdot\Gamma(n-x+b)}{\Gamma(n+a+b)}$. Furthermore, recall that

$$\binom{n}{x} = \frac{\Gamma(n+1)}{\Gamma(x+1) \cdot \Gamma(n-x+1)}$$

(see Equation (11.18)), so we have

$$Pr(S = x) = \frac{\Gamma(n+1) \cdot \Gamma(a+b) \cdot \Gamma(x+a) \cdot \Gamma(n-x+b)}{\Gamma(x+1) \cdot \Gamma(n-x+1) \cdot \Gamma(a) \cdot \Gamma(b) \cdot \Gamma(n+a+b)}.$$

(b) Now let S have the negative binomial-beta mixture. Its PF is given by

$$Pr(S=x) = \int_0^1 Pr(S=x \mid P=p) \cdot f_P(p)\, dp$$

$$= \int_0^1 \binom{x+r-1}{r-1} \cdot p^r (1-p)^x \cdot \frac{\Gamma(a+b)}{\Gamma(a) \cdot \Gamma(b)} p^{a-1}(1-p)^{b-1}\, dp$$

$$= \binom{x+r-1}{r-1} \cdot \frac{\Gamma(a+b)}{\Gamma(a) \cdot \Gamma(b)} \int_0^1 p^{r+a-1} (1-p)^{x+b-1}\, dp.$$

This time the integral evaluates to $\frac{\Gamma(r+a)\cdot\Gamma(x+b)}{\Gamma(r+x+a+b)}$ and the combinatorial factor is $\frac{\Gamma(x+r)}{\Gamma(r)\cdot\Gamma(x+1)}$, so we have

$$Pr(S=x) = \frac{\Gamma(x+r) \cdot \Gamma(a+b) \cdot \Gamma(r+a) \cdot \Gamma(x+b)}{\Gamma(r) \cdot \Gamma(x+1) \cdot \Gamma(a) \cdot \Gamma(b) \cdot \Gamma(r+x+a+b)}.$$

11-19 From Equation (11.31a) we have

$$p_{ZM}(x) = \left(1 - p_{ZM}(0)\right) \cdot \frac{p(x)}{1 - p(0)} = \left(1 - p_{ZM}(0)\right) \cdot p_{ZT}(x),$$

from Equation (11.31b).

11-20 The given relationship can be written as
$$p(n) = \frac{m!}{n!} \cdot p(m).$$
Since it holds for all $m \geq 0$ and all $n \geq 0$, we can let $m = n-1$ to obtain
$$p(n) = \frac{(n-1)!}{n!} \cdot p(n-1) = \frac{1}{n} \cdot p(n-1) = \left(0 + \frac{1}{n}\right) \cdot p(n-1).$$
Reference to Table 11.1 tells us that the distribution is Poisson with $\alpha = 0$ and $\beta = \lambda = 1$, so $p(0) = p(1) = e^{-1}$. Then from Equation (11.31a) we have
$$p_{ZM}(1) = \left(\frac{1 - p_{ZM}(0)}{1 - p(0)}\right) \cdot p(1) = \left(\frac{1 - .10}{1 - e^{-1}}\right) \cdot e^{-1} = .52378.$$

11-21 (a) From Equation (11.31b) we have
$$p_{ZT}(x) = \frac{p(x)}{1 - p(0)} = \frac{\frac{e^{-\lambda}\lambda^x}{x!}}{1 - e^{-\lambda}} = \left(\frac{e^{-\lambda}}{1 - e^{-\lambda}}\right)\left(\frac{\lambda^x}{x!}\right),$$
for $x = 1, 2, \cdots$.

(b) From Equation (11.31a) we have
$$p_{ZM}(x) = \left(\frac{1 - p_{ZM}(0)}{1 - p(0)}\right) \cdot p(x)$$
$$= \left(\frac{.65}{1 - e^{-\lambda}}\right)\left(\frac{e^{-\lambda}\lambda^x}{x!}\right) = \left(\frac{.65 e^{-\lambda}}{1 - e^{-\lambda}}\right)\left(\frac{\lambda^x}{x!}\right),$$
for $x = 1, 2, \cdots$.

11-22 Since total claims is Poisson, then the number of claims N that exceed 30,000 is also Poisson, with rate $\lambda = (.02)(100) = 2$ per month, or $\lambda = 2n$ over an n-month period. We seek the value of n such that $Pr(N \geq 3) > .90$, or that $Pr(N \leq 2) < .10$. We have

CHAPTER ELEVEN 153

$$Pr(N \leq 2) = p(0) + p(1) + p(2) = e^{-2n}\left(1 + 2n + \frac{(2n)^2}{2!}\right),$$

and we seek the value of n such that

$$e^{-2n}(1 + 2n + 2n^2) < .10.$$

At $n = 2$ we have

$$e^{-4}(1+4+8) = .23810$$

and at $n = 3$ we have

$$e^{-6}(1+6+18) = .06197,$$

so we conclude that $n = 3$ full months of data are needed.

11-23 The number of losses in a two-year period is Poisson with $\lambda = 200$. A loss is a claim if it exceeds 100, the probability of which is

$$Pr(X > 100) = e^{-100/500} = .81873,$$

since X is exponential with mean 500. Then the number of claims is Poisson with

$$\lambda = (200)(.81873) = 163.75,$$

which is also the expected number of claims.

11-24 The second event occurs after one hour has passed if there are exactly none or one event in the first hour. The number of events in the first hour is Poisson with $\lambda = 2$, so the desired probability is

$$p(0) + p(1) = e^{-2}(1+2) = .40601.$$

11-25 (a) The waiting time for the tenth event, denoted S_{10}, has a gamma distribution with parameters $\alpha = 10$ and $\beta = \lambda = 2$. Then

$$E[S_{10}] = \frac{\alpha}{\beta} = \frac{10}{2} = 5.$$

(b) The interarrival time for the eleventh event, denoted T_{11}, has an exponential distribution with parameter $\beta = \lambda = 2$. Then

$$Pr(T_{11} > 2) = e^{-2\beta} = e^{-4} = .01832.$$

11-26 Simply replace X and each X_i by $X(t)$ and $X_i(t)$, respectively. Otherwise the argument is identical to that presented in Section 11.1.2.

11-27 The Poisson rate is .50 per minute, so it is 30 per hour. Let P, N and D denote the random variables for number of pennies, nickels, and dimes, respectively. By the Poisson decomposition property, we know that P, N and D are mutually independent and have Poisson distributions with rates $\lambda_P = (.60)(30) = 18$ and $\lambda_N = \lambda_D = (.20)(30) = 6$.

(a) The value (in cents) of the coins found is

$$V = 1 \cdot P + 5 \cdot N + 10 \cdot D.$$

In this case we are given that $N = 10$, so we have

$$V = P + 50 + 10D$$

so

$$E[V] = E[P] + 50 + 10 \cdot E[D]$$
$$= 18 + 50 + 10(6) = 128.$$

(b) This time no additional information is given. Again

$$V = P + 5N + 10D,$$

so

$$Var(V) = Var(P) + 25 \cdot Var(N) + 100 \cdot Var(D)$$
$$= 18 + 25(6) + 100(6) = 768.$$

(c) The Poisson rate of finding dimes is 6 per hour, or 1 per ten-minute interval. If three or more are found in the first ten minutes, then both events are satisfied. If two are found in

CHAPTER ELEVEN

the first ten minutes, then at least one more is needed in the second ten minutes to satisfy both events. The overall probability is

$$P = Pr\{3 \text{ or more in } (0,10)\}$$
$$+ Pr\{2 \text{ in } (0,10) \cap 1 \text{ or more in } (10,20)\}.$$

Recall that non-overlapping intervals are independent. Thus we have

$$P = (1 - p(0) - p(1) - p(2)) + (p(2) \cdot [1 - p(0)]),$$

where the probability values are Poisson with $\lambda = 1$. This evaluates to

$$P = (1 - e^{-1} - e^{-1} - .50e^{-1}) + (.50e^{-1})(1 - e^{-1})$$
$$= 1 - 2e^{-1} - .50e^{-2} = .19657.$$

11-28 Note first that the sixth minute is like any other minute by the Poisson property of stationary increments. We know (see Section 11.2.2) that a Poisson-gamma mixture is negative binomial. Here the gamma mixing distribution has mean

$$E[\Lambda] = \frac{\alpha}{\beta} = 2$$

and variance

$$Var(\Lambda) = \frac{\alpha}{\beta^2} = \left(\frac{\alpha}{\beta}\right)\left(\frac{1}{\beta}\right) = 4,$$

which implies $\beta = .50$ and $\alpha = 1.00$. Then the negative binomial parameters are $p = \frac{\beta}{1+\beta} = \frac{1}{3}$ and $r = \alpha = 1$, which is therefore a geometric distribution. Finally the probability of the event $x = 1$ is $p \cdot q = 2/9$.

11-29 The distribution of the number of events occurring in the interval $(9.0, 9.1)$ is Poisson with parameter

$$\lambda = \int_{9.0}^{9.1} t \, dt = \left.\frac{1}{2}t^2\right|_{9.0}^{9.1} = .905.$$

Then the 51st event occurs in $(9.0, 9.1)$ if one or more such events occur, the probability of which is

$$1 - e^{-.905} = .59546.$$

11-30 The nth event will occur before (or at) time t if the number of events occurring by time t is at least n. That is, the event $S_n \leq t$ is equivalent to the event $N(t) \geq n$, so their probabilities are equal. We have

$$Pr(S_n \leq t) = F_{S_n}(t) = Pr[N(t) \geq n].$$

But $N(t)$ is non-homogeneous Poisson, so

$$Pr[N(t) = r] = \frac{e^{-m(t)}[m(t)]^r}{r!},$$

and therefore

$$Pr[N(t) \geq n] = \sum_{r=n}^{\infty} \frac{e^{-m(t)}[m(t)]^r}{r!},$$

which is also $F_{S_n}(t)$. We find the PDF of S_n by differentiating its CDF, obtaining

$$f_{S_n}(t) = \frac{d}{dt} \sum_{r=n}^{\infty} \frac{e^{-m(t)}[m(t)]^r}{r!}$$

$$= \sum_{r=n}^{\infty} \frac{[m(t)]^r}{r!} \cdot \frac{d}{dt} e^{-m(t)} + \sum_{r=n}^{\infty} e^{-m(t)} \cdot \frac{d}{dt} \frac{[m(t)]^r}{r!}.$$

The derivatives are

$$\frac{d}{dt} e^{-m(t)} = -m'(t) \cdot e^{-m(t)}$$

and

$$\frac{d}{dt} \frac{[m(t)]^r}{r!} = \frac{r[m(t)]^{r-1} \cdot m'(t)}{r!} = \frac{m'(t) \cdot [m(t)]^{r-1}}{(r-1)!}.$$

Then we have

Chapter Eleven

$$f_{S_n}(t) = m'(t) \cdot e^{-m(t)} \sum_{r=n}^{\infty} \frac{[m(t)]^{r-1}}{(r-1)!} - m'(t) \cdot e^{-m(t)} \sum_{r=n}^{\infty} \frac{[m(t)]^{r}}{r!}$$

$$= m'(t) \cdot e^{-m(t)} \left[\sum_{r=n}^{\infty} \left(\frac{[m(t)]^{r-1}}{(r-1)!} - \frac{[m(t)]^{r}}{r!} \right) \right]$$

$$= m'(t) \cdot e^{-m(t)} \left(\frac{[m(t)]^{n-1}}{(n-1)!} \right).$$

Finally, since $m(t) = \int_0^t \lambda(s)\,ds$, then $m'(t) = \lambda(t)$, and the given expression is derived.

11-31 Clearly the process is nonstationary with process rate function given by $\lambda(t) = 3t+6$, where $t=0$ denotes 1:00 pm and $t=1$ denotes 2:00 pm. Then the mean value for the interval $(0,1)$ is

$$m(1) = \int_0^1 \lambda(t)\,dt = \int_0^1 (3t+6)\,dt = 7.50,$$

and the probability of the event $N(1) = 2$ is

$$\frac{e^{-7.50}(7.50)^2}{2!} = .01556.$$

11-32 Note that the process counting the number of infections occurring is a standard (homogeneous) Poisson process with $\lambda = 20$ (per day), so the expected number of infections would be 200 in a 10-day period. But we wish to count the number of *identifications* in the 10-day period, not the number of actual infections. Let $t = 0$ denote the start of the 10-day period.

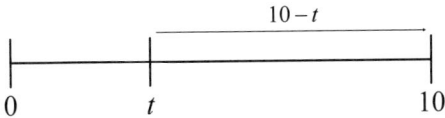

For an infection occurring at time t, the probability of being identified by time 10 is $1 - e^{-(10-t)/7}$, since the time-to-identification has an exponential distribution with mean 7. Thus the rate function for the process counting all occurring infections is the constant $\lambda(t) = 20$, but the rate function for the process counting only infections that get identified by time 10 is the non-constant

$$\lambda'(t) = 20(1 - e^{-(10-t)/7}),$$

which identifies this process as a nonstationary (nonhomogeneous) Poisson process. Then the expected number of identifications in the interval from $t=0$ to $t=10$ is given by

$$\begin{aligned}
m(10) &= \int_0^{10} \lambda'(t)\, dt \\
&= \int_0^{10} 20(1 - e^{-(10-t)/7})\, dt \\
&= \int_0^{10} 20\, dt - 20 \int_0^{10} e^{-10/7} \cdot e^{t/7}\, dt \\
&= 20t \Big|_0^{10} - 20 \cdot e^{-10/7} (7 e^{t/7}) \Big|_0^{10} \\
&= 200 - 20(.23965)(7)(4.17273 - 1) = 93.55161.
\end{aligned}$$

CHAPTER TWELVE
CLAIM SEVERITY MODELS

12-1 $F_X(x) = \int_0^x f_X(y)\,dy = \alpha\cdot\theta^\alpha \int_0^x (y+\theta)^{-(\alpha+1)}\,dy$

$= \alpha\cdot\theta^\alpha \left[-\frac{1}{\alpha}\cdot(y+\theta)^{-\alpha}\Big|_0^x \right]$

$= \alpha\cdot\theta^\alpha \left[\frac{\theta^{-\alpha}}{\alpha} - \frac{(x+\theta)^{-\alpha}}{\alpha} \right]$

$= 1 - \left(\frac{\theta}{x+\theta}\right)^\alpha$

12-2 From Exercise 12-1 we have $S_X(x) = \left(\dfrac{\theta}{x+\theta}\right)^\alpha$. Then

$E[X] = \int_0^\infty S_X(y)\,dy$

$= \theta^\alpha \int_0^\infty (y+\theta)^{-\alpha}\,dy$

$= \theta^\alpha \left(\dfrac{(y+\theta)^{-\alpha+1}}{-\alpha+1} \Big|_0^\infty \right).$

Provided $\alpha > 1$, then $-\alpha+1 < 0$ so the upper limit is zero. Then

$E[X] = \theta^\alpha \left(-\dfrac{\theta^{-\alpha+1}}{-\alpha+1} \right) = \dfrac{\theta}{\alpha-1}.$

12-3 The second moment is

$$E[X^2] = \int_0^\infty x^2 \cdot f_X(x)\,dx$$

$$= \alpha \cdot \theta^\alpha \int_0^\infty \frac{x^2}{2x} \frac{\left|(x+\theta)^{-\alpha-1}\,dx\right.}{\left.\begin{array}{c}(x+\theta)^{-\alpha}\\ -\alpha\end{array}\right.}$$

$$= \alpha \cdot \theta^\alpha \left[\left.\frac{x^2 \cdot (x+\theta)^{-\alpha}}{-\alpha}\right|_0^\infty + \frac{2}{\alpha}\int_0^\infty x(x+\theta)^{-\alpha}\,dx \right].$$

If $\alpha > 1$ the first term in brackets goes to zero at both limits, so we have

$$E[X^2] = 2\cdot\theta^\alpha \int_0^\infty \frac{x}{dx} \frac{\left|(x+\theta)^{-\alpha}\,dx\right.}{\left.\begin{array}{c}(x+\theta)^{-\alpha+1}\\ -\alpha+1\end{array}\right.}$$

$$= \frac{2\cdot\theta^\alpha}{\alpha-1}\left[\left.-x(x+\theta)^{-\alpha+1}\right|_0^\infty + \int_0^\infty (x+\theta)^{-\alpha+1}\,dx \right].$$

Again the first term goes to zero at both limits, so we have

$$E[X^2] = \frac{2\cdot\theta^\alpha}{\alpha-1}\int_0^\infty (x+\theta)^{-\alpha+1}\,dx = \frac{2\cdot\theta^\alpha}{\alpha-1}\left[\left.\frac{(x+\theta)^{-\alpha+2}}{-\alpha+2}\right|_0^\infty \right].$$

This time we require $\alpha > 2$ for the term in brackets to go to zero at the upper limit. Finally we have

$$E[X^2] = \frac{2\cdot\theta^\alpha}{\alpha-1}\left(\frac{\theta^{-\alpha+2}}{\alpha-2}\right) = \frac{2\cdot\theta^2}{(\alpha-1)(\alpha-2)}.$$

CHAPTER TWELVE   161

12-4   By use of L'Hospital's rule, we have

$$\lim_{x\to\infty}\frac{S_X(x)}{S_Y(x)} = \lim_{x\to\infty}\frac{S'_X(x)}{S'_Y(x)} = \lim_{x\to\infty}\frac{-f_X(x)}{-f_Y(x)} = \lim_{x\to\infty}\frac{f_X(x)}{f_Y(x)}.$$

When X is Pareto and Y is exponential, we have

$$\lim_{x\to\infty}\frac{S_X(x)}{S_Y(x)} = \lim_{x\to\infty}\frac{\left(\frac{\theta}{x+\theta}\right)^\alpha}{e^{-\beta x}} = \theta^\alpha\cdot\lim_{x\to\infty}\frac{e^{\beta x}}{(x+\theta)^\alpha} = \infty,$$

by the same steps as described in the solution to Example 12.1.

12-5 (a) With $\beta=\frac{1}{\theta}$ the mean is

$$E[X] = \frac{\alpha}{\beta} = \alpha\theta.$$

(b) The variance is

$$Var(X) = \frac{\alpha}{\beta^2} = \alpha\theta^2.$$

(c) The MGF is

$$M_X(t) = \left(\frac{\beta}{\beta-t}\right)^\alpha = \left(\frac{\frac{1}{\theta}}{\frac{1}{\theta}-t}\right)^\alpha = \left(\frac{1}{1-\theta t}\right)^\alpha.$$

(d) See Section 2.3.4, substituting $\frac{1}{\theta}$ for β.

12-6   If X has a normal distribution with mean μ and standard deviation σ, then $Y=\theta X$ (for $\theta>0$) has CDF

$$F_Y(y) = Pr(Y\le y) = Pr(\theta X\le y) = Pr\left(X\le\frac{y}{\theta}\right) = F_X\left(\frac{y}{\theta}\right).$$

But X is normal, so

$$F_X\left(\frac{y}{\theta}\right) = \Phi\left(\frac{\frac{y}{\theta}-\mu}{\sigma}\right) = \Phi\left(\frac{y-\theta\mu}{\theta\sigma}\right).$$

The last expression is the CDF of a normal distribution with mean $\theta\mu$ and standard deviation $\theta\sigma$, so the set of normal distributions is closed under scalar multiplication and forms a scale family. Note that since both parameters μ and σ change for $Y = \theta X$, then neither is a scale parameter

12-7 If X has a Pareto distribution with parameters α and θ, then $Y = cX$ has CDF

$$F_Y(y) = Pr(Y \leq y) = Pr(cX \leq y) = Pr\left(X \leq \frac{y}{c}\right) = F_X\left(\frac{y}{c}\right).$$

But X is Pareto with CDF given by Equation (12.2), so we have

$$F_X\left(\frac{y}{c}\right) = 1 - \left(\frac{\theta}{\frac{y}{c} + \theta}\right)^\alpha = 1 - \left(\frac{c\theta}{y + c\theta}\right)^\alpha,$$

which is the CDF of a Pareto distribution with parameter α and $c\theta$, which shows that θ is a scale parameter for this scale family of distribution.

12-8 The demonstration follows that given in Example 12.2(b) for the exponential distribution. For the gamma we have

$$f_Y(y) = f_X\left(\frac{y}{c}\right) \cdot \frac{1}{c}$$

$$= \frac{\left(\frac{y/c}{\theta}\right)^\alpha \cdot e^{-y/c\theta}}{\frac{y}{c} \cdot \Gamma(\alpha)} \cdot \frac{1}{c}$$

$$= \frac{(y/c\theta)^\alpha \cdot e^{-y/c\theta}}{y \cdot \Gamma(\alpha)}$$

$$= \frac{(y/\theta')^\alpha \cdot e^{-y/\theta'}}{y \cdot \Gamma(\alpha)},$$

which is gamma with $\theta' = c \cdot \theta$, so gamma is a scale family and θ is a scale parameter.

CHAPTER TWELVE

12-9 The Weibull PDF is given by Equation (12.12b) as

$$f_X(x) = \frac{\tau(x/\theta)^\tau \cdot e^{-(x/\theta)^\tau}}{x},$$

with y replaced by x. Then we let $y = cx$, so $x = \frac{y}{c}$ and $\frac{dx}{dy} = \frac{1}{c}$, and find

$$f_Y(y) = \frac{\tau(y/c\theta)^\tau \cdot e^{-(y/c\theta)^\tau}}{y/c} \cdot \frac{1}{c}$$

$$= \frac{\tau(y/\theta')^\tau \cdot e^{-(y/\theta')^\tau}}{y},$$

which is again a Weibull distribution with θ replaced by $\theta' = c \cdot \theta$. These are the criteria for being a scale family with a scale parameter.

12-10 The inverse Weibull distribution is the distribution of $Y = X^{-1}$, where X has a Weibull distribution. We have

$$F_Y(y) = \Pr(Y \leq y) = \Pr(X^{-1} \leq y) = \Pr\left(X > \frac{1}{y}\right) = S_X\left(\frac{1}{y}\right).$$

But X is Weibull with SDF given by

$$S_X(x) = e^{-(x/\theta)^\tau},$$

so we have

$$S_X\left(\frac{1}{y}\right) = e^{-(1/y\theta)^\tau}$$

and the CDF of Y is therefore

$$F_Y(y) = S_X\left(\frac{1}{y}\right) = e^{-(1/y\theta)^\tau}.$$

In this form, θ is not a scale parameter. To have a scale parameter, let $\beta = \frac{1}{\theta}$ and then replace β with θ to obtain

$$F_Y(y) = e^{-(\theta/y)^\tau}.$$

The PDF is found by differentiation as

$$\begin{aligned}
f_Y(y) &= \frac{d}{dy} F_Y(y) \\
&= \frac{d}{dy} e^{-(\theta/y)^\tau} \\
&= e^{-(\theta/y)^\tau} \left(-\tau \left(\frac{\theta}{y}\right)^{\tau-1}\right)\left(-\frac{\theta}{y^2}\right) \\
&= e^{-(\theta/y)^\tau} \left(\frac{\tau \cdot \theta^{\tau-1}}{y^{\tau-1}}\right)\left(\frac{\theta}{y^2}\right) \\
&= e^{-(\theta/y)^\tau} \left(\frac{\tau \cdot \theta^\tau}{y^{\tau+1}}\right) \\
&= \frac{\tau}{y} \cdot e^{-(\theta/y)^\tau} \cdot \left(\frac{\theta}{y}\right)^\tau = \frac{\tau \cdot (\theta/y)^\tau \cdot e^{-(\theta/y)^\tau}}{y}.
\end{aligned}$$

12-11 (a) Recall that when the domain of X is $(0,\infty)$ the expected value can be found as $\int_0^\infty S(x)\,dx$. For the Weibull distribution, with SDF given by Equation (12.12a), we have

$$E[X] = \int_0^\infty e^{-(x/\theta)^\tau}\,dx.$$

We make the variable change $y = (x/\theta)^\tau$, so

$$dy = \tau(x/\theta)^{\tau-1} \cdot \frac{1}{\theta}\,dx$$

and therefore

CHAPTER TWELVE

$$dx = \frac{\theta}{\tau} \cdot (x/\theta)^{1-\tau} \, dy = \frac{\theta}{\tau} \cdot (y^{1/\tau})^{1-\tau} \, dy = \frac{\theta}{\tau} \cdot y^{(1/\tau)-1} \, dy.$$

Then we have

$$E[X] = \int_0^\infty e^{-y} \cdot \frac{\theta}{\tau} \cdot y^{(1/\tau)-1} \, dy$$

$$= \theta \cdot \frac{1}{\tau} \cdot \Gamma\left(\frac{1}{\tau}\right),$$

using the gamma function as defined by Equation (2.56). Then we use the gamma recursive relationship $\Gamma(\alpha) = (\alpha-1)\cdot\Gamma(\alpha-1)$ to finally reach

$$E[X] = \theta \cdot \Gamma(1+\tfrac{1}{\tau}).$$

(b) This time we use the PDF to find $E[X]$. For the inverse Weibull we have

$$E[X] = \int_0^\infty x \cdot f_X(x) \, dx$$

$$= \int_0^\infty \tau(\theta/x)^\tau \cdot e^{-(\theta/x)^\tau} \, dx$$

$$= \int_0^\infty \tau(x/\theta)^{-\tau} \cdot e^{-(x/\theta)^{-\tau}} \, dx,$$

where the PDF is given by Exercise 12-10. We then substitute $y = (x/\theta)^{-\tau}$, so

$$dy = -\tau(x/\theta)^{-\tau-1} \cdot \frac{1}{\theta} \, dx = -\tau \cdot y^{1+(1/\tau)} \cdot \frac{1}{\theta} \, dx$$

and

$$dx = -\frac{\theta}{\tau} \cdot y^{-1-(1/\tau)} \, dy.$$

Note that $y = \infty$ when $x = 0$ and $y = 0$ when $x = \infty$, so the limits reverse in the variable change. Then we have

$$E[X] = \int_\infty^0 \tau \cdot y \cdot e^{-y} \cdot -\frac{\theta}{\tau} \cdot y^{-1-(1/\tau)} \, dy$$

$$= \theta \cdot \int_0^\infty y^{-1/\tau} \cdot e^{-y} \, dy$$

$$= \theta \cdot \int_0^\infty y^{1-(1/\tau)-1} \cdot e^{-y} \, dy$$

$$= \theta \cdot \Gamma(1-\tfrac{1}{\tau}).$$

12-12 For an inverse distribution, the transformation is $Y = X^{-1}$, so that $x = g^{-1}(y) = y^{-1}$. The transformation is decreasing, so from Equation (12.6b), we have

$$F_Y(y) = 1 - F_X[g^{-1}(y)]$$

$$= \left(\frac{\theta}{x+\theta}\right)^\alpha \bigg|_{x=y^{-1}}$$

$$= \left(\frac{\theta y}{1+\theta y}\right)^\alpha.$$

Again to have θ be a scale parameter, we let $\lambda = \frac{1}{\theta}$ to reach

$$F_Y(y) = \left(\frac{y}{\lambda + y}\right)^\alpha,$$

and then change λ back to θ. Then the PDF is

$$f_Y(y) = \frac{d}{dy} F_Y(y)$$

$$= \alpha \left(\frac{y}{\theta + y}\right)^{\alpha-1} \cdot \left(\frac{(\theta+y) - y}{(\theta+y)^2}\right)$$

$$= \frac{\alpha \theta \cdot y^{\alpha-1}}{(\theta+y)^{\alpha+1}}.$$

12-13 Y has a lognormal distribution if $Y = e^X$, where X is normal with mean μ and standard deviation σ. Then

$$F_Y(y) = Pr(Y \le y) = Pr(e^X \le y) = Pr(X \le \ln y) = F_X(\ln y).$$

But X is normal, so

$$F_Y(y) = F_X(\ln y)$$

$$= \Phi\left(\frac{\ln y - \mu}{\sigma}\right).$$

12-14 The lognormal PDF is given by Equation (12.15) as

$$f_X(x) = \frac{1}{x} \cdot \frac{1}{\sigma\sqrt{2\pi}} \cdot e^{-\frac{1}{2}\left(\frac{\ln x - \mu}{\sigma}\right)^2},$$

with y replaced by x. Then we let $y = cx$, so $x = \frac{y}{c}$ and $\frac{dx}{dy} = \frac{1}{c}$, and find

$$f_Y(y) = \frac{1}{y/c} \cdot \frac{1}{\sigma\sqrt{2\pi}} \cdot e^{-\frac{1}{2}\left(\frac{\ln(y/c) - \mu}{\sigma}\right)^2} \cdot \frac{1}{c}$$

$$= \frac{1}{y} \cdot \frac{1}{\sigma\sqrt{2\pi}} \cdot e^{-\frac{1}{2}\left(\frac{\ln y - \ln c - \mu}{\sigma}\right)^2}$$

$$= \frac{1}{y} \cdot \frac{1}{\sigma\sqrt{2\pi}} \cdot e^{-\frac{1}{2}\left(\frac{\ln y - \mu'}{\sigma}\right)^2},$$

where $\mu' = (\mu + \ln c)$. Clearly $f_Y(y)$ is again a lognormal density, so the lognormal forms a scale family, but $\mu' \ne c \cdot \mu$ so μ is not a scale parameter. (Clearly σ is also not a scale parameter.)

12-15 For this mixture distribution, we find

$$Pr(X > .50) = \int_1^{11} Pr(X > .50 \mid \beta) \cdot f_B(\beta) \, d\beta$$

$$= \int_1^{11} e^{-.50\beta}(.10) \, d\beta,$$

since $X \mid \beta$ is exponential and B is uniform. Then

$$Pr(X > .50) = .10 \int_1^{11} e^{-.50\beta} \, d\beta$$

$$= .10 \left[-2e^{-.50\beta} \Big|_1^{11} \right]$$

$$= .20(e^{-.50} - e^{-5.50}) = .12049.$$

12-16 This follows directly from Equation (12.17a), a simple application of the first part of the double expectation theorem. We have, unconditionally,

$$E[X^k] = E_\Lambda \left[E[X^k \mid \Lambda] \right]$$

$$= \sum_\lambda E\left[X^k \mid \Lambda = \lambda \right] \cdot p_\Lambda(\lambda).$$

12-17 This is another application of conditional expectation. Let X denote the repair costs. We have $E[X \mid W] = 60$ and $E[X \mid D] = 75$. The conditional variances are

$$Var(X \mid W) = 3600$$

and

$$Var(X \mid D) = \frac{(150)^2}{12} = 1875,$$

so the conditional second moments are

$$E[X^2 \mid W] = 3600 + (60)^2 = 7200$$

and
$$E[X^2 | D] = 1875 + (75)^2 = 7500.$$

(a) The unconditional first moment is
$$E[X] = (60)(.70) + (75)(.30) = 64.50.$$

(b) The unconditional second moment is
$$E[X^2] = (7200)(.70) + (7500)(.30) = 7290,$$
so the unconditional variance is
$$Var(X) = 7290 - (64.50)^2 = 3129.75.$$

(c) $Pr(X < 60) = Pr(X < 60 | W) \cdot Pr(W)$
$$+ Pr(X < 60 | D) \cdot Pr(D)$$
$$= (1 - e^{-60/60})(.70) + \left(\frac{60}{150}\right)(.30)$$
$$= (.63212)(.70) + (.40)(.30) = .56248$$

12-18 We seek
$$Pr(X < 200) = Pr(X < 200 | P_1) \cdot Pr(P_1)$$
$$+ Pr(X < 200 | P_2) \cdot Pr(P_2).$$

Using Equation (12.2) for the Pareto CDF we have
$$Pr(X < 200) = (.80)\left[1 - \left(\frac{100}{300}\right)^2\right] + (.20)\left[1 - \left(\frac{3000}{3200}\right)^4\right]$$
$$= (.80)(.88889) + (.20)(.22752) = .75662.$$

12-19 (a) Both the conditional density of X, given $\Theta = \theta$, and the density of Θ (the mixing distribution) are normal, so by Equation (12.16a) the unconditional density of X is

$$f_X(x) = \int_{-\infty}^{\infty} \frac{1}{\sigma_1\sqrt{2\pi}} \cdot e^{-\frac{1}{2}\left(\frac{x-\theta}{\sigma_1}\right)^2} \cdot \frac{1}{\sigma_2\sqrt{2\pi}} \cdot e^{-\frac{1}{2}\left(\frac{\theta-\mu}{\sigma_2}\right)^2} d\theta.$$

First we see that the product of the constants produces $\sigma_1 \cdot \sigma_2$ in the denominator, which can be written as

$$\sigma_1 \cdot \sigma_2 = \sqrt{\sigma_1^2 \cdot \sigma_2^2} = \sqrt{\frac{(\sigma_1^2 \cdot \sigma_2^2)(\sigma_1^2 + \sigma_2^2)}{\sigma_1^2 + \sigma_2^2}}$$

$$= \sqrt{\sigma_1^2 + \sigma_2^2} \cdot \sqrt{\frac{\sigma_1^2 \cdot \sigma_2^2}{\sigma_1^2 + \sigma_2^2}}.$$

Then we have

$$\frac{1}{\sigma_1\sqrt{2\pi}} \cdot \frac{1}{\sigma_2\sqrt{2\pi}} = \frac{1}{\sqrt{\sigma_1^2 + \sigma_2^2} \cdot \sqrt{2\pi}} \cdot \frac{1}{s \cdot \sqrt{2\pi}},$$

where we let s stand for $\sqrt{\dfrac{\sigma_1^2 \cdot \sigma_2^2}{\sigma_1^2 + \sigma_2^2}}$ for convenience.

When we multiply the two exponential terms we add their exponents to obtain

$$-\frac{1}{2}\left[\frac{(x-\theta)^2}{\sigma_1^2} + \frac{(\theta-\mu)^2}{\sigma_2^2}\right]$$

$$= -\frac{1}{2}\left[\frac{\sigma_2^2(x-\theta)^2 + \sigma_1^2(\theta-\mu)^2}{\sigma_1^2 \cdot \sigma_2^2}\right]$$

$$= -\frac{1}{2}\left[\frac{\sigma_2^2(x^2-2x\theta+\theta^2) + \sigma_1^2(\theta^2-2\theta\mu+\mu^2)}{(\sigma_1^2+\sigma_2^2)\left(\dfrac{\sigma_1^2 \cdot \sigma_2^2}{\sigma_1^2+\sigma_2^2}\right)}\right].$$

Now we do some rearranging in the numerator of the last expression. We have

$$\sigma_2^2(x^2-2x\theta+\theta^2)+\sigma_1^2(\theta^2-2\theta\mu+\mu^2)$$
$$= \sigma_2^2 x^2 + \sigma_1^2 \mu^2 - 2\theta(\sigma_2^2 x+\sigma_1^2 \mu)+\theta^2(\sigma_1^2+\sigma_2^2)$$
$$= \sigma_2^2 x^2 \left(\frac{\sigma_1^2}{\sigma_1^2+\sigma_2^2}\right)\left(\frac{\sigma_1^2+\sigma_2^2}{\sigma_1^2}\right) + \sigma_1^2 \mu^2 \left(\frac{\sigma_2^2}{\sigma_1^2+\sigma_2^2}\right)\left(\frac{\sigma_1^2+\sigma_2^2}{\sigma_2^2}\right)$$
$$\quad - 2\theta(\sigma_2^2 x+\sigma_1^2 \mu)\left(\frac{\sigma_1^2+\sigma_2^2}{\sigma_1^2+\sigma_2^2}\right) + \theta^2(\sigma_1^2+\sigma_2^2)$$
$$= \left(\frac{\sigma_1^2 \cdot \sigma_2^2}{\sigma_1^2+\sigma_2^2}\right)\left[x^2\left(\frac{\sigma_1^2+\sigma_2^2}{\sigma_1^2}\right) + \mu^2\left(\frac{\sigma_1^2+\sigma_2^2}{\sigma_2^2}\right)\right]$$
$$\quad + (\sigma_1^2+\sigma_2^2)\left[\theta^2 - 2\theta\left(\frac{\sigma_1^2 \mu+\sigma_2^2 x}{\sigma_1^2+\sigma_2^2}\right)\right].$$

Next we add and subtract the quantity $\dfrac{(\sigma_1^2 \mu+\sigma_2^2 x)^2}{\sigma_1^2+\sigma_2^2}$, placing the subtracted term inside the first set of brackets and the added term inside the second set of brackets. This gives us

$$\left(\frac{\sigma_1^2 \cdot \sigma_2^2}{\sigma_1^2+\sigma_2^2}\right)\left[x^2\left(\frac{\sigma_1^2+\sigma_2^2}{\sigma_1^2}\right) - \frac{(\sigma_1^2\mu+\sigma_2^2 x)^2}{\sigma_1^2 \cdot \sigma_2^2} + \mu^2\left(\frac{\sigma_1^2+\sigma_2^2}{\sigma_2^2}\right)\right]$$
$$\quad + (\sigma_1^2+\sigma_2^2)\left[\theta^2 - 2\theta\left(\frac{\sigma_1^2\mu+\sigma_2^2 x}{\sigma_1^2+\sigma_2^2}\right) + \frac{(\sigma_1^2\mu+\sigma_2^2 x)^2}{(\sigma_1^2+\sigma_2^2)^2}\right]$$
$$= \left(\frac{\sigma_1^2 \cdot \sigma_2^2}{\sigma_1^2+\sigma_2^2}\right)\left[x^2\left(\frac{\sigma_1^2+\sigma_2^2}{\sigma_1^2}\right)\right.$$
$$\quad \left. -\frac{(\sigma_1^2)^2 \mu^2 + 2\sigma_1^2\sigma_2^2 x\mu + (\sigma_2^2)^2 x^2}{\sigma_1^2 \cdot \sigma_2^2} + \mu^2\left(\frac{\sigma_1^2+\sigma_2^2}{\sigma_2^2}\right)\right]$$
$$\quad + (\sigma_1^2+\sigma_2^2)(\theta^2-2\theta m+m^2),$$

substituting m for $\dfrac{\sigma_1^2\mu+\sigma_2^2 x}{\sigma_1^2+\sigma_2^2}$. Finally the expression inside the brackets simplifies to $(x^2-2x\mu+\mu^2)$, so our numerator has become

$$\left(\frac{\sigma_1^2 \cdot \sigma_2^2}{\sigma_1^2+\sigma_2^2}\right)(x^2-2x\mu+\mu^2)+(\sigma_1^2+\sigma_2^2)(\theta^2-2\theta m+m^2).$$

Then the exponent in the e term is

$$-\frac{1}{2}\left[\frac{\left(\frac{\sigma_1^2 \cdot \sigma_2^2}{\sigma_1^2+\sigma_2^2}\right)(x-\mu)^2+\left(\sigma_1^2+\sigma_2^2\right)(\theta-m)^2}{\left(\sigma_1^2+\sigma_2^2\right)\left(\frac{\sigma_1^2 \cdot \sigma_2^2}{\sigma_1^2+\sigma_2^2}\right)}\right]$$

$$=-\frac{1}{2}\left[\frac{(x-\mu)^2}{\sigma_1^2+\sigma_2^2}+\frac{(\theta-m)^2}{(\sigma_1^2 \cdot \sigma_2^2)/(\sigma_1^2+\sigma_2^2)}\right].$$

The product of the original two exponential terms has now become

$$\exp\left[-\frac{1}{2}\left(\frac{(x-\mu)^2}{\sigma_1^2+\sigma_2^2}\right)\right] \cdot \exp\left[-\frac{1}{2}\left(\frac{(\theta-m)^2}{s^2}\right)\right]$$

and the original expression for $f_X(x)$ has become

$$f_X(x) = \frac{1}{\sqrt{\sigma_1^2+\sigma_2^2} \cdot \sqrt{2\pi}} \cdot \exp\left[-\frac{1}{2}\left(\frac{(x-\mu)^2}{\sigma_1^2+\sigma_2^2}\right)\right]$$

$$\cdot \int_{-\infty}^{\infty} \frac{1}{s \cdot \sqrt{2\pi}} \cdot \exp\left[-\frac{1}{2}\left(\frac{(\theta-m)^2}{s^2}\right)\right] d\theta.$$

The integrand is a normal density for the random variable θ, with mean m and standard deviation s, so the integral evaluates to unity. Then the marginal distribution of X is normal with mean μ and variance $\sigma_1^2+\sigma_2^2$, as expected.

CHAPTER TWELVE

(b) We seek the value of

$$Pr(X<90 \mid X>65) = \frac{Pr(65<X<90)}{Pr(X>65)}.$$

Using the result of part (a), we know that X is normal with mean $\mu = 75$, the mean of the mixing distribution, and variance $\sigma_1^2 + \sigma_2^2 = 64+36 = 100$. Then we have

$$\frac{Pr(65<X<90)}{1-Pr(X<65)} = \frac{Pr\left(\frac{65-75}{10}<Z<\frac{90-75}{10}\right)}{1-Pr\left(Z<\frac{65-75}{10}\right)}$$

$$= \frac{Pr(-1.00<Z<1.50)}{1-Pr(Z<-1.00)}$$

$$= \frac{\Phi(1.50)-\Phi(-1.00)}{1-\Phi(-1.00)}$$

$$= \frac{\Phi(1.50)-1+\Phi(1.00)}{\Phi(1.00)}$$

$$= \frac{.9332-1+.8413}{.8413} = .92060.$$

12-20 The spliced model has density $f_1(x) = \frac{1}{3}$ over the interval $(0,3)$. The initial exponential model had density $.25e^{-.25x}$, so the new spliced model has density $f_2(x) = .25r \cdot e^{-.25x}$ where r is the constant of proportionality. In order that $f_2(x)$ be a proper density over the interval $(3,\infty)$, we require

$$\int_3^\infty f_2(x)\,dx = -r \cdot e^{-.25x}\Big|_3^\infty = r \cdot e^{-.75} = 1,$$

which implies $r = e^{.75}$. Then the spliced distribution is

$$f_X(x) = \begin{cases} k/3 & \text{for } 0<x<3 \\ .25e^{.75}(1-k) \cdot e^{-.25x} & \text{for } 3<x<\infty \end{cases}.$$

To have continuity at $x = 3$, where $f_1(x) = \frac{k}{3}$, we require

$$.25e^{.75}(1-k) \cdot e^{-(.25)(3)} = .25(1-k) = \frac{k}{3},$$

which solves for $k = \frac{.75}{1.75} = \frac{3}{7}$, so $f_1(x) = \frac{1}{7}$. Then

$$Pr(X < 3) = \int_0^3 f_1(x)\,dx = \int_0^3 \frac{1}{7}\,dx = \frac{3}{7}.$$

12-21 We want to show that the limit, as $\alpha \to \infty$, $\theta \to 0$, and $\alpha\theta \to c$, a constant, of $\frac{\alpha\theta \cdot x^{\alpha-1}}{(\theta+x)^{\alpha+1}}$ is $\frac{c \cdot e^{-c/x}}{x^2}$. Using a similar approach as in Example 12.10, we substitute c/α for θ, so that $\theta \to 0$ as $\alpha \to \infty$, reaching

$$\frac{\alpha(\frac{c}{\alpha}) \cdot x^{\alpha-1}}{(x+\frac{c}{\alpha})^{\alpha+1}} = \frac{c}{x^2} \cdot \frac{x^{\alpha+1}}{(x+\frac{c}{\alpha})^{\alpha+1}} = \frac{c}{x^2} \cdot \frac{1}{(1+\frac{c}{\alpha x})^{\alpha+1}}.$$

Then we want to show that

$$\lim_{\alpha \to \infty}\left[\left(1+\frac{c}{\alpha x}\right)^{-(\alpha+1)}\right] = e^{-c/x}$$

or

$$\lim_{\alpha \to \infty} \ln\left[\left(1+\frac{c}{\alpha x}\right)^{-(\alpha+1)}\right] = -\frac{c}{x}$$

or

$$\lim_{\alpha \to \infty}\left[-(\alpha+1) \cdot \ln\left(1+\frac{c}{\alpha x}\right)\right] = -\frac{c}{x}$$

or

$$\lim_{\alpha \to \infty} \left(\frac{\ln\left(1+\frac{c}{\alpha x}\right)}{\frac{-1}{\alpha+1}} \right) = -\frac{c}{x}$$

or (applying L'Hospital)

$$\lim_{\alpha \to \infty} \left(\frac{\left(\frac{\alpha x}{\alpha x+c}\right)\left(\frac{-c}{\alpha^2 x}\right)}{\frac{1}{(\alpha+1)^2}} \right) = -\frac{c}{x}$$

or

$$\lim_{\alpha \to \infty} \left(\frac{-c(\alpha+1)^2}{\alpha(\alpha x+c)} \right) = -\frac{c}{x}$$

or (applying L'Hospital again)

$$\lim_{\alpha \to \infty} \left(\frac{-2c(\alpha+1)}{2\alpha x + c} \right) = -\frac{c}{x}$$

or (applying L'Hospital a third time)

$$\lim_{\alpha \to \infty} \left(\frac{-2c}{2x} \right) = -\frac{c}{x},$$

as required.

12-22 The mean excess loss function is the expected value of the amount paid per payment event random variable Z. Recall that

$$E[Z] = \frac{E[Y]}{Pr(Y>0)} = \frac{E[Y]}{1-F_X(d)}.$$

(a) $E[Y] = E[(X-100)_+]$

$= \int_{100}^{500} (x-100) \cdot f_X(x)\, dx$

$= \dfrac{1}{500} \int_{100}^{500} (x-100)\, dx$

$= \dfrac{1}{500} \left(\dfrac{1}{2}x^2 - 100x \right) \Big|_{100}^{500}$

$= \dfrac{1}{500}(125{,}000 - 50{,}000 - 5{,}000 + 10{,}000) = 160$

Then $E[Z] = \dfrac{160}{S_X(100)} = \dfrac{160}{.80} = 200.00$.

(b) This time we use $Y = X - (X \wedge d)$, so

$$E[Y] = E[X] - E[(X \wedge d)] = E[X] - \int_0^d S_X(x)\, dx.$$

Since X is Pareto with $\theta = 1000$, and since

$$E[X] = \dfrac{\theta}{\alpha - 1} = 500,$$

then we have $\alpha - 1 = 2$ so $\alpha = 3$. Recall also that for the Pareto distribution

$$1 - F_X(x) = \left(\dfrac{\theta}{x+\theta} \right)^{\alpha} = \left(\dfrac{1000}{x+1000} \right)^3.$$

Then

$E[(X \wedge d)] = \int_0^{100} (1000)^3 \cdot (x+1000)^{-3}\, dx$

$= (1000)^3 \cdot -\dfrac{1}{2}(x+1000)^{-2} \Big|_0^{100}$

$= \dfrac{1}{2}(1000)^3 \left[(1000)^{-2} - (1100)^{-2} \right] = 86.77686,$

and

$$E[Y] = 500 - 86.77686 = 413.22314.$$

Chapter Twelve

Finally,

$$E[Z] = \frac{413.22314}{1 - F_X(100)} = \frac{413.22314}{.75131} = 550.00.$$

(c) This time we have

$$E[Y] = E[(X-100)_+]$$
$$= (50)(.30) + (150)(.20) + (250)(.20) + (400)(.10)$$
$$= 135,$$

and

$$1 - F_X(100) = 1 - .20 = .80,$$

so

$$E[Z] = \frac{135}{.80} = 168.75.$$

12-23 From first principles, using Equation (12.26a), we have

$$E[Y^k] = \int_{100}^{\infty} (x-100)^k \cdot f_X(x)\, dx,$$

for $k = 1, 2$. Then

$$E[Y] = .001 \int_{100}^{\infty} (x-100) \cdot e^{-.001x}\, dx$$

$$= .001 \left[\frac{(x-100) \cdot e^{-.001x}}{-.001} \bigg|_{100}^{\infty} + 1000 \int_{100}^{\infty} e^{-.001x}\, dx \right]$$

$$= \frac{e^{-.001x}}{-.001} \bigg|_{100}^{\infty} = 1000 e^{-.10} = 904.84$$

and

$$E[Y^2] = .001 \int_{100}^{\infty} (x-100)^2 \cdot e^{-.001x} \, dx$$

$$= .001 \left[\frac{(x-100)^2 \cdot e^{-.001x}}{-.001} \bigg|_{100}^{\infty} + 2000 \int_{100}^{\infty} (x-100) \cdot e^{-.001x} \, dx \right]$$

$$= 2000 \left[.001 \int_{100}^{\infty} (x-100) \cdot e^{-.001x} \, dx \right]$$

$$= 2000(904.84) = 1,809,680.$$

Then

$$Var(Y) = E[Y^2] - (E[Y])^2 = 990,944.57.$$

Because the distribution is exponential, we can take advantage of the memoryless property. That is, given that $X > 100$, the distribution of $X - 100$ is the same exponential distribution as that of X itself. Here

$$Pr(X > 100) = e^{-(100)(.001)} = e^{-.10} = .90484.$$

Then

$$E[Y] = E[X \mid X > 100] \cdot Pr(X > 100)$$
$$= (1000)(.90484) = 904.84$$

and

$$E[Y^2] = E[X^2 \mid X > 100] \cdot Pr(X > 100)$$
$$= 2(1000)^2 (.90484) = 1,809,680,$$

as before, and the variance follows.

CHAPTER TWELVE 179

12-24 This is a straightforward application of Equation (12.28a). We have

$$E[Z] = \frac{\int_4^{10}(x-4)\cdot f_X(x)\, dx}{\int_4^{10} f_X(x)\, dx}$$

$$= \frac{.02\int_4^{10}(x-4)\cdot x\, dx}{.02\int_4^{10} x\, dx}$$

$$= \frac{x^3/3 - 2x^2\big|_4^{10}}{x^2/2\big|_4^{10}} = 3.42857.$$

12-25 Deductibles are easily handled with a short discrete loss distribution. If the loss is $X = 100, 200, 300$ the payment is $Y = 0, 50, 150$ with probabilities .20, .20, .60. The probability of payment is $Pr(X=200 \text{ or } 300) = .80$. Then

$$E[Y \mid X=200 \text{ or } 300] = \frac{(50)(.20) + (150)(.60)}{.80} = 125$$

and

$$E[Y^2 \mid X=200 \text{ or } 300] = \frac{(50)^2(.20) + (150)^2(.60)}{.80} = 17,500$$

so

$$Var(Y \mid X=200 \text{ or } 300) = 17,500 - (125)^2 = 1875.$$

12-26 (a) Recall from Equation (12.34) that

$$E[X \wedge d] = \int_0^d [1 - F_X(x)]\, dx.$$

For the Pareto distribution we have

$$1 - F_X(x) = \left(\frac{\theta}{x+\theta}\right)^\alpha,$$

so

$$E[X \wedge d] = \theta^\alpha \int_0^d (x+\theta)^{-\alpha} \, dx$$

$$= \theta^\alpha \left[\frac{(x+\theta)^{-\alpha+1}}{-(\alpha-1)} \right]_0^d$$

$$= \frac{\theta^\alpha}{\alpha-1} \left[\theta^{-\alpha+1} - (d+\theta)^{-\alpha+1} \right]$$

$$= \frac{\theta}{\alpha-1} \left[1 - \theta^{\alpha-1}(d+\theta)^{-(\alpha-1)} \right]$$

$$= \frac{\theta}{\alpha-1} \left[1 - \left(\frac{\theta}{d+\theta}\right)^{\alpha-1} \right],$$

as required.

(b) When $\alpha = 1$, we have $1 - F_X(x) = \frac{\theta}{x+\theta}$. Then

$$E[X \wedge d] = \int_0^d \frac{\theta}{x+\theta} \, dx = \theta \cdot \ln(x+\theta)\big|_0^d$$

$$= \theta \left[\ln(d+\theta) - \ln(\theta) \right]$$

$$= \theta \cdot \ln\left(\frac{d+\theta}{\theta}\right).$$

(c) We know from Equation (12.36) that

$$E[(X-d)_+] = E[X] - E[X \wedge d].$$

For the Pareto distribution, $E[X]$ is given by Equation (12.3a) and $E[X \wedge d]$ by part (a) of this exercise. Then we have

$$E[(X-d)_+] = \frac{\theta}{\alpha-1} - \frac{\theta}{\alpha-1}\left[1 - \left(\frac{\theta}{d+\theta}\right)^{\alpha-1}\right]$$

$$= \left(\frac{\theta}{\alpha-1}\right)\left(\frac{\theta}{d+\theta}\right)^{\alpha-1} = \frac{\theta^\alpha}{(\alpha-1)(d+\theta)^{\alpha-1}},$$

as required.

CHAPTER TWELVE

12-27 From Equation (12.28a) we know that

$$E[X-d \mid X > d] = \frac{E[(X-d)_+]}{1-F_X(d)},$$

where here $1-F_X(d) = \left(\frac{\theta}{d+\theta}\right)^2$, from Equation (12.2), and $E[(X-d)_+] = \frac{\theta^2}{d+\theta}$, from Exercise 12-26(a), since $\alpha = 2$. Then

$$E[X-d \mid X > d] = \frac{\theta^2/(d+\theta)}{\theta^2/(d+\theta)^2} = d+\theta,$$

so the given relationship tells us that

$$100 + \theta = \frac{5}{3}(50+\theta),$$

which solves for $\theta = 25$. Then

$$E[X-150 \mid X > 150] = 150 + \theta = 175.$$

12-28 The policy has a coverage maximum at $u = 1000$, but no deductible. The expected payment is

$$E[Y] = E[X \wedge 1000] = \int_0^{1000} S_X(x) \, dx,$$

by Equation (12.34). Then we have

$$\begin{aligned}
E[Y] &= \int_0^{1000} (.80e^{-.02x} + .20e^{-.001x}) \, dx \\
&= \left[.80\left(\frac{e^{-.02x}}{-.02}\right) + .20\left(\frac{e^{-.001x}}{-.001}\right)\right]_0^{1000} \\
&= .80\left(\frac{1-e^{-20}}{.02}\right) + .20\left(\frac{1-e^{-1}}{.001}\right) \\
&= (.80)(50) + (.20)(632.12) = 166.42.
\end{aligned}$$

12-29 (a) From Exercise 12-26(a) we have

$$E[X \wedge d] = \frac{\theta}{\alpha - 1}\left[1 - \left(\frac{\theta}{d+\theta}\right)^{\alpha-1}\right]$$

$$= \frac{2000}{1}\left[1 - \left(\frac{2000}{2500}\right)\right]$$

$$= 400.$$

For this Pareto distribution,

$$E[X] = \frac{\theta}{\alpha - 1} = 2000,$$

so

$$LER = \frac{E[X \wedge d]}{E[X]} = \frac{400}{2000} = .20.$$

(b) First we find

$$E[X] = .01\int_0^{80} x\, dx + .00025\int_{80}^{120}(120x - x^2)\, dx$$

$$= .01(x^2/2)\Big|_0^{80} + .00025(60x^2 - x^3/3)\Big|_{80}^{120}$$

$$= .01(3200)$$

$$\quad + .00025(864,000 - 576,000 - 384,000 + 170,667)$$

$$= 50.67,$$

and then we find

$$E[X \wedge 20] = \int_0^{20} x \cdot f(x)\, dx + \int_{20}^{120} 20 \cdot f(x)\, dx$$

$$= .01\int_0^{20} x\, dx + (20)(.01)\int_{20}^{80} dx$$

$$\quad + (20)(.00025)\int_{80}^{120}(120 - x)\, dx$$

$$= .01(x^2/2)\Big|_0^{20} + .20x\Big|_{20}^{80} + .005(120x - x^2/2)\Big|_{80}^{120}$$

$$= 18.$$

Then

$$LER = \frac{E[X \wedge 20]}{E[X]} = \frac{18}{50.67} = .35524.$$

12-30 For an exponential severity, the limited expected value is

$$E[X \wedge d] = \theta(1-e^{-d/\theta}),$$

from Example 12.10(a), and the expected value is $E[X] = \theta$, using the scale parameter form. Then the *LER* is

$$\frac{E[X \wedge d]}{E[X]} = \frac{\theta(1-e^{-d/\theta})}{\theta} = 1-e^{-d/\theta} = .70,$$

so $e^{-d/\theta} = .30$. When the deductible is increased to $\frac{4}{3}d$, the *LER* becomes

$$1-e^{-4d/3\theta} = 1-(.30)^{4/3} = .79917.$$

12-31 The payment is $.80(x-20)$. If the maximum payment is 60, then the maximum covered loss is u, where $.80(u-20) = 60$, which solves for $u = 95$. Then the expected payment, given $X > 20$, is

$$E[Y \mid X > 20] = \frac{E[Y]}{1-F_X(20)} = \frac{.80E[(X \wedge 95)-(X \wedge 20)]}{1-F_X(20)}.$$

From text Equation (12.34),

$$E[X \wedge 95] = \int_0^{95}(1-.0001x^2)\,dx = x - \frac{.0001}{3}x^3 \Big|_0^{95} = 66.42,$$

and

$$E[X \wedge 20] = \int_0^{20}(1-.0001x^2)\,dx = x - \frac{.0001}{3}x^3 \Big|_0^{20} = 19.73.$$

Directly,

$$1 - F_X(20) = 1 - .0001(20)^2 = .96.$$

Then

$$E[Y \mid X > 20] = \frac{(.80)(66.42 - 19.73)}{.96} = 38.91.$$

12-32 Under the deductible, the payment is 0 if the loss is 0, 1, or 2, the payment is 1 if the loss is 3, and so on. Then the expected payment is

$$\begin{aligned}E[P] &= 1 \cdot p(3) + 2 \cdot p(4) + 3 \cdot p(5) + \cdots \\ &= p(1) + 2 \cdot p(2) + 3 \cdot p(3) + 4 \cdot p(4) + \cdots \\ &\quad - \big(p(1) + 2 \cdot p(2) + 2 \cdot p(3) + 2 \cdot p(4) + \cdots\big).\end{aligned}$$

Note that the additive line above is $E[X] = 3$. Thus we have

$$\begin{aligned}E[P] &= 3 - p(1) - 2[1 - p(0) - p(1)] \\ &= 1 + 2 \cdot p(0) + p(1) \\ &= 1 + 2 \cdot e^{-3} + 3 \cdot e^{-3} = 1.24894.\end{aligned}$$

Under coinsurance, the expected payment is α times the expected loss, or simply 3α. Equating and solving for α we have

$$\alpha = \frac{1.24894}{3} = .41631.$$

12.33 When annual costs reach 2250, the insured will have paid a total of $250 + .25(2250 - 250) = 750$. To reach 3600 she must pay the next 2850, which brings the total costs to $2250 + 2850 = 5100$.

Therefore the plan pays 75% of costs between 250 and 2250 plus 95% of costs in excess of 5100, so the plan's payment is

$$Y = .75[(X \wedge 2250) - (X \wedge 250)] + .95[(X-5100)_+]$$
$$= .75[(X \wedge 2250) - (X \wedge 250)] + .95[X - (X \wedge 5100)]$$

and the plan's expected payment is

$$E[Y] = .75(E[X \wedge 2250] - E[X \wedge 250])$$
$$+ .95(E[X] - E[X \wedge 5100]).$$

From text Exercise 12-26(a) we know that

$$E[X \wedge d] = \frac{\theta}{\alpha - 1}\left[1 - \left(\frac{\theta}{d+\theta}\right)^{\alpha-1}\right]$$

for the Pareto distribution. Here $\alpha = 2$ and $\theta = 2000$, so we have

$$E[X \wedge d] = 2000\left[1 - \left(\frac{2000}{2000+d}\right)\right] = \frac{2000d}{2000+d}.$$

Then

$$E[Y] = .75\left(\frac{(2000)(2250)}{4250} - \frac{(2000)(250)}{2250}\right)$$
$$+ .95\left(2000 - \frac{(2000)(5100)}{7100}\right)$$
$$= .75(1058.82 - 222.22) + .95(2000 - 1436.22) = 1162.22.$$

12-34 The amount by which claims are under 400 is $(400-X)_+$, and the bonus is c times this amount. Therefore the expected bonus is

$$E[B] = 100 = c \cdot E[(400-X)_+] = c(400 - E[400 \wedge X]).$$

Since X is Pareto with $\alpha = 2$ and $\theta = 300$, we have

$$E[400 \wedge X] = 300\left[1 - \left(\frac{300}{300+400}\right)\right] = \frac{(300)(400)}{700} = 171.43.$$

Then we have

$$c = \frac{100}{400 - 171.43} = .43750.$$

12-35 In Year Z the expected payment, with a deductible of 1500, is

$$E[Y] = \frac{1}{6}(0 + 500 + 1500 + 2500 + 3500 + 4500) = \frac{12,500}{6}.$$

In Year Z+1 each loss amount is larger by a multiple of 1.05, but the deductible remains at 1500, so the expected payment is

$$E[Y^*] = \frac{1}{6}(0 + 600 + 1650 + 2700 + 3750 + 4800) = \frac{13,500}{6}.$$

Then the percentage increase from Year Z to Year Z+1 is

$$\frac{13,500/6 - 12,500/6}{12,500/6} = \frac{1,000}{12,500} = .08,$$

or 8%.

12-36 From Exercise 12-6 we know that the family of normal distributions is a scale family, so that if $X^* = 1.05X$, where X is normal with parameters μ and σ, then X^* is also normal with parameters 1.05μ and 1.05σ. In this case, the normal parameters are

$$\mu^* = (1.05)(1000) = 1050$$

and

$$\sigma^* = (1.05)(100) = 105.$$

12-37 Since N_0 is negative binomial, then

$$M_{N_0}(z) = \left(\frac{p}{1-qe^z}\right)^r,$$

where $q = 1-p$. Then the MGF of N_d is

$$M_{N_d}(t) = \left(\frac{p}{1-qe^z}\right)^r\bigg|_{z=\ln(1-k+ke^t)}$$

$$= \left(\frac{p}{1-(1-p)(1-k+ke^t)}\right)^r$$

$$= \left(\frac{p}{1-(1-p)(1-k)-k(1-p)e^t}\right)^r$$

$$= \left(\frac{p}{k+p(1-k)-k(1-p)e^t}\right)^r$$

$$= \left(\frac{\frac{p}{k+p(1-k)}}{1-\frac{k(1-p)}{k+p(1-k)}\cdot e^t}\right)^r$$

$$= \left(\frac{p^*}{1-q^*e^t}\right)^{r^*},$$

where $q^* = 1-p^*$, $p^* = \dfrac{p}{k+p(1-k)} = \dfrac{p}{p+k(1-p)}$, and $r^* = r$. Therefore N_d has a negative binomial distribution with parameters $r^* = r$ and $p^* = \dfrac{p}{p+k(1-p)}$.

12-38 (a) From Equation (2.31) we have

$$E[X] = \frac{rq}{p} = r\left(\frac{\beta}{1+\beta}\right)(1+\beta) = r\beta.$$

(b) From Equation (2.32) we have

$$Var(X) = \frac{rq}{p^2} = r\left(\frac{\beta}{1+\beta}\right)(1+\beta)^2 = r\beta(1+\beta).$$

(c) From Equation (2.33) we have

$$M_X(t) = \left(\frac{p}{1-qe^t}\right)^r = \left(\frac{\frac{1}{1+\beta}}{1-\frac{\beta}{1+\beta}\cdot e^t}\right)^r$$

$$= \left(\frac{1}{1+\beta-\beta\cdot e^t}\right)^r = [1-\beta(e^t-1)]^{-r}.$$

(d) From Example 11.6 we have

$$P_X(s) = M_X(t)|_{t=\ln s} = [1-\beta(s-1)]^{-r}.$$

(e) From Exercise 12-37 we have

$$M_{N_d}(t) = \left(\frac{p*}{1-q*e^t}\right)^{r*} = \left(\frac{\frac{1}{1+\beta*}}{1-\frac{\beta*}{1+\beta*}\cdot e^t}\right)^{r*}$$

$$= \left(\frac{1}{1+\beta*-\beta*\cdot e^t}\right)^{r*}$$

$$= [1-\beta*(e^t-1)]^{-r*},$$

where

$$\beta* = \frac{1-p*}{p*} = \frac{\frac{k(1-p)}{p+k(1-p)}}{\frac{p}{p+k(1-p)}} = \frac{k(1-p)}{p} = k\cdot\beta.$$

CHAPTER TWELVE

12-39 For the coefficient of the exponential term, we multiply both numerator and denominator by $(1-e^{-k\lambda})$ to obtain

$$\frac{(1-p_{ZM}(0))(1-e^{-k\lambda})}{(1-e^{-\lambda})(1-e^{-k\lambda})} = \frac{1-p_{ZM}(0)-e^{-k\lambda}+p_{ZM}(0)\cdot e^{-k\lambda}}{(1-e^{-\lambda})(1-e^{-k\lambda})},$$

and then subtract and add $e^{-\lambda}$ in the numerator to obtain

$$\frac{1-e^{-\lambda}-p_{ZM}(0)+e^{-\lambda}-e^{-k\lambda}+p_{ZM}(0)\cdot e^{-k\lambda}}{(1-e^{-\lambda})(1-e^{-k\lambda})}.$$

Then we divide both numerator and denominator by $(1-e^{-\lambda})$ to obtain

$$\frac{\frac{(1-e^{-\lambda})-(p_{ZM}(0)-e^{-\lambda}+e^{-k\lambda}-p_{ZM}(0)\cdot e^{-k\lambda})}{1-e^{-\lambda}}}{1-e^{-k\lambda}} = \frac{1-p_{ZM}^*(0)}{1-e^{-\lambda^*}},$$

where $\lambda^* = k\cdot\lambda$ and

$$p_{ZM}^*(0) = p_{ZM}(0)-e^{-\lambda}+e^{-k\lambda}-p_{ZM}(0)\cdot e^{-k\lambda},$$

as required.

12-40 We are given that N_{100} is Poisson with $\lambda = 6$. From Equation (12.52) we then know that N_{150} will be Poisson with parameter $\lambda^* = k\cdot\lambda$, where

$$k = \frac{1-F_X(150)}{1-F_X(100)} = \frac{S_X(150)}{S_X(100)}.$$

Since X is Pareto, we easily find

and

$$S_X(100) = \left(\frac{1000}{1100}\right)^2 = .82644$$

$$S_X(150) = \left(\frac{1000}{1150}\right)^2 = .75614,$$

so

$$k = \frac{.75614}{.82644} = .91494$$

and therefore N_{150} is Poisson with parameter

$$\lambda^* = k \cdot \lambda = (.91494)(6) = 5.48964.$$

Finally the probability of 5 claims is

$$Pr(N_{150} = 5) = \frac{e^{-5.48964} \cdot (5.48964)^5}{5!} = .17156.$$

12-41 Defining $\overset{o}{e}_x$ by Equation (12.55a), we have

$$\lim_{x \to \infty} \overset{o}{e}_x = \lim_{x \to \infty} \frac{\int_x^\infty S_X(y)\, dy}{S_X(x)}.$$

Applying L'Hospital's rule we have

$$\lim_{x \to \infty} \overset{o}{e}_x = \lim_{x \to \infty} \left(\frac{\frac{d}{dx}\int_x^\infty S_X(y)\, dy}{\frac{d}{dx} S_X(x)} \right)$$

$$= \lim_{x \to \infty} \left(\frac{-S_X(x)}{-f_X(x)} \right) = \lim_{x \to \infty} \left(\frac{1}{\lambda_X(x)} \right),$$

since $\lambda_X(x) = \frac{f_X(x)}{S_X(x)}.$

Chapter Twelve

12-42 (a) Under exponential, $S_X(x) = e^{-\beta x}$ so

$$\int_x^\infty S_X(y)\,dy = \int_x^\infty e^{-\beta y}\,dy = \frac{e^{-\beta x}}{\beta}.$$

Then from Equation (12.57a) we have

$$\overset{o}{e}_x = \frac{\int_x^\infty S_X(y)\,dy}{S_X(x)} = \frac{\frac{1}{\beta}\cdot e^{-\beta x}}{e^{-\beta x}} = \frac{1}{\beta}.$$

(Note: Given $X > x$, the distribution of $T = X - x$ is the same as that of X itself, so the conditional expected value is $E[X] = \frac{1}{\beta}$.)

(b) Under Weibull, $S_X(x) = e^{-(x/\theta)^\tau}$ so

$$\overset{o}{e}_x = \frac{\int_x^\infty e^{-(y/\theta)^\tau}\,dy}{e^{-(x/\theta)^\tau}}.$$

To evaluate the integral we make the variable change $z = (y/\theta)^\tau$, so $y = \theta \cdot z^{1/\tau}$ and $dy = \frac{\theta}{\tau} \cdot z^{(1/\tau)-1}\,dz$. Then the integral becomes

$$\int_{(x/\theta)^\tau}^\infty e^{-z} \cdot \frac{\theta}{\tau} \cdot z^{(1/\tau)-1}\,dz$$

$$= \frac{\theta}{\tau}\left[\int_0^\infty z^{(1/\tau)-1} e^{-z}\,dz - \int_0^{(x/\theta)^\tau} z^{(1/\tau)-1} e^{-z}\,dz\right]$$

$$= \frac{\theta}{\tau}\left[\Gamma(\tfrac{1}{\tau}) - \Gamma(\tfrac{1}{\tau}) \cdot \Gamma\!\left(\tfrac{1}{\tau};(x/\theta)^\tau\right)\right]$$

$$= \frac{\theta}{\tau} \cdot \Gamma(\tfrac{1}{\tau}) \cdot \left[1 - \Gamma\!\left(\tfrac{1}{\tau};(x/\theta)^\tau\right)\right].$$

(See Appendix E for a discussion of the incomplete gamma function.) Dividing the evaluated integral by $S_X(x)$ we have

$$\overset{o}{e}_x = \frac{\frac{\theta}{\tau} \cdot \Gamma\left(\frac{1}{\tau}\right) \cdot \left[1 - \Gamma\left(\frac{1}{\tau}; (x/\theta)^\tau\right)\right]}{e^{-(x/\theta)^\tau}}.$$

Alternatively, we can use Equation (12.56), with x in place of d, taking $E[X]$ and $S_X(x)$ from Table 12.1 and $E[X \wedge x]$ from Table 12.2. This directly gives us

$$\overset{o}{e}_x = \frac{\theta \cdot \Gamma\left(1+\frac{1}{\tau}\right) - \theta \cdot \Gamma\left(1+\frac{1}{\tau}\right) \cdot \Gamma\left(\frac{1}{\tau}; (x/\theta)^\tau\right)}{e^{-(x/\theta)^\tau}}.$$

Since $\Gamma\left(1+\frac{1}{\tau}\right) = \frac{1}{\tau} \cdot \Gamma\left(\frac{1}{\tau}\right)$, it is easy to see that the two expressions for $\overset{o}{e}_x$ are identical.

12-43 Using Equation (12.59c), and substituting from Tables 12.1 and 12.2, we have

$$\begin{aligned}
CTE_x &= \frac{\frac{\omega}{2} - \left(x - \frac{x^2}{2\omega}\right) + x\left(1 - \frac{x}{\omega}\right)}{1 - \frac{x}{\omega}} \\
&= \frac{\frac{\omega}{2} - \frac{2x\omega - x^2}{2\omega} + \frac{x\omega - x^2}{\omega}}{\frac{\omega - x}{\omega}} \\
&= \frac{\frac{\omega^2}{2} - x\omega + \frac{x^2}{2} + x\omega - x^2}{\omega - x} \\
&= \frac{\omega^2 - x^2}{2(\omega - x)} = \frac{\omega + x}{2}.
\end{aligned}$$

CHAPTER TWELVE

12-44 Again we use Equation (12.59c) and Tables 12.1 and 12.2. Note that the second term in the expression for $E[X \wedge x]$ in Table 12.2 is itself $x \cdot S_X(x)$, so Equation (12.59c) gives

$$CTE_x = \frac{e^{\mu+\sigma^2/2} - e^{\mu+\sigma^2/2} \cdot \Phi\left(\frac{\ln x - \mu - \sigma^2}{\sigma}\right)}{1 - \Phi\left(\frac{\ln x - \mu}{\sigma}\right)}$$

$$= \frac{e^{\mu+\sigma^2/2}\left[1 - \Phi\left(\frac{\ln x - \mu - \sigma^2}{\sigma}\right)\right]}{1 - \Phi\left(\frac{\ln x - \mu}{\sigma}\right)}.$$

12-45 We seek the value of x for which

$$F_X(x) = e^{-\beta/x} = .90.$$

Then

$$x = \frac{\beta}{-\ln .90} = 9.49122\beta.$$

12-46 Recall that

$$DRM = \int_0^\infty g[S_X(x)]\, dx$$

and also that

$$E[X] = \int_0^\infty S_X(x)\, dx.$$

Then $DRM = E[X]$ if $g[S_X(x)] = S_X(x)$, which implies that $g(t) = t$.

12-47 Referring to Figure 12.9, for all $x \geq x_\alpha$ we have $S_X(x) \leq 1-\alpha$, so

$$S_X^*(x) = g[S_X(x)] = \frac{S_X(x)}{1-\alpha} = \frac{S_X(x)}{S_X(x_\alpha)}$$

for $x \geq x_\alpha$. Similarly, for $0 \leq x < x_\alpha$ we have $S_X(x) > 1-\alpha$, so

$$S_X^*(x) = g[S_X(x)] = 1$$

for $0 \leq x < x_\alpha$. Then the distortion risk measure is

$$DRM = \int_0^\infty S_X^*(x)\, dx = \int_0^{x_\alpha} 1\, dx + \int_{x_\alpha}^\infty \frac{S_X(x)}{S_X(x_\alpha)}\, dx = x_\alpha + \overset{o}{e}_{x_u},$$

from Equation (12.57a). But from Equation (12.59b) we know that

$$CTE_\alpha = CTE_{x_\alpha} = x_\alpha + \overset{o}{e}_{x_\alpha},$$

and the desired result is established.

12-48 The distorted survival function is

$$S_X^*(x) = 1 - \left(1 - S_X(x)\right)^k = 1 - \left(\tfrac{x}{\omega}\right)^k,$$

so the distortion risk measure is

$$DRM = \int_0^\omega \left[1 - \left(\tfrac{x}{\omega}\right)^k\right] dx$$

$$= x - \frac{x^{k+1}}{(k+1)\omega^k}\bigg|_0^\omega$$

$$= \omega - \frac{\omega^{k+1}}{(k+1)\omega^k} = \omega - \frac{\omega}{k+1} = \frac{\omega k}{k+1}.$$

CHAPTER TWELVE

12-49 The Pareto survival function is $S(x)=\left(\dfrac{1000}{x+1000}\right)^4$, so the distorted survival function is

$$S^*(x) = g[S(x)] = \left[\left(\dfrac{1000}{x+1000}\right)^4\right]^{1/2} = \left(\dfrac{1000}{x+1000}\right)^2,$$

which is still Pareto but with $\alpha = 2$. Then

$$DRM = \int_0^\infty S^*(x)\,dx = E[X^*] = \dfrac{1000}{\alpha-1} = 1000.$$

12-50 The value of $x_{.90}$ is 4, the smallest value of x satisfying $F_X(x) \geq .90$. Since $F_X(4) = .94721$, we observe that 4 is also the smallest value of x satisfying $F_X(x) \geq .94721$, so $\beta = .94721$. Then we have

$$E[X \mid X > 4] = \dfrac{5 \cdot p(5) + 6 \cdot p(6) + \cdots}{p(5) + p(6) + \cdots}$$

$$= \dfrac{E[X] - 1 \cdot p(1) - 2 \cdot p(2) - 3 \cdot p(3) - 4 \cdot p(4)}{1 - p(0) - p(1) - p(2) - p(3) - p(4)}$$

$$= \dfrac{2 - .27061 - (2)(.27061) - (3)(.18045) - (4)(.09020)}{1 - .13534 - .27061 - .27061 - .18045 - .09020}$$

$$= \dfrac{.28602}{.05279} = 5.41807.$$

Finally we have

$$CTE_{.90} = \left(\dfrac{.94721 - .90}{1 - .90}\right)(4) + \left(\dfrac{1 - .94721}{1 - .90}\right)(5.41807)$$

$$= (.47210)(4) + (.52790)(5.41807) = 4.74860.$$

12-51 First note that X is still a continuous random variable, but without an assumed parametric distribution. From the empirical data we have calculated the given values of $F_X(x)$, and the given values of $E[X \wedge x]$. To find the expected payment per loss event we use the form $Y = X - (X \wedge d)$, to take advantage of the given data. Then

$$E[Y] = E[X] - E[X \wedge d].$$

Note that $E[X] = E[X \wedge 1000] = 331$, since the smaller of X or 1000 is always X. Then

$$E[Z] = \frac{E[Y]}{1 - F_X(d)} = \frac{331 - 91}{.80} = 300.00.$$

CHAPTER THIRTEEN
MODELS FOR AGGREGATE PAYMENTS

13-1 For the compound model $S = X_1 + X_2 + \cdots + X_N$, the double expectation theorem tells us that

$$E[S] = E[X] \cdot E[N]$$

and

$$Var(S) = Var(X) \cdot E[N] + Var(N) \cdot (E[X])^2.$$

In the special case where N has a Poisson distribution with $E[N] = Var(N) = \lambda$, we have

$$E[S] = \lambda \cdot E[X]$$

and

$$Var(S) = \lambda \left[Var(X) + (E[X])^2 \right] = \lambda \cdot E[X^2].$$

13-2 From the distribution of N we find

$$E[N] = (1)(.30) + (2)(.20) = .70,$$
$$E[N^2] = (1)(.30) + (4)(.20) = 1.10,$$

and

$$Var(N) = 1.10 - (.70)^2 = .61.$$

From the distribution of X we find

$$E[X] = \frac{\theta}{\alpha - 1} = 2500,$$
$$E[X^2] = \frac{2\theta^2}{(\alpha-1)(\alpha-2)} = (5000)^2,$$

and

$$Var(X) = (5000)^2 - (2500)^2 = 18,750,000.$$

Then from the double expectation theorem,

$$E[S] = E[X] \cdot E[N] = (2500)(.70) = 1750$$

and

$$Var(S) = Var(X) \cdot E[N] + Var(N) \cdot (E[X])^2$$
$$= (18,750,000)(.70) + (.61)(2500)^2$$
$$= 16,937,500$$

so

$$SD(S) = \sqrt{Var(S)} = 4115.52.$$

Finally,

$$CV(S) = \frac{SD(S)}{E[S]} = \frac{4115.52}{1750} = 2.35.$$

13-3 The number of days of rain has a binomial distribution with $n = 30$ and $p = .10$, so we have

$$E[N] = np = 3.00$$

and

$$Var(N) = npq = 2.70.$$

Then

$$S = X_1 + X_2 + \cdots + X_N$$

has a compound distribution with $E[X] = Var(X) = .50$.

(a) From the double expectation theorem we have

$$E[S] = E[X] \cdot E[N] = (.50)(3.00) = 1.50.$$

(b) Similarly,

$$Var(S) = Var(X) \cdot E[N] + Var(N) \cdot (E[X])^2$$
$$= (.50)(3.00) + (2.70)(.50)^2 = 2.175.$$

(c) Recall that $M_S(t) = M_N[\ln M_X(t)]$. Here we have

$$M_N(t) = (q + p \cdot e^t)^n$$

and

$$M_X(t) = \left(\frac{\beta}{\beta-t}\right)^\alpha.$$

To find α and β, recall that $E[X] = \frac{\alpha}{\beta}$ and $Var(X) = \frac{\alpha}{\beta^2}$, so

$$Var(X) = \frac{\alpha}{\beta^2} = \left(\frac{\alpha}{\beta}\right)\left(\frac{1}{\beta}\right) = (.50)\left(\frac{1}{\beta}\right) = .50,$$

which implies $\beta = 1$ and $\alpha = .50$, so $M_X(t) = \left(\frac{1}{1-t}\right)^{.50}$.

Finally,

$$M_S(t) = \left(q + p \cdot e^{\ln M_X(t)}\right)^n$$

$$= \left(q + p \cdot M_X(t)\right)^n = \left[.90 + .10\left(\frac{1}{1-t}\right)^{.50}\right]^{30}.$$

13-4 (a) The aggregate claim random variable is

$$S = X_1 + X_2 + \cdots + X_{40} + Y_1 + Y_2 + \cdots + Y_{60},$$

where X_i denotes the claim from the ith male and Y_j denotes the claim from the jth female. We have

$$E[S] = 40 \cdot E[X] + 60 \cdot E[Y] = (40)(2) + (60)(4) = 320$$

and

$$Var(S) = 40 \cdot Var(X) + 60 \cdot Var(Y) = (40)(4) + (60)(10) = 760.$$

(b) Let N denote the number of males in the group of 100 members. When the value of N is given, as in part (a), then $E[S]$ and $Var(S)$ are easily found. Here we find first the conditional mean and variance of S, given $N = n$.

From part (a) we can write

$$S = X_1 + X_2 + \cdots + X_n + Y_1 + Y_2 + \cdots + Y_{100-n}.$$

Then

$$E[S|N=n] = n \cdot E[X] + (100-n) \cdot E[Y]$$
$$= 2n + 4(100-n) = 400 - 2n,$$

or $E[S|N] = 400 - 2N$, in terms of random variables.

Then by the first part of the double expectation theorem we have

$$E[S] = E_N[E[S|N]] = E_N[400 - 2N] = 400 - 2 \cdot E[N].$$

But N is binomial, so $E[N] = (100)(.40) = 40$, leading to

$$E[S] = 400 - 2(40) = 320.$$

Similarly,

$$Var(S|N=n) = n \cdot Var(X) + (100-n) \cdot Var(Y)$$
$$= 4n + 10(100-n) = 1000 - 6n,$$

or $Var(S|N) = 1000 - 6N$, in terms of random variables. Then by the second part of the double expectation theorem we have

$$Var(S) = E_N[Var(S|N)] + Var_N(E[S|N])$$
$$= E_N[1000 - 6N] + Var_N(400 - 2N)$$
$$= 1000 - 6 \cdot E[N] + 4 \cdot Var(N)$$
$$= 1000 - 6(40) + 4(24) = 856.$$

13-5 Aggregate claim is modeled by the individual risk model as

$$S = X_1 + X_2 + \cdots + X_{10},$$

where the X_i's are independent. For the ith ship, the expected claim is 500 if a claim occurs, which happens with probability .01. Therefore

$$E[X] = E[X|claim] \cdot Pr(claim) = (500)(.01) = 5.$$

Similarly, the second moment of claim amount is $2500 + (500)^2 = 252{,}500$ if a claim occurs, so

$$E[X^2] = E[X^2 \,|\, claim] \cdot Pr(claim) = (252{,}500)(.01) = 2525.$$

Then
$$Var(X) = 2525 - (5)^2 = 2500.$$

Finally,
$$E[S] = 10 \cdot E[X] = 50$$

and
$$Var(S) = 10 \cdot Var(X) = 25{,}000.$$

Alternatively, we can model aggregate claims by the collective risk model as

$$S = X_1 + X_2 + \cdots + X_N,$$

where N is the number of ships producing a claim. Assuming independence among ships, the number of claims is clearly binomial with $E[N] = (10)(.01) = .10$ and $Var(N) = (10)(.01)(.99) = .099$.

Then
$$E[S] = E[X] \cdot E[N] = (500)(.10) = 50$$
and
$$Var(S) = Var(X) \cdot E[N] + Var(N) \cdot (E[X])^2$$
$$= (2500)(.10) + (.099)(500)^2 = 25{,}000$$

as before.

13-6 The total payment can be modeled as
$$S = X_1 + X_2 + \cdots + X_N,$$

where X_i denotes the total payment for the ith individual claim. In turn,
$$X = Y + .80Z,$$

where Y denotes the room charge and Z denotes other charges. We have

$$E[X] = E[Y] + .80E[Z] = 1000 + (.80)(500) = 1400$$

and

$$\begin{aligned} Var(X) &= Var(Y) + (.80)^2 \cdot Var(Z) + 2(.80) \cdot Cov(Y, Z) \\ &= (500)^2 + (.80)^2 (300)^2 + 2(.80)(100,000) \\ &= 250,000 + 57,600 + 160,000 = 467,600. \end{aligned}$$

Note that N is Poisson, so $E[N] = Var(N) = 4$. Then

$$\begin{aligned} Var(S) &= Var(X) \cdot E[N] + Var(N) \cdot (E[X])^2 \\ &= (467,600)(4) + (4)(1400)^2 \\ &= 9,710,400. \end{aligned}$$

13-7 The aggregate repair cost is

$$\begin{aligned} S &= S_1 + S_2 + S_3 \\ &= (X_1 + X_2 + \cdots + X_{N_1}) + (Y_1 + Y_2 + \cdots + Y_{N_2}) + (Z_1 + Z_2 + \cdots + Z_{N_3}), \end{aligned}$$

where N_1 is the number of powerboat repairs, N_2 is the number of sailboat repairs, and N_3 is the number of luxury yacht repairs. Note that N_1, N_2, N_3 all have binomial distributions. We have

$$\begin{aligned} E[N_1] &= (100)(.30) = 30, \\ E[N_2] &= (300)(.10) = 30, \\ E[N_3] &= (50)(.60) = 30, \\ Var(N_1) &= (100)(.30)(.70) = 21, \\ Var(N_2) &= (300)(.10)(.90) = 27, \end{aligned}$$

and

$$Var(N_3) = (50)(.60)(.40) = 12.$$

From these values we find

$$E[S_1] = (300)(30) = 9,000,$$
$$E[S_2] = (1000)(30) = 30,000,$$
$$E[S_3] = (5000)(30) = 150,000,$$
$$Var(S_1) = (300)^2(21) + (10,000)(30) = 2,190,000,$$
$$Var(S_2) = (1000)^2(27) + (400,000)(30) = 39,000,000,$$

and

$$Var(S_3) = (5000)^2(12) + (2,000,000)(30) = 360,000,000.$$

Then

$$E[S] = 9,000 + 30,000 + 150,000 = 189,000$$

and

$$Var(S) = 2,190,000 + 39,000,000 + 360,000,000 = 401,190,000$$

so

$$SD(S) = \sqrt{401,190,000} = 20,029.73$$

and the annual repair budget is

$$E[S] + SD(S) = 189,000 + 20,029.73 = 209,029.73.$$

13-8 The number of insurance purchases, N, is binomial with $n = 10$ and $p = .10$, so $E[N] = np = 1$ and $Var(N) = npq = .90$. The random present value of payment for the ith insurance purchase is $X_i = 1000 Z_{22}$, with expected value $E[X_i] = 1000 A_{22}$ and variance $Var(X_i) = (1000)^2 \cdot (^2A_{22} - A_{22}^2)$, using notation defined in Section 5.1.2. The present value of total payments is therefore given by the collective risk model as

$$S = X_1 + X_2 + \cdots + X_N,$$

with the moments of X and N given above. Then we have

$$\begin{aligned} Var(S) &= Var(X) \cdot E[N] + Var(N) \cdot (E[X])^2 \\ &= (1000)^2 \cdot (^2A_{22} - A_{22}^2) + .90\big((1000)^2 \cdot A_{22}^2\big) \\ &= (1000)^2 \cdot (^2A_{22} - .10 A_{22}^2) \\ &= (1000)^2 \cdot [.01587 - (.10)(.07135)^2] = 15{,}361. \end{aligned}$$

13-9 At $k = 0$ we have

$$p_X^{*(0)}(x) = \begin{cases} 1 & \text{for } x = 0 \\ 0 & \text{for } x > 0 \end{cases}.$$

At $k = 1$ we have $p_X^{*(1)}(x) = p_X(x)$.

At $k = 2$ we have $p_S(x) = p_X^{*(2)}(x)$, where $S = X_1 + X_2$. We find

$$\begin{aligned} p_S(0) &= (.30)(.30) = .09 \\ p_S(1) &= (.30)(.30) + (.30)(.30) = .18 \\ p_S(2) &= (.30)(.30) = .09 \\ p_S(3) &= (.30)(.40) + (.40)(.30) = .24 \\ p_S(4) &= (.30)(.40) + (.40)(.30) = .24 \\ p_S(5) &= 0 \\ p_S(6) &= (.40)(.40) = .16 \end{aligned}$$

(Check: $.09 + .18 + .09 + .24 + .24 + .16 = 1.00$, as required.)

At $k = 3$ we have $p_S(x) = p_X^{*(3)}(x)$, where $S = (X_1 + X_2) + X_3$. We find

$$p_S(0) = (.09)(.30) = .027$$
$$p_S(1) = (.09)(.30) + (.18)(.30) = .081$$
$$p_S(2) = (.09)(.30) + (.18)(.30) = .081$$
$$p_S(3) = (.24)(.30) + (.09)(.30) + (.09)(.40) = .135$$
$$p_S(4) = (.24)(.30) + (.24)(.30) + (.18)(.40) = .216$$
$$p_S(5) = (0)(.30) + (.24)(.30) + (.09)(.40) = .108$$
$$p_S(6) = (.16)(.30) + (0)(.30) + (.24)(.40) = .144$$
$$p_S(7) = (.16)(.30) + (.24)(.40) = .144$$
$$p_S(8) = 0$$
$$p_S(9) = (.16)(.40) = .064$$

(Check: .027+.081+.081+.135+.216+.108+.144+.144+.064 = 1.00, as required.)

13-10 The expression for $p_S(x)$ shows us that N has a Poisson distribution with $\lambda = 50$. The distribution of X produces

$$E[X] = (1)(.40) + (2)(.50) + (3)(.10) = 1.70$$

and

$$E[X^2] = (1)(.40) + (4)(.50) + (9)(.10) = 3.30.$$

Then

$$Var(S) = \lambda \cdot E[X^2] = (50)(3.30) = 165.$$

13-11 The convolutions of X, as far as $x = 2$, are as follows:

$$p^{*(0)}(0) = 1, \quad p^{*(0)}(1) = 0, \quad p^{*(0)}(2) = 0$$
$$p^{*(1)}(0) = 0, \quad p^{*(1)}(1) = .20, \quad p^{*(1)}(2) = .30$$
$$p^{*(2)}(0) = 0, \quad p^{*(2)}(1) = 0, \quad p^{*(2)}(2) = .04$$
$$p^{*(3)}(0) = p^{*(3)}(1) = p^{*(3)}(2) = 0$$

Then

$$p_S(0) = p^{*(0)}(0) \cdot p_N(0) = e^{-\lambda}$$
$$p_S(1) = p^{*(1)}(1) \cdot p_N(1) = (.20)(\lambda \cdot e^{-\lambda})$$
$$p_S(2) = p^{*(1)}(2) \cdot p_N(1) + p^{*(2)}(2) \cdot p_N(2)$$
$$= (.30)(\lambda \cdot e^{-\lambda}) + (.04)\left(\frac{1}{2}\lambda^2 \cdot e^{-\lambda}\right).$$

Then

$$\begin{aligned}Pr(S \geq 3) &= 1 - Pr(S \leq 2) \\ &= 1 - [p_S(0) + p_S(1) + p_S(2)] \\ &= 1 - e^{-.60}\left[1 + (.20)(.60) + (.30)(.60) + (.02)(.60)^2\right] \\ &= 1 - e^{-.60}(1 + .12 + .18 + .0072) = .28259.\end{aligned}$$

13-12 The model for aggregate benefits is the collective risk model. From the given distribution of N we find $E[N] = .70$ and $Var(N) = 1.21$, and from the given distribution of X we find $E[X] = 2$ and $Var(X) = 16$. Then we have

$$E[S] = (.70)(2) = 1.40,$$

$$Var(S) = (.70)(16) + (1.21)(2)^2 = 16.04,$$

and

$$SD(S) = \sqrt{16.04} = 4.005.$$

The expected value plus two standard deviations is 9.41, so we seek

$$Pr(S > 9.41) = 1 - Pr(S < 9.41) = 1 - Pr(S = 0),$$

since there are no possible values of S between 0 and 10. In turn, $S = 0$ if there are no claims or if any occurring claim produces a benefit of 0. Therefore

$$Pr(S=0) = p_N(0) + p_N(1) \cdot p_X(0) + p_N(2) \cdot (p_X(0))^2$$
$$= .70 + (.20)(.80) + (.10)(.80)^2 = .924,$$

so
$$Pr(S > 9.41) = 1 - .924 = .076.$$

13-13 From Equation (13.13) we have

$$f_S(x) = \sum_{k=1}^{\infty} p_N(k) \cdot f_X^{*(k)}(x),$$

for $x > 0$. (Note that $f_X^{*(0)}(x) = 0$ for $x > 0$, so the term in the summation at $k = 0$ can be ignored.) When N is Poisson and X is exponential we have

$$f_S(x) = \sum_{k=1}^{\infty} \frac{e^{-\lambda} \lambda^k}{k!} \cdot \frac{\beta^k}{\Gamma(k)} \cdot x^{k-1} e^{-\beta x},$$

since the k-fold convolution of the exponential is gamma with $\alpha = k$. This simplifies to

$$f_S(x) = e^{-\lambda} \cdot e^{-\beta x} \cdot \lambda \beta \sum_{k=1}^{\infty} \frac{(\lambda \beta x)^{k-1}}{k! \cdot (k-1)!},$$

since $\Gamma(k) = (k-1)!$. In this case $\lambda = 5$ and $\beta = .01$, so we find

$$f_S(100) = .05 e^{-5} \cdot e^{-1} \sum_{k=1}^{\infty} \frac{5^{k-1}}{k!(k-1)!}$$

$$= .05 e^{-6} \left[1 + \frac{5}{2!} + \frac{5^2}{3!2!} + \frac{5^3}{4!3!} + \cdots \right]$$

$$= (.00012394)(1 + 2.5 + 2.08333 + .86806 + .21701 + \cdots)$$

$$= .00083 + \cdots.$$

(Including the sixth term in the summation does not change the value of $f_S(100)$ within five places.)

13-14 The distribution of number of fires is binomial with $n=4$ and $p=.05$, so the probability values are

$$p_N(0) = (.95)^4 = .81451,$$

$$p_N(1) = 4(.05)(.95)^3 = .17148,$$

$$p_N(2) = 6(.05)^2(.95)^2 = .01354,$$

$$p_N(3) = 4(.05)^3(.95) = .00046,$$

and

$$p_N(4) = (.05)^4 = .00001.$$

We can calculate $Pr(S > 2000) = 1 - F_S(2000)$ from Equation (13.21c) as

$$Pr(S > x) = e^{-\beta x} \sum_{r=0}^{3} \frac{(\beta x)^r}{r!} \left(1 - \sum_{k=0}^{r} p_N(k)\right).$$

Here $x = 2000$ and $\beta = .001$ so $\beta x = 2$. Then we have

$$\begin{aligned}Pr(S > 2000) &= e^{-2} \sum_{r=0}^{3} \frac{2^r}{r!}\left(1 - \sum_{k=0}^{r} p_N(k)\right) \\ &= e^{-2}[(1-.81451) + 2(1-.81451-.17148) \\ &\quad + 2(1-.81451-.17148-.01354) \\ &\quad + \tfrac{8}{6}(1-.81451-.17148-.01354-.00046)] \\ &= e^{-2}(.18549+.02802+.00094+.00001) = .02902.\end{aligned}$$

(Note that the sum of the $p_N(k)$ values is 1 for all $r \geq n$, so the summation on r can stop at $r = n-1 = 3$ in this case.)

13-15 $S = X_1 + X_2 + \cdots + X_N$, where $E[N] = Var(N) = 2$. The distribution of X is lognormal, with

$$E[X] = E[e^Y] = M_Y(1)$$

and

$$E[X^2] = E[e^{2Y}] = M_Y(2).$$

Recall that the MGF of the normal random variable is

$$M_Y(t) = e^{\mu t + \sigma^2 t^2 / 2}.$$

In this problem $\mu = 1$ and $\sigma = 2$, so we have

$$E[X] = M_Y(1) = e^{1+4/2} = e^3 = 20.08554$$

and

$$E[X^2] = M_Y(2) = e^{2+16/2} = e^{10} = 22{,}026.46579.$$

Then
$$\begin{aligned}
E[S] &= (20.08554)(2) &&= 40.17108 \\
Var(S) &= (22{,}026{,}46579)(2) &&= 44{,}052.93159 \\
SD(S) &= \sqrt{44{,}052.93159} &&= 209.88790.
\end{aligned}$$

Finally,

$$CV(S) = \frac{SD(S)}{E[S]} = \frac{209.88790}{40.17108} = 5.22485.$$

13-16 This question involves convolution of continuous densities. Note that $N = 2$ at most, so we need only $f_X^{*(1)}(x)$ and $f_X^{*(2)}(x)$, where $f_X^{*(1)}(x) = f_X(x) = .01$ for $0 < x < 100$. To find $f_X^{*(2)}(x)$, we convolute $S = X_1 + X_2$.

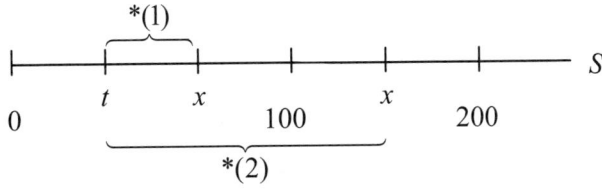

Note that the domain of S is $(0, 200)$, but any one X can only go up to 100. This means we will have separate $f_X^{*(2)}(x)$ for $0 < x < 100$ and $100 < x < 200$.

If $0 < x < 100$, then one X takes on value t (with density .01) and the other takes on value $x - t$, also with density .01. Then

$$f_X^{*(2)}(x) = \int_0^x f_{X_1}(t) \cdot f_{X_2}(x-t)\, dt = \int_0^x (.01)^2\, dt = .0001x.$$

For $100 < x < 200$, the value t cannot be less than $x - 100$ nor more than 100. Then

$$f_X^{*(2)}(x) = \int_{x-100}^{100} f_{X_1}(t) \cdot f_{X_2}(x-t)\, dt$$

$$= \int_{x-100}^{100} (.01)^2\, dt = .0001t \Big|_{x-100}^{100} = .02 - .0001x.$$

Recall that $f_X^{*(1)}(x) = f_X(x) = .01$ only applies in $0 < x < 100$. In general, $f_S(x) = .60 f_X^{*(1)}(x) + .40 f_X^{*(2)}(x)$. Specifically,

$$f_S(x) = (.60)(.01) + (.40)(.0001x) = .006 + .00004x$$

for $0 < x < 100$, and

$$f_S(x) = (.40)(.02 - .0001x) = .008 - .00004x$$

for $100 < x < 200$. We seek $Pr(S > 75) = 1 - Pr(S < 75)$, so we only need $f_S(x)$ for $0 < x < 100$. Then

$$Pr(S > 75) = 1 - Pr(S < 75)$$
$$= 1 - \int_0^{75} (.006 + .00004x)\, dx$$
$$= 1 - (.006x + .00002x^2)\Big|_0^{75}$$
$$= 1 - (.006)(75) - (.00002)(75)^2$$
$$= 1 - .45 - .1125 = .4375.$$

Chapter Thirteen 211

13-17 This is the usual collective risk model with $E[N]=3$, $E[X]=10$, $Var(N)=3.60$, and $Var(X)=\frac{400}{12}$. Then

$$E[S] = E[X] \cdot E[N] = (10)(3) = 30$$

and

$$Var(S) = E[N] \cdot Var(X) + Var(N) \cdot (E[X])^2$$
$$= (3)(\tfrac{400}{12}) + (3.60)(100) = 460.$$

Then

$$Pr(S<k) = Pr\left(Z < \frac{k-30}{\sqrt{460}}\right) = .95$$

so $\frac{k-30}{\sqrt{460}} = 1.645$, which solves for

$$k = 1.645\sqrt{460} + 30 = 65.28132.$$

13-18 If the dam is open for k hours, the expected number of salmon is $E[N]=100k$ with variance $Var(N)=900k$ (due to independence). We are also given $E[X]=Var(X)=5$. Then S, the total number of eggs released, has moments

$$E[S] = E[N] \cdot E[X] = (100k)(5) = 500k$$

and

$$Var(S) = E[N] \cdot Var(X) + Var(N) \cdot (E[X])^2$$
$$= (100k)(5) + (900k)(5)^2 = 23,000k.$$

Then

$$Pr(S>10,000) = Pr\left(Z > \frac{10,000-500k}{\sqrt{23,000k}}\right) = .95$$

implies

$$\frac{10,000-500k}{\sqrt{23,000k}} = -1.645.$$

Letting $x = \sqrt{k}$ we have the quadratic

$$10{,}000 - 500x^2 = -249.48x,$$

which solves for $x = 4.72857$. Then $k = x^2 = 22.36$.

13-19 By eliminating coverage on certain vehicles, the number of losses is now Poisson with $\lambda = 16$. Furthermore, only losses in excess of 100 produce payments. The probability of this is

$$Pr(X > 100) = e^{-(100)(.005)} = .60653,$$

so the number of payments is Poisson with

$$\lambda = (16)(.60653) = 9.70449.$$

The expected payment per payment event is

$$\begin{aligned} E[Z] &= \frac{E[(X-100)_+]}{Pr(X > 100)} \\ &= \frac{200 e^{-(100)(.005)}}{e^{-(100)(.005)}} \\ &= 200 \end{aligned}$$

(As already known from the memoryless property of the exponential distribution). Then the expected aggregate payment after the modifications is

$$E[S] = E[N] \cdot E[Z] = (200)(9.70449) = 1940.89.$$

13-20 First we note that the deductible is per loss, so only losses in excess of 30 will produce claims. Total number of losses is Poisson with $\lambda = 20$, so total number of claims is also Poisson with $\lambda = 20 \cdot Pr(X > 30) = (20)(.75) = 15$. Then the aggregate payment is

$$S = Z_1 + Z_2 + \cdots + Z_N,$$

where Z_i is the amount paid on the ith payment event, and N is the number of payment events. Since N is Poisson, then the variance of S is

$$Var(S) = \lambda \cdot E[Z^2] = 15 \cdot E[Z^2].$$

Now Z is the random variable for the amount of payment, given that payment occurs, which is given that the loss X exceeds 30, so $Z = X-30 \,|\, X > 30$. Therefore

$$\begin{aligned} E[Z^2] &= E[(X-30)^2 \,|\, X > 30] \\ &= E[X^2 - 60X + 900 \,|\, X > 30] \\ &= E[X^2 - 60X + 1800 - 900 \,|\, X > 30] \\ &= E[X^2 - 60(X-30) - 900 \,|\, X > 30] \\ &= E[X^2 \,|\, X > 30] - 60 \cdot E[X-30 \,|\, X > 30] - E[900 \,|\, X > 30]. \end{aligned}$$

The value of the first conditional expectation is given as 9000, and the value of the third one is 900. For the second one, recall that

$$\begin{aligned} E[X-30 \,|\, X > 30] &= \frac{E[(X-30)_+]}{Pr(X > 30)} \\ &= \frac{E[X] - E[X \wedge 30]}{Pr(X > 30)} \\ &= \frac{70 - 25}{.75} = 60, \end{aligned}$$

so we have

$$E[Z^2] = 9000 - 60(60) - 900 = 4500.$$

Finally

$$Var(S) = 15 \cdot E[Z^2] = (15)(4500) = 67{,}500.$$

13-21 (a) The PF of S follows from the set of $p_X^{*(k)}(x)$, as

$$p_S(x) = \sum_k p_X^{*(k)}(x) \cdot Pr(N=k).$$

Thus we have

$$p_S(0) = p_X^{*(1)}(0) \cdot p_N(1) + p_X^{*(2)}(0) \cdot p_N(2) + p_X^{*(3)}(0) \cdot p_N(3)$$
$$= (.30)(.60) + (.09)(.30) + (.027)(.10) = .2097,$$
$$p_S(1) = (.30)(.60) + (.18)(.30) + (.081)(.10) = .2421,$$

and so on to complete the set of $p_S(x)$ shown in the textbook answers. The CDF of S follows by summation.

(b) Note that
$$E[X] = (1)(.30) + (3)(.40) = 1.50$$
and
$$E[N] = (1)(.60) + (2)(.30) + (3)(.10) = 1.50.$$
Then
$$E[S] = E[N] \cdot E[X] = (1.50)(1.50) = 2.25.$$

Then we use Equation (13.15) recursively to find, at $d = 0$,

$$E[(S-0)_+] = [1 - F_S(0)] + E[(S-1)_+],$$

so

$$E[(S-1)_+] = E[S] - [1 - F_S(0)]$$
$$= 2.25 - (1 - .2097) = 1.4597.$$

At $d = 1$ we have $E[(S-1)_+] = [1 - F_S(1)] + E[(S-2)_+]$,
so

$$E[(S-2)_+] = [(S-1)_+] - [1 - F_S(1)]$$
$$= 1.4597 - (1 - .4518) = .9115.$$

At $d = 2$ we have $E[(S-2)_+] = [1 - F_S(2)] + E[(S-3)_+]$,
so

$$E[(S-3)_+] = E[(S-2)_+] - [1 - F_S(2)]$$
$$= .9115 - (1 - .4869) = .3984.$$

(c) We use Equation (13.17) to find

$$E[(S-2.70)_+] = (.70) \cdot E[(S-3)_+] + (.30) \cdot E[(S-2)_+]$$
$$= (.70)(.3984) + (.30)(.9115) = .55233.$$

(d) Clearly $E[(S-d)_+]$ decreases as d increases, so the value of d for which $E[(S-d)_+] = 1$ satisfies $1 < d < 2$. Again using Equation (13.17) we have

$$E[(S-d)_+] = E[(S-(1+r))_+]$$
$$= (r) \cdot E[(S-2)_+] + (1-r) \cdot E[(S-1)_+]$$
$$= .9115r + 1.4597(1-r)$$
$$= 1.4597 - .5482r = 1.00,$$

so $r = \dfrac{.4597}{.5482} = .83856$, and therefore $d = 1 + r = 1.83856$.

13-22 We seek the value of $E[(S-8)_+]$, which can be calculated directly from the distribution of S as

$$E[(S-8)_+] = (0)(.90) + (0)(.05) + (2)(.03) + (7)(.02)$$
$$= .06 + .14$$
$$= .20 \text{ million, or } 200,000.$$

13-23 Since x does not assume consecutive integral values, Equations (13.14) and (13.15) do not hold. Starting with Equation (13.13b) we have

$$E[(S-5,000)_+] = \sum_{x>5,000} (x-d) \cdot p_S(x)$$
$$= (10,000-5,000) \cdot p_S(10,000)$$
$$+ \sum_{x>10,000} (x-5,000) \cdot p_S(x),$$

since $x+10,000$ is the next possible value of x greater than 5,000. Add and subtract 5,000 inside the latter summation to reach

$$E[(S-5,000)_+] = 5,000 \cdot p_S(10,000)$$
$$+ \sum_{x>10,000}(x-10,000)\cdot p_S(x)$$
$$+ \sum_{x>10,000} 5,000 \cdot p_S(x)$$
$$= 5,000\cdot p_S(10,000) + 5,000\sum_{x>10,000} p_S(x)$$
$$+ E[(S-10,000)_+]$$
$$= 5,000[1-F_S(5,000)] + E[(S-10,000)_+].$$

Then

$$Pr(S>5,000) = 1 - F_S(5,000)$$
$$= \frac{E[(S-5,000)_+] - E[(S-10,000)_+]}{5000}$$
$$= \frac{2000-1500}{5000} = .10.$$

13-24 Recall that

$$E[(X-d)_+] = \sum_{x>d}(x-d)\cdot p_X(x) = E[X] - E[X\wedge d].$$

We are given $E[(X-d)_+] = 2$ and $E[X] = 4$, so $E[X\wedge d] = 2$, where $(X\wedge d) = \min(X,d)$.

At the low end, x will be less than d so the expectation starts building up with

$$(0)(.05) + (1)(.06) + (2)(.25) + (3)(.22) + \cdots,$$

and at the high end d will be less than x so we will have $d(.12) + d(.05) + d(.05) + \cdots$.

Then $E[X\wedge d] = 2 = .06 + .50 + .66 + .40 + \cdots$.

CHAPTER THIRTEEN   **217**

If $d = 4$, then $E[X \wedge 4] = 1.62 + 4(.32) = 2.90$,
which is too big, so $d < 4$.
If $d = 3$, then $E[X \wedge 3] = 1.22 + 3(.42) = 2.48$,
which is too big, so $d < 3$.
If $d = 2$, then $E[X \wedge 2] = .56 + 2(.64) = 1.84$,
which is too small, so $d > 2$.

Then $E[X \wedge d] = .56 + d(.64) = 2$, so $d = 2.25$.

13-25 The distribution of S is exponential. We have

$$E[(S-d)_+] = E[S] - E[S \wedge d]$$
$$= \int_0^\infty S_S(x)\, dx - \int_0^d S_S(x)\, dx$$
$$= \int_d^\infty e^{-\beta x}\, dx$$
$$= -\frac{1}{\beta} \cdot e^{-\beta x}\Big|_d^\infty = \frac{1}{\beta} \cdot e^{-\beta d}.$$

13-26 The convolutions of X are as follows:

x	$p^{*(0)}(x)$	$p^{*(1)}(x)$	$p^{*(2)}(x)$	$p^{*(3)}(x)$
0	1	0	0	0
2000		.30	0	0
3000		.70	0	0
4000			$(.3)(.3) = .09$	0
5000			$2(.3)(.7) = .42$	0
6000			$(.7)(.7) = .49$	$(.09)(.3) = .027$
7000				$(.42)(.3)+(.09)(.7) = .189$
8000				$(.49)(.3)+(.42)(.7) = .441$
9000				$(.49)(.7) = .343$

Next we find the distribution of S as follows:

$$p_S(0) = p_N(0) = .3500$$

$p_S(2000) = p^{*(1)}(2000) \cdot p_N(1) = (.30)(.35) = .1050$

$p_S(3000) = p^{*(1)}(3000) \cdot p_N(1) = (.70)(.35) = .2450$

$p_S(4000) = p^{*(2)}(4000) \cdot p_N(2) = (.09)(.20) = .0180$

$p_S(5000) = p^{*(2)}(5000) \cdot p_N(2) = (.42)(.20) = .0840$

$p_S(6000) = p^{*(2)}(6000) \cdot p_N(2) + p^{*(3)}(6000) \cdot p_N(3)$
$\quad\quad\quad = (.49)(.20) + (.027)(.10) = .1007$

$p_S(7000) = p^{*(3)}(7000) \cdot p_N(3) = (.189)(.10) = .0189$

$p_S(8000) = p^{*(3)}(8000) \cdot p_N(3) = (.441)(.10) = .0441$

$p_S(9000) = p^{*(3)}(9000) \cdot p_N(3) = (.343)(.10) = .0343$

The employer's retained claim cost, R, is S, if $S \le 4000$, or 4000, if $S \ge 4000$. Then we have

$E[R] = (2000)(.1050) + (3000)(.2450)$
$\quad\quad\quad\quad + (4000)(1 - .3500 - .1050 - .2450)$
$\quad\quad = 210 + 735 + 1200 = 2145.$

Along with the reinsurance cost of 750, the employer's total cost is

$$2145 + 750 = 2895.$$

(Note that it was only necessary to develop the distribution of S as far as $s = 3000$.)

13-27 If the maximum coverage is u, then the maximum payment is $.80(u-1000) = 300$, which solves for $u = 1375$.

Recall that when there is both a deductible and a maximum coverage, as well as a coinsurance factor, then the expected payment is

$E[P] = \alpha[E[X \wedge u] - E[X \wedge d]]$
$\quad\quad = (.80)(E[X \wedge 1375] - E[X \wedge 1000]).$

From Equation (13.17) we find

CHAPTER THIRTEEN 219

$$E[(X-1375)_+] = \frac{125}{500} \cdot E[(X-1000)_+] + \frac{375}{500} \cdot E[(X-1500)_+].$$

Recall also that $E[(X-r)_+] = E[X] - E[X \wedge r]$.
Therefore $E[X \wedge r] = E[X] - E[(X-r)_+]$. Then

$$\begin{aligned}
E[P] &= (.80)\big(E[X] - E[(X-1375)_+] - E[X] + E[(X-1000)_+]\big) \\
&= (.80)\big(E[(X-1000)_+] - E[(X-1375)_+]\big) \\
&= (.80)\left[400 - \left(\frac{125}{500}\right)(400) - \left(\frac{375}{500}\right)(200)\right] \\
&= (.80)(400 - 100 - 150) = 120.
\end{aligned}$$

13-28 The total loss amount is modeled by the individual risk model as

$$S = X_1 + X_2 + X_3.$$

We convolute the given distribution of X to obtain the following distribution for $R = X_1 + X_2$:

r	0	1	2	3	4	5	6
$p(r)$	.16	.24	.25	.20	.10	.04	.01

Next we convolute R with X_3 to obtain the following distribution for S:

s	0	1	2	3	4	5	6	7	8	9
$p(s)$	.064	.144	.204	.219	.174	.111	.056	.021	.006	.001

Then we note that the payment, P, will be $S-1$, due to the group deductible. Its expected value is

$$\begin{aligned}
E[P] &= (1)(.204) + (2)(.219) + (3)(.174) + (4)(.111) + (5)(.056) \\
&\quad + (6)(.021) + (7)(.006) + (8)(.001) \\
&= .204 + .438 + .522 + .444 + .280 + .126 + .042 + .008 \\
&= 2.064.
\end{aligned}$$

13-29 If the aggregate loss is S, the aggregate payment is $P=(S-3)_+$, in light of the aggregate deductible, and we seek the value of $E[P]=E[(S-3)_+]$. We will use the recursive relationship given by Equation (13.26), so we will need the values of $E[S]$ and $F_S(x)$ for $x=0,1,2$. First we find

$$E[X] = (1)(.60)+(2)(.40) = 1.40$$

so

$$E[S] = E[X]\cdot E[N] = (1.40)(2) = 2.80.$$

Next we calculate

$$p_S(0) = Pr(N=0) = e^{-2} = .13534,$$

$$p_S(1) = Pr(N=1)\cdot Pr(X=1) = 2\cdot e^{-2}(.60) = .16240,$$

and

$$p_S(2) = Pr(N=1)\cdot Pr(X=2)+Pr(N=2)\cdot [Pr(X=1)]^2$$
$$= 2\cdot e^{-2}(.40)+2\cdot e^{-2}(.60)^2 = .20571,$$

which then gives us

$$F_S(0) = p_S(0) = .13534,$$

$$F_S(1) = F_S(0)+p_S(1) = .29774,$$

and

$$F_S(2) = F_S(1)+p_S(2) = .50345.$$

Now we use Equation (13.26) recursively to find

$$E[(S-0)_+] = E[S] = 2.80,$$

$$E[(S-1)_+] = E[(S-0)_+]-[1-F_S(0)] = 1.93534,$$

$$E[(S-2)_+] = E[(S-1)_+]-[1-F_S(1)] = 1.23308,$$

and finally,

$$E[(S-3)_+] = E[(S-2)_+] - [1 - F_S(2)] = .73653.$$

13-30   If X has a binomial distribution (see Section 2.2.2), its MGF is

$$M_X(t) = (q + pe^t)^n.$$

For any positive integer k we have

$$M_X(t) = (q + pe^t)^n = [(q + pe^t)^{n/k}]^k.$$

In order that $(q + pe^t)^{n/k}$ be the MGF of a binomial random variable, it is necessary that n/k be a positive integer, which will not be the case for *every* positive integer k as required to meet the definition of infinite divisibility.

CHAPTER FOURTEEN
PROCESS MODELS

14-1   Recall that
$$M_{S(t)}(r) = M_{N(t)}[\ln M_X(r)].$$

Here $N(t)$ is a Poisson process with $\lambda = 2$, so $M_{N(t)}(r) = e^{2t(e^r - 1)}$ and therefore
$$M_{S(t)}(r) = e^{2t[M_X(r)-1]} = \exp\left[\frac{8t}{(r-2)^2} - 2t\right].$$

Then
$$2t \cdot M_X(r) - 2t = \frac{8t}{(r-2)^2} - 2t,$$

so
$$M_X(r) = \frac{4}{(r-2)^2} = \frac{2^2}{(2-r)^2} = \left(\frac{2}{2-r}\right)^2.$$

This shows us that X has a gamma distribution with $\beta = 2$ and $\alpha = 2$, so its variance is $Var(X) = \frac{\alpha}{\beta^2} = \frac{2}{4} = .50$.

14-2   The distribution of X is uniform over $(1,10)$, so $E[X] = 5.50$ and $Var(X) = \frac{(10-1)^2}{12} = \frac{81}{12} = \frac{27}{4} = 6.75$. Then
$$E[S(t)] = \lambda t \cdot E[X] = 5.50 \lambda t$$

and
$$Var[S(t)] = \lambda t \cdot E[X^2] = \lambda t[6.75 + (5.50)^2] = 37\lambda t.$$

Finally,
$$\frac{Var[S(t)]}{E[S(t)]} = \frac{37\lambda t}{5.50\lambda t} = \frac{74}{11}.$$

14-3 The waiting time until the next claim has an exponential distribution with parameter λ. We are given
$$Pr(T \geq 2) = e^{-2\lambda} = .60,$$
or $e^{-\lambda} = (.60)^{1/2}$. Then the number of claims has a Poisson distribution with parameter λ per unit time (i.e., per year), so the number of claims in a five-year period is Poisson with parameter 5λ. Then
$$Pr(N=4) = \frac{e^{-5\lambda} \cdot (5\lambda)^4}{4!} = \frac{(.60)^{5/2} \cdot \left[-\ln(.60)^{5/2}\right]^4}{4!}$$
$$= \frac{(.278855)(2.659811)}{24}$$
$$= .03090.$$

14-4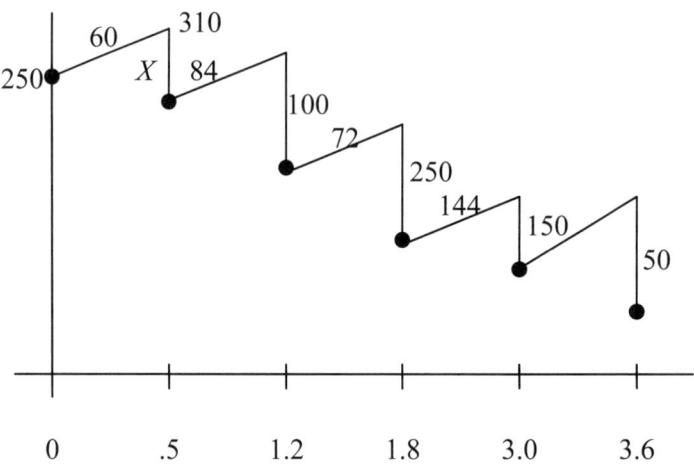

To avoid ruin at $t = 0.5$, $X \not> 310$.
To avoid ruin at $t = 1.2$, $X \not> 394 - 100 = 294$.
To avoid ruin at $t = 1.8$, $X \not> 466 - 350 = 116$.
To avoid ruin at $t = 3.0$, $X \not> 610 - 500 = 110$.
To avoid ruin at $t = 3.6$, $X \not> 682 - 550 = 132$.

To avoid ruin in $(0, 3.6)$, $X \not> 110$.

14-5 We start with $u=200$, so the first two claims cannot cause ruin. To avoid ruin at $t=1.8$, the premium must exceed $375-200=175$. Then $(1+\theta)(80)(1.8)=175$, which implies $\theta \not< .21527$.

To avoid ruin at $t=3.0$, the premium must exceed $575-200=375$. Then $(1+\theta)(80)(3)=375$, which implies $\theta \not< .5625$.

To avoid ruin at $t=3.6$, the premium must exceed 425. Then $(1+\theta)(80)(3.6)=425$, which implies $\theta \not< .4757$.

To avoid ruin any time in $0 \le t \le 3.6$, θ cannot be less than $.5625$.

14-6

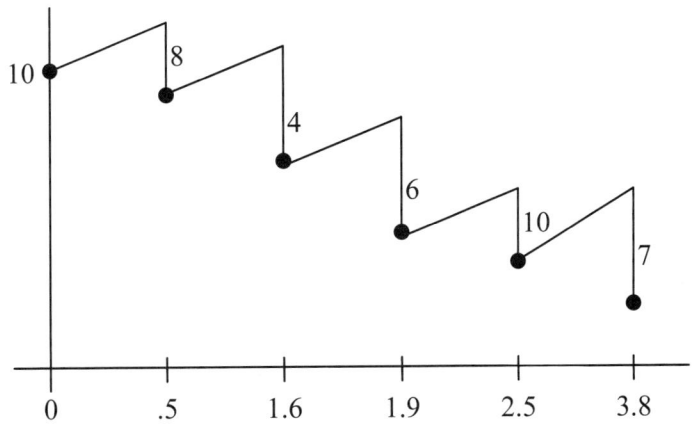

Since $u=10$ exceeds $X_1=8$, ruin cannot occur at $t=.5$.

To avoid ruin at $t=1.6$, $10+1.6c$ must exceed 12, so c must exceed 1.25.

To avoid ruin at $t=1.9$, $10+1.9c$ must exceed 18, so c must exceed 4.21.

To avoid ruin at $t=2.5$, $10+2.5c$ must exceed 28, so c must exceed 7.20.

To avoid ruin at $t=3.8$, $10+3.8c$ must exceed 35, so c must exceed 6.57.

To avoid ruin any time in $0 \le t \le 3.8$, c must exceed 7.20.

14-7 Since the premium comes in at rate 20, then by time $t=2$ the surplus is $60+2(20)=100$ and by time $t=7$ the surplus is $60+7(20)=200$. This means that ruin will occur if the claim occurs before $t=2$, and is of either possible size, or if the claim occurs between $t=2$ and $t=7$, and is of size 200. Under any other outcome, ruin does not occur. Therefore the probability of ruin is

$$\left(1-\frac{1}{3}\right)+\left(\frac{1}{3}-\frac{1}{8}\right)(.40) = \frac{2}{3}+\left(\frac{5}{24}\right)\left(\frac{4}{10}\right) = \frac{3}{4}.$$

14-8 When all claims are of the same size, x, then $E[X]=x$ and $M_X(r)=E[e^{Xr}]=e^{xr}$. Then the adjustment coefficient is given by

$$e^{xr} = 1+(1+\theta)xr.$$

Here $\theta = \dfrac{3-\ln 4}{\ln 4}$ and $x = \ln 2$, so

$$e^{r\cdot \ln 2} = 1+\left(1+\frac{3-\ln 4}{\ln 4}\right)\cdot r \cdot \ln 2$$

$$2^r = 1+\left(\frac{3}{\ln 4}\right)\cdot \ln 2^r = 1+3\left(\frac{r\cdot \ln 2}{2\cdot \ln 2}\right) = 1+\frac{3}{2}r.$$

By inspection, $r^* = 2$.

14-9 The adjustment coefficient is the non-zero root of

$$M_X(r) = 1+r(1+\theta)\mu.$$

When X is exponential, then $\dfrac{\beta}{\beta-r} = 1+(1+\theta)r\left(\frac{1}{\beta}\right).$

I. True: As $r \to \infty$, $M_X(r) \to \infty$ so $r^* \not> \beta$.

II. True: As θ increases, the line moves upward, so the intersection point r^* increases.

III. False: $\psi(u) = \dfrac{1}{1+\theta}\left(e^{-\theta\beta u/(1+\theta)}\right)$, which depends on β.

I and II are true.

CHAPTER FOURTEEN

14-10 Here X is exponential with $\beta = 2$ and $r^* = 1$. For exponential X,

$$r^* = \frac{\theta\beta}{1+\theta} = \frac{2\theta}{1+\theta} = 1,$$

from which we find $\theta = 1$. Also for exponential X,

$$\psi(u) = \frac{1}{1+\theta} \cdot e^{-r^*u} = \frac{1}{2} \cdot e^{-u} = .10$$

$$e^{-u} = .20$$

$$u = -\ln.20 = -\ln\left(\frac{1}{5}\right) = -\ln 1 + \ln 5 = \ln 5.$$

14-11

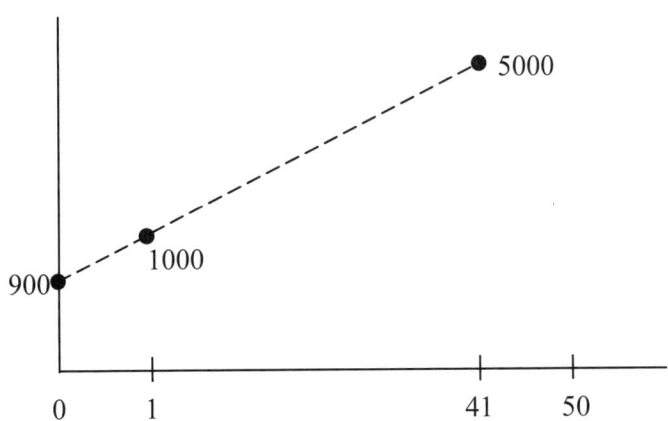

Ruin occurs if there is a claim of either size in $(0,1)$, since $u + ct$ is not yet up to 1000. If there is no claim in $(0,1)$, then ruin can still occur if there is a claim of 5000 in $(1, 41)$, since $u + ct$ does not reach 5000 until $t = 41$. The probability of any claim in $(0,1)$ is $\frac{1}{50}$, given claim at all.

The probability of claim in $(1,41)$ is $\frac{40}{50}$, given claim at all, and the (independent) probability of the claim being size 5000 is $\frac{1}{5}$.

The probability of claim at all is $\frac{1}{10}$. Therefore

$$\psi(900) = \frac{1}{10}\left[\frac{1}{50} + \frac{40}{50}\left(\frac{1}{5}\right)\right] = \frac{45}{2500} = .018.$$

14-12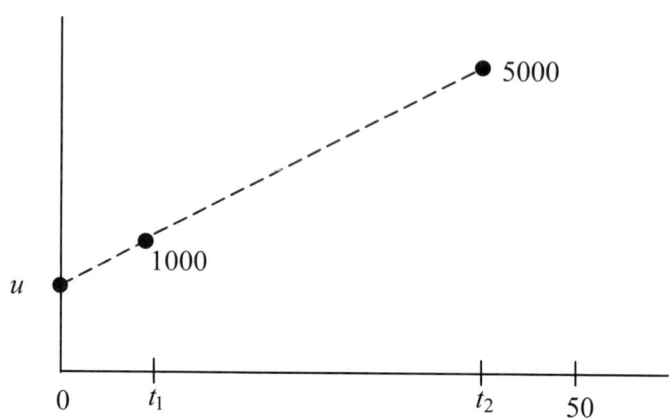

$u+ct = u+100t$ reaches 1000 at time $t_1 = \frac{1000-u}{100}$, and reaches 5000 (if no prior claim) at time $t_2 = \frac{5000-u}{100}$. Just as in Exercise 14-11, ruin occurs if any claim in $(0,t)$ or if claim of size 5000 in (t_1,t_2). The probabilities of claim in these intervals, *given any claim at all*, are $\frac{t_1}{50}$ and $\frac{t_2-t_1}{50}$, and the probability of any claim at all is $\frac{1}{10}$. The (independent) probability of claim being of size 5000, given claim occurring, is $\frac{1}{5}$. Then

$$\psi(u) = \frac{1}{10}\left[\frac{t_1}{50} + \frac{t_2-t_1}{50}\left(\frac{1}{5}\right)\right]$$
$$= \frac{1}{10}\left[\frac{1000-u}{5000} + \frac{4000}{5000}\left(\frac{1}{5}\right)\right] = .02.$$

The last equation solves for $u = 800$.

14-13 When X is exponential, the adjustment coefficient and the probability of ruin do *not* depend on the parameter λ of the claims number distribution, so they do *not* depend on the parameter n. We know that $r^* = \frac{\theta\beta}{1+\theta}$. In this case, $E[X] = 100,000$ so

$$\beta = \frac{1}{E[X]} = .00001 = 10^{-5}.$$

Chapter Fourteen

$$r^* = \frac{\theta}{1+\theta} \times 10^{-5} = \frac{.10}{1.10} \times 10^{-5} < .10 \times 10^{-5} = 10^{-6}, \text{ so II is true.}$$

$$\psi(u) = \frac{1}{1+\theta} \cdot e^{-r^*u}$$

$$= \frac{1}{1.1} \cdot \exp\left[-\frac{.10}{1.10}(.00001)(1,100,000)\right]$$

$$= \frac{1}{1.1} \times e^{-1} < e^{-1},$$

so I is true.

$\psi(u)$ is independent of n, so $\psi_{10}(u) = \psi_{20}(u)$, so, for given u, $\psi_{10}(u) > (.95)\psi_{20}(u)$, so III is false.

I and II are true.

14-14 We are given that X is exponential with $\beta = .20$, $\theta = .20$, and $u = 10$. Then

$$r^* = \frac{\theta\beta}{1+\theta} = \frac{(.20)(.20)}{1.20} = \frac{4}{120} = \frac{1}{30},$$

and $\psi(u) = \frac{1}{1+\theta}(e^{-r^*u})$, so $\psi(10) = \frac{1}{1.20}(e^{-10/30})$. If surplus is increased by the Δ, then $\psi(10+\Delta) = \frac{1}{1.20}(e^{-(10+\Delta)/30})$. We seek the value of Δ such that $\psi(10+\Delta) = \frac{1}{2}\psi(10)$.

$$\frac{1}{1.20} \cdot e^{-(10+\Delta)/30} = \frac{1}{2}\left(\frac{1}{1.20} \cdot e^{-10/30}\right)$$

$$e^{-\Delta/30} = \frac{1}{2}$$

$$-\frac{\Delta}{30} = \ln\left(\frac{1}{2}\right) = -\ln 2$$

$$\Delta = 30\ln 2$$

14-15 $E[Y] = \dfrac{p_2}{2p_1}$, where X is gamma with $\alpha = \beta = 2$.

$p_1 = E[X] = 2$

$p_2 = E[X^2] = Var(X) + p_1^2 = 6$

$E[Y] = \dfrac{6}{2(2)} = 1.50$

14-16

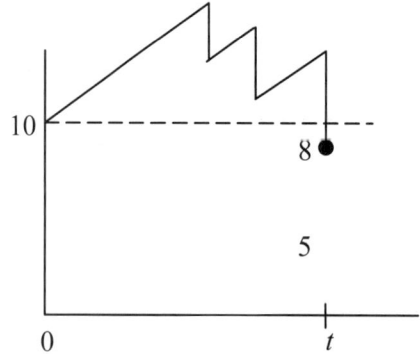

The claim that drops surplus below $u = 10$ is of size 5, so the new surplus level cannot be less than 5. If the surplus level is to be less than 8, then we are saying $5 < U(t) < 8$.

Recall that Y is the random variable for distance below 10, so we seek $Pr(2<Y<5)$.

Recall that when X is distributed as $Pr(X=x) = 1.00$, then Y is uniform over $(0,x)$. In this case Y is uniform over $(0,5)$, so $Pr(2 < Y < 5) = \dfrac{3}{5} = .60$.

14-17 Recall that if X is exponential, then Y is the same exponential. Here $E[X] = 2$, so $\beta = \tfrac{1}{2}$. $Pr(Y > u) = e^{-\beta u} = e^{-u/2} = e^{-2}$. Therefore $\tfrac{u}{2} = 2$ and $u = 4$.

(Note that $\lambda = 100$ and $\theta = .20$ are not needed.)

CHAPTER FOURTEEN

14-18 Since $u = 0$, then event of ruin is event of surplus dropping below u, so deficit at ruin is Y. We know that $E[Y] = \dfrac{p_2}{2p_1}$.

Here X is uniform over $(0,30)$, so $f(x) = \dfrac{1}{30}$, and

$$p_1 = E[X] = \int_0^{30} \dfrac{x}{30}\, dx = \dfrac{x^2}{60}\bigg|_0^{30} = 15$$

and

$$p_2 = E[X^2] = \int_0^{30} \dfrac{x^2}{30}\, dx = \dfrac{x^3}{90}\bigg|_0^{30} = 300.$$

Then $E[Y] = \dfrac{300}{2(15)} = 10$.

14-19 $L = Y_1 + Y_2 + \cdots + Y_N$, so $M_L(r) = M_N\big[\ln M_Y(r)\big]$.

Here $M_N(t) = \dfrac{\frac{\theta}{1+\theta}}{1 - \frac{1}{1+\theta} \cdot e^t} = \dfrac{\theta}{1+\theta - e^t}$, so

$$M_L(r) = \dfrac{\theta}{1+\theta - M_Y(r)} = \dfrac{\theta}{1+\theta - \frac{e^r - 1}{r}} = \dfrac{\theta r}{(1+\theta)r - e^r + 1}.$$

14-20 Gamma distribution with $\alpha = 1$ is really exponential, so X is exponential with $\beta = 2$, so $p_1 = E[X] = \frac{1}{2}$ and $M_X(r) = \dfrac{2}{2-r}$.

    I.   False:

$$M_L(r) = \dfrac{\theta}{1+\theta - M_Y(r)} = \dfrac{.20}{1.20 - \frac{2}{2-r}} = \dfrac{.20(2-r)}{.40 - 1.20r} = \dfrac{2-r}{2-6r}$$

    II.   True:

$$M_Y(r) = \dfrac{1}{p_1 r}[M_X(r) - 1] = \dfrac{2}{r}\left(\dfrac{2}{2-r} - 1\right) = \dfrac{2r}{r(2-r)} = \dfrac{2}{2-r}$$

    III. True:

$$r^* = \dfrac{\theta \beta}{1+\theta} = \dfrac{.20(2)}{1.20} = \dfrac{1}{3}$$

II and III are true.

14-21 The integral in the second line of Equation (14.23) is evaluated by parts. We have

$$\int_0^\infty \frac{S_X(y)}{-f_X(y)\,dy} \left|\begin{array}{c} e^{ry}\,dy \\ \frac{1}{r}\cdot e^{ry} \end{array}\right. = \frac{1}{r}\cdot e^{ry}\cdot S_X(y)\Big|_0^\infty + \frac{1}{r}\int_0^\infty e^{ry}\cdot f_X(y)\,dy$$

$$= -\frac{1}{r} + \frac{1}{r}\cdot M_X(r) = \frac{1}{r}[M_X(r)-1],$$

as required, since $S_X(\infty)=0$, $S_X(0)=1$, and the second integral defines $M_X(r)$.

14-22 We take $\psi(u)$ from Equation (14.19), substitute $\frac{1}{\beta}$ for μ, and differentiate to obtain

$$\psi'(u) = \frac{1}{1+\theta}\cdot\exp\left[-\frac{\beta\theta u}{1+\theta}\right]\cdot-\frac{\beta\theta}{1+\theta}.$$

Multiplying by e^{ru} gives

$$e^{ru}\cdot-\psi'(u) = \frac{1}{1+\theta}\cdot\exp\left[-\frac{\beta\theta u}{1+\theta}+ru\right]\cdot\frac{\beta\theta}{1+\theta},$$

so the left side of Equation (14.32) becomes

$$\int_0^\infty e^{ru}\cdot-\psi'(u)\,du$$

$$= \int_0^\infty \frac{1}{1+\theta}\cdot\exp\left[-\left(\frac{[\beta\theta-r(1+\theta)]u}{1+\theta}\right)\right]\cdot\frac{\beta\theta}{1+\theta}\,du$$

$$= \left(\frac{1}{1+\theta}\right)\left(\frac{\beta\theta}{1+\theta}\right)\left(\frac{1+\theta}{[r(1+\theta)-\beta\theta]}\right)$$

$$\cdot\int_0^\infty \exp\left[-\left(\frac{[\beta\theta-r(1+\theta)]u}{1+\theta}\right)\right]\cdot\frac{r(1+\theta)-\beta\theta}{1+\theta}\,du$$

$$= \frac{\beta\theta}{(1+\theta)\cdot[r(1+\theta)-\beta\theta]}\cdot\exp\left[-\left(\frac{[\beta\theta-r(1+\theta)]u}{1+\theta}\right)\right]\Big|_0^\infty.$$

Chapter Fourteen

The exponential function evaluates to 0 at the upper limit and 1 at the lower limit, so the overall left side of Equation (14.32) becomes $\dfrac{\beta\theta}{(1+\theta)\cdot[\beta\theta-r(1+\theta)]}$.

More simply, by substituting $\dfrac{\beta}{\beta-r}$ for $M_X(r)$ and $\dfrac{1}{\beta}$ for μ, the right side of Equation (14.32) becomes

$$\dfrac{\theta\left[\dfrac{\beta}{\beta-r}-1\right]}{(1+\theta)\cdot\left[1+\dfrac{(1+\theta)r}{\beta}-\dfrac{\beta}{\beta-r}\right]}$$

$$=\dfrac{\beta\theta r}{(1+\theta)\cdot[\beta(\beta-r)+(1+\theta)(\beta-r)r-\beta^2]},$$

by multiplying both numerator and denominator by $\beta(\beta-r)$. The bracketed expression in the denominator simplifies to

$$\beta^2-\beta r+\beta r+\beta\theta r-r^2-\theta r^2-\beta^2 = r[\beta\theta-(1+\theta)r],$$

and the entire right side becomes $\dfrac{\beta\theta}{(1+\theta)\cdot[\beta\theta-(1+\theta)r]}$, the same as the left side.

14-23 (Note that this model is like Example 14.6, but with a third year to consider.)

The initial surplus plus premium produces a fund of 5, before claims. After claims the fund is 5, 4, 3, or 1, with respective probabilities .15, .25, .40, and .20. If the fund is either 5 or 4, the first year dividend drops it to 3, so, after dividend, the fund at $t=1$ is either 3 or 1 with probabilities .80 and .20, respectively. (Note that ruin in the first year is not possible, so $\psi(3,1)=0$.)

In the second year, the fund plus premium is either 5 or 3, before claims. Ruin occurs *only* if the fund is 3 and the claim is 4, so the probability of ruin by time 2 is $\psi(3,2)=(.20)(.20)=.04$, and the probability of surviving to time 2 is $1-\psi(3,2)=.96$.

The possible surviving values of the fund at $t=2$, after claims and after dividend, are as follows:

Fund at $t=1$, after Premium	Second Year Claim	Fund at $t=2$, after Dividend	Probability of Outcome
5	0	3	$(.80)(.15) = .12$
5	1	3	$(.80)(.25) = .20$
5	2	3	$(.80)(.40) = .32$
5	4	1	$(.80)(.20) = .16$
3	0	3	$(.20)(.15) = .03$
3	1	2	$(.20)(.25) = .05$
3	2	1	$(.20)(.40) = .08$

After the third year premium, the fund is either 5 (with probability .67), 4 (with probability .05), or 3 (with probability .24). Note that these add to .96, the value of $1-\psi(3,2)$.

Finally, the fund fails in the third year only if it starts at 3 or 4, and has claim of 4. The probability of this is $(.29)(.20) = .058$, so the probability of surviving the third year, given survival through the second year, is $1-.058 = .942$. Finally, the unconditional probability of survival to $t=3$ is

$$1-\psi(3,3) = (.96)(.942) = .90432.$$

14-24 The initial surplus plus premium and interest produces a fund at the end of the first year, before losses, of $3(1.10) = 3.30$. After deducting the year-end loss, the surplus at $t=1$ is 3.30 (with probability .60), 1.30 (with probability .30), or negative (with probability .10). Therefore the probability of ruin in the first year is $\psi(1,1) = .10$ and the probability of survival to $t=1$ is $1-\psi(1,1) = .90$.

Including premium and interest, the fund at the end of the second year, before losses, is $(5.30)(1.10) = 5.83$ (with probability .60), $(3.30)(1.10) = 3.63$ (with probability .30), or ruined (with probability .10). After loss, the distribution of surplus at $t=2$ is as follows:

Amount	Probability
5.83	(.60)(.60) = .36
3.83	(.60)(.30) = .18
Negative	(.60)(.10) = .06
3.63	(.30)(.60) = .18
1.63	(.30)(.30) = .09
Negative	(.30)(.10) = .03

Along with the 10% probability of ruin in the first year, we find $\psi(1,2) = .10 + .06 + .03 = .19$ as the probability of ruin by time $t = 2$.

Including premium and interest, the fund at the end of the third year, before losses, is $(7.83)(1.10) = 8.613$ (with probability .36), $(5.83)(1.10) = 6.413$ (with probability .18), $(5.63)(1.10) = 6.193$ (with probability .18), $(3.63)(1.10) = 3.993$ (with probability .09), or ruined (with probability .19).

Ruin occurs in the third year only with a loss of 6 against a fund of 3.993, so the probability of ruin in the third year is $(.10)(.09) = .009$. Along with the 19% probability of ruin in the first two years we finally have

$$\psi(1,3) = .19 + .009 = .199.$$